VISION SYSTEMS: SEGMENTATION AND PATTERN RECOGNITION

VISION SYSTEMS: SEGMENTATION AND PATTERN RECOGNITION

Editor

Bilroy Muller

scitus
academics

Vision Systems: Segmentation and Pattern Recognition
Edited by **Bilroy Muller**

ISBN: 978-1-68117-589-8
Library of Congress Control Number: 2016946444

Notice

Printed in United States of America on Acid Free Paper

PREFACE

In the development of autonomous navigation systems for interaction with the planet, computer vision is the key. In addition, it makes us amazed at the performance of our own vision system. Computer vision research has improved exponentially in the last two decades due to the convenience of fast processors and cheap cameras. This increase was accompanied by a blurring of the boundaries between the different vision applications, making it truly interdisciplinary. Vision systems can be regarded as eye computers that can identify, inspect and communicate information that is critical to eliminating costly errors, improving efficiency and improving customer satisfaction through the regular supply of quality products. Vision systems are primarily used for online inspection and can perform complex or perhaps mundane repetitive tasks at high speeds with high consistency and high accuracy.

This book attempts to compile state-of-the-art research and innovative developments in segmentation and pattern recognition techniques.

TABLE OF CONTENTS

1

ROBOT GUIDANCE USING MACHINE VISION TECHNIQUES IN INDUSTRIAL ENVIRONMENTS: A COMPARATIVE REVIEW

Luis Pérez [1,*], Íñigo Rodríguez [1,†], Nuria Rodríguez [1,†], Rubén Usamentiaga [2] and Daniel F. García [2]

[1] Fundación PRODINTEC, Avda. Jardín Botánico 1345, 33203 Gijón (Asturias), Spain

[2] Department of Computer Science and Engineering, Universidad de Oviedo, Campus de Viesques, 33203 Gijón (Asturias), Spain

ABSTRACT

In the factory of the future, most of the operations will be done by autonomous robots that need visual feedback to move around the working space avoiding obstacles, to work collaboratively with humans, to identify and locate the working parts, to complete the information provided by other sensors to improve their positioning accuracy,*etc.* Different vision techniques, such as photogrammetry, stereo vision, structured light, time of flight and laser triangulation, among others, are widely used for inspection and quality control processes in the industry and now for robot guidance. Choosing which type of vision system to use is highly dependent on the parts that need to be located or measured. Thus, in this paper a comparative review of different machine vision techniques for robot guidance is presented. This work analyzes accuracy, range and weight of the sensors, safety, processing time and environmental influences. Researchers and developers can take it as a background information for their future works.

KEYWORDS

machine vision; 3D sensors; perception for manipulation; robot guidance; robot pose; part localization

1. INTRODUCTION

Since the end of the 18th century with the first Industrial Revolution through the introduction of mechanical production facilities powered by water and steam, factories have experimented big changes in their production systems [1]. The second Industrial Revolution, in the start of the 20th Century, introduced mass production based on the division of labor powered by electrical energy [2]. The third Industrial Revolution of the start of 1970s introduced the use of electronics and information technologies for a further automatization of production [3]. Nowadays, we are involved in the fourth Industrial Revolution, commonly called "Industry 4.0", based on cyber-physical production systems (CPS) and embracing automation, data exchange and manufacturing technologies. These cyber-physical systems monitor the physical processes, make decentralized decisions and trigger actions, communicating and cooperating with each other and with humans in real time. This facilitates fundamental improvements to the industrial processes involved in manufacturing, engineering, material usage and supply chain and life cycle management [4].

Inside each revolution, several milestones have been achieved incrementing the innovation level. For instance, inside Industry 4.0, robot-based automatization has experimented its own revolutions. The first robotic revolution was the industrial automatization, the second one was the introduction of sensitive robots for safe automatization, the third one was the mobility with mobile manipulators, and the fourth and the last one is based on intelligent and perceptive robot systems [5].

The European Commission has set as objective for the Horizon 2020 Work Programme to achieve the leadership in industrial technologies (*i.e.*, Public-Private Partnership Factories of the Future or PPP FoF [6]). For this purpose, process automation and decreased accident rates are both important. Productivity and safety were limited by manual processes in the traditional industry; automatization and intelligent robots drive modern industry towards efficiency, resulting in a rapid increase in productivity, major material and energy savings and safer working conditions. Manufacturing demonstrates a huge potential to generate wealth and to create high-quality and highly skilled jobs [7]. In fact, several technology enablers have been identified within PPP FoF, such as advanced manufacturing processes and technologies, mechatronics for advanced manufacturing systems, including robotics, information and communication technologies (ICT), manufacturing strategies, knowledge-workers and modelling, simulation and forecasting methods and tools. Moreover, the European Commission has identified robotics as a key issue due to its importance for European economy: Europe is one of the world leading regions in industrial robotics with a share of more than 25% of supply and use. It is expected that robotics growth reaches 32 B$ by 2016 and a direct impact on job creation as forecasts determine that each industrial robot needs at least four people to run, maintain and service it [8]. Robotics directly improves society and better living conditions as it addresses global concerns such as climate change, sustainable transport, affordable renewable energy, food safety and security, and coping with an ageing population. Some examples of European projects in this area are TAPAS [9,10], VALERI [11,12] and SYMBIO-TIC [13].

Vision systems are widely used in industry, mainly for inspection and quality control processes [14]. Their use has been increased in applications related to improving the safety of workers in the industrial environment and for robot guidance [15]. Robots need machine vision to move around the working space avoiding obstacles, to work collaboratively with humans, to identify and locate the working parts, to improve their positioning accuracy, *etc*. Depending on the objective, the vision system can be scene-related or object-related [16]. In scene-related tasks the camera is usually mounted on a mobile robot and applied for mapping, localization and obstacle detection. In object-related tasks, the camera is usually attached to the end-effector of the robot manipulator (eye-in-hand configuration), so that new images can be acquired by changing the point of view of the camera.

Industrial robots are able to move to a position repeatedly with a small error of 0.1 mm, although their absolute accuracy can be several mm due to tolerances, eccentricities, elasticities, play, wear-out, load, temperature and insufficient knowledge of model parameters for the transformation from poses into robot axis angles [17,18,19]. In the automotive industry the accuracy requirement for operations such as spot welding will be of the order of 1 mm. The aerospace industry provides a challenging environment to apply robotics as its accuracy requirements are at least a factor of ten- to twenty-fold higher [20]. Conventional robots are not capable of achieving this accuracy. To improve the accuracy, optical calibration methods, such as laser tracker systems, photogrammetry or vision systems with multiple high resolution cameras, are used to detect the spatial position of the tool tip and to correct the robot motion. The combination of a measurement system with a robot is an optimal solution as it makes use of the robot ability for precise movement and overcomes the accuracy deficiencies. Moreover, working parts can be positioned slightly different from what the robot is expecting. In order to successfully navigate a mobile robot, obtaining detailed information on its immediate environment is the main concern. If the collected data is correct and sufficiently detailed, the creation of a 3D appearance model is possible and developers are given the opportunity to create accordingly sophisticated navigation software.

At this point, machine vision techniques and robotics become the main actors in the industrial scenarios. Thus, this work is a comparative review of different machine vision techniques and their applications for robot guidance, studying and analyzing the state of the art and the different approaches. The suitability of each vision technique depends on its final application, as requirements differ in terms of accuracy, range and weight of the sensors, safety for human workers, acquisition and processing time, environmental conditions, integration with other systems (mainly the robot), and budget. Main challenges are found in textureless surfaces for the correspondence problem, lighting conditions that may cause brightness, occlusions due to the camera point of view, undetermined moving objects, *etc.* Other comparatives can be found in the literature although they are oriented to commercial purposes, centered in one vision technique, or focused on software and algorithms. They are also analyzed in this work.

The rest of the paper is organized as follows: Section 2 resumes the fundamentals of vision-based 3D reconstruction,Section 3 reviews a wide range of robot guidance applications using machine vision, Section 4 performs a comparative analysis according to the application requirements and discusses advantages and drawbacks, and finally main conclusions are found in Section 5.

2. FUNDAMENTALS OF 3D RECONSTRUCTION

Three-dimensional perception is one of the key technologies for robots. A 3D view of the surroundings of the robot is crucial for accomplishing navigation and manipulation tasks in a fully autonomous way in incompletely known environments. Moreover, tele-operation of robots requires a visualization of the environment in a human-readable way, which is important for an intuitive user interface. Thus, vision systems for robot guidance generally need to obtain 3D information.

Given a point in the scene, its corresponding point in the image can be obtained by mathematical models [21]. This is the direct problem. As it determines a set of parameters that describe the mapping between 3D points in the world coordinate system and the 2D image coordinates, this process is also known as camera calibration. The perspective projection of the world coordinates onto the image is generally modeled using the pinhole camera model [22]. Figure 1 shows a graphical representation. Using this model, the image of a 3D point, *P*, is formed by an optical ray passing through the optical center and intersecting the image plane. The result is the point *P'* in the image plane, which is located at a distance *f* (focal length) behind the optical center.

The first step to mathematically describe the projection of 3D points on the 2D image plane is the transformation from the world coordinate system *W* to the camera coordinate system *C*. This transformation is given by Equation (1). Using this equation, the camera coordinates of a point $P_c = (x_c, y_c, z_c)^T$ are calculated from its world coordinate $P_w = (x_w, y_w, z_w)^T$ using the rigid transformation $H_{w \to c}$:

$$\begin{pmatrix} p^c \\ 1 \end{pmatrix} = H_{w \to c} \begin{pmatrix} p^w \\ 1 \end{pmatrix} \quad (1)$$

The homogeneous transformation matrix $H_{w \to c}$ includes three translations (t_x, t_y, tz) and three rotations (α, β, γ). These six parameters are called the extrinsic camera parameters and describe the rotation $(R_{w \to c})$ and translation $(t_{w \to c})$ from *W* to *C*. Thus, Equation (1) can also be expressed as Equation (2):

$$\begin{pmatrix} x^c \\ y^c \\ z^c \\ 1 \end{pmatrix} = \begin{pmatrix} R_{w \to c} & t_{w \to c} \\ 0 \;\; 0 \;\; 0 & 1 \end{pmatrix} \begin{pmatrix} x^w \\ y^w \\ z^w \\ 1 \end{pmatrix} \quad (2)$$

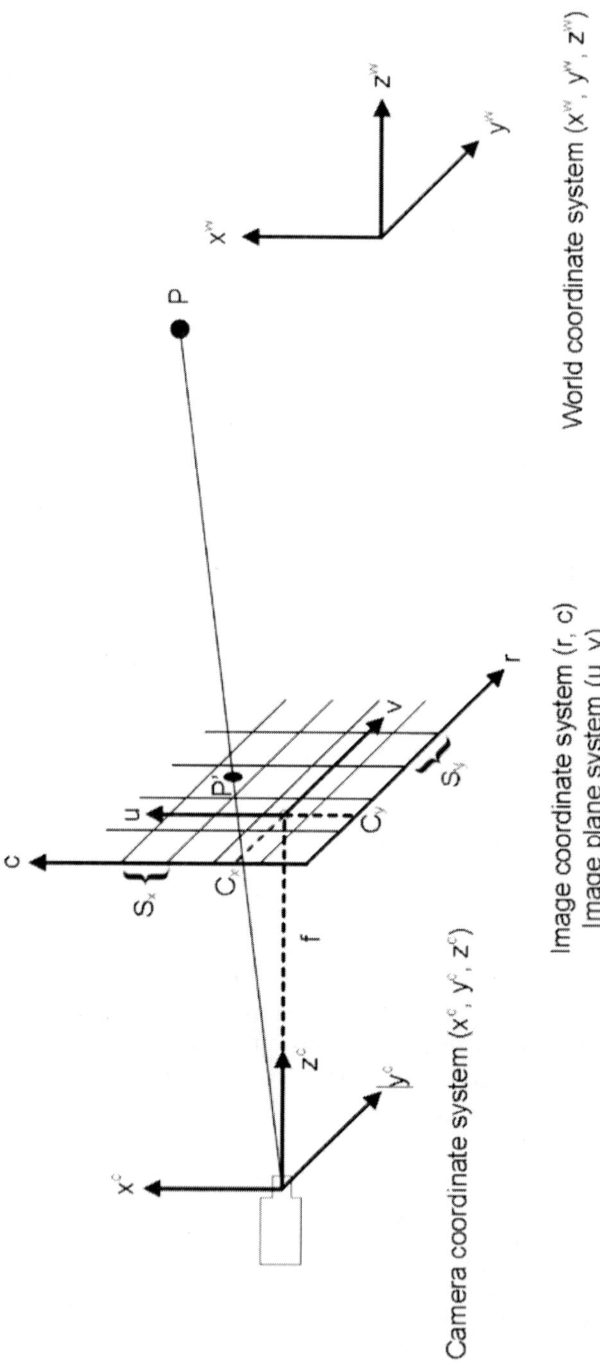

Figure 1. Pinhole camera model [23].

Based on the pinhole model, the projection of the point in the camera coordinate system *C* onto the image coordinate system is calculated using Equation (3):

$$\begin{pmatrix} u \\ v \end{pmatrix} = \frac{f}{z^c}\begin{pmatrix} x^c \\ y^c \end{pmatrix} \tag{3}$$

The pinhole model is only an ideal approximation of the real camera projection. Imaging devices introduce a certain amount of nonlinear distortion [24]. Thus, when high accuracy is required, lens distortion must be taken into account [25]. The final step is the transformation from the image plane coordinate system *(u, v)* to the image coordinate system *(r, c)*, which is the pixel coordinate system. This transformation is achieved using Equation (4), where S_x and S_y are scaling factors that represent the horizontal and vertical distances between the sensor elements on the CCD chip of the camera and the point $(C_x, C_y)^T$, which is the perpendicular projection of the optical center onto the image plane. Equation (4) reflects the calibration matrix:

$$\begin{pmatrix} r \\ c \end{pmatrix} = \begin{pmatrix} \frac{v}{S_y} + C_y \\ \frac{u}{S_x} + C_x \end{pmatrix} \tag{4}$$

The projection of a point in the scene on the image can be mathematically calculated as shown in Figure 2a. However, given a point of the image it is not possible to obtain directly its original point in the space, as it is not a one-to-one relationship, but one-to-several, thus the inverse problem is ill-defined [26]. In algebraic terms, the projection of a 3D point on the image is not an injective application. Different points can be projected on the same pixel. What is really obtained by solving the inverse problem is a straight line formed by all points that are represented on the same pixel of the image. This is the projection line shown in Figure 2b.

Passive techniques, such as stereo vision or photogrammetry, which only require ambient lighting, solve the problem by looking for the same point in multiple images and computing the intersection of the projection lines. Others project a visible or infrared pattern onto the scene and estimate the depth information from the returning time (time of flight), the deformation of the pattern (light coding) or trigonometric calculations (laser triangulation and structured light). They are active vision. This difference in illumination method is important since the less well-defined features an object may have, the less accurate the system will be when passive vision is used. This is not the case with active vision systems, since a known pattern is used to illuminate the object. Nevertheless, using active vision can result in measurement inaccuracies, especially in the edges or in objects with varying surface finishes [27]. The main disadvantage of non-contact measurement systems is their high sensitivity to various external factors inherent to the measurement process or the optical characteristics of the object [28]. Passive vision techniques need multiple cameras for 3D reconstruction and active ones only use a single camera. However, as it will be shown, some techniques can be passive or active vision or use one or several cameras depending on the application. In addition, some of them are in fact evolutions or improvements of others. Thus, depending on the authors different classifications can be found over the literature. Table 1 shows one possible classification and points out that some technique can be included in more than one group.

Table 1. Vision techniques classification.

	Single Camera	Multiple Cameras
Passive vision	2D	Stereo vision Photogrammetry
Active vision	Time of flight Structured light Light coding Laser triangulation	Structured light Projected texture stereo vision

Numerous sensor technologies are available, and each of them provide unique advantages for its use in specific environments or situations. In the following subsections, different 3D vision techniques are presented.

2.1. Stereo Vision and Photogrammetry

Literally photogrammetry consists of measuring real dimensions from a photo of an object. It is a 3D reconstruction technique based on conventional 2D images commonly used in architecture [29,30,31,32], topography [33,34], geology [35], archaeology [36], engineering [37,38], and manufacturing [39].

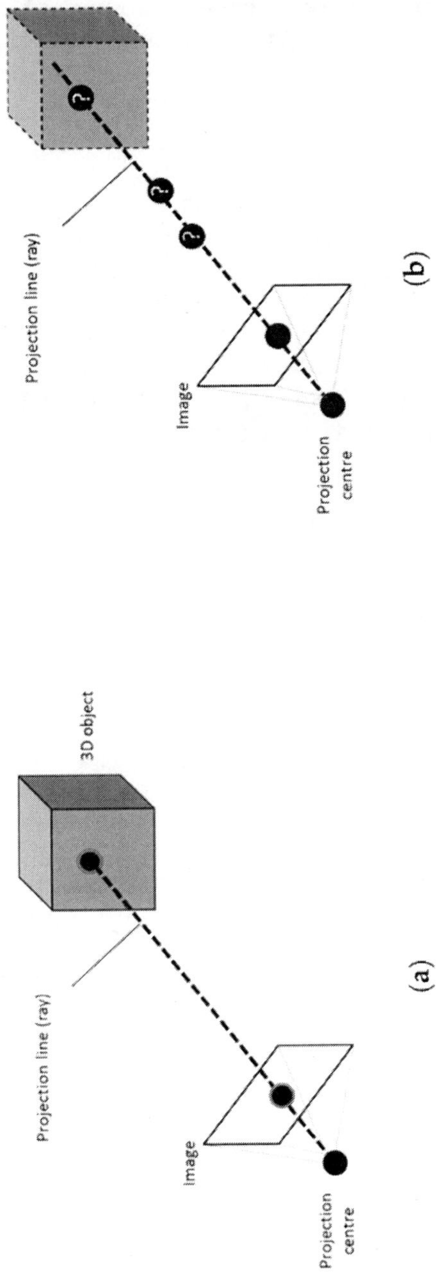

Figure 2. From 3D to 2D. (**a**) Direct problem; (**b**) Inverse problem.

In stereo vision and photogrammetric techniques, the same point has to be found in other image to calculate the intersection of the projection lines and to obtain the 3D position (Figure 3). However, it is recommended that every point could be found at least in three images in order to ensure the detection and to improve the accuracy. The selected points must be the homologous and not any other ones in order to get the right 3D position.

Physical marks, such as stickers or laser points (Figure 4), are necessary over and around the object (the more, the better) and they must be of high contrast in order to ensure the detection. In Figure 5 two images of the same marked part have been taken and processed. The detected marks are printed in red. If the spatial position of the cameras and their calibration parameters are known, the marks can be paired using epipolar geometry and their projection lines and their intersections can be calculated to find the 3D position [40]. Notice that only those marked points are detected and used for the model (marker-based stereo vision).

In some cases, it is desirable to avoid these physical marks in order to save time and to automate the process. Feature tracking algorithms find, extract and match intrinsic characteristics of the objects between similar or consecutive images- avoiding physical marks, as can be seen in Figure 6 (markerless stereo vision).

The extracted features depend on the problem or the type of application. In fact, a characteristic feature is a region of interest in the image that provides important information, such as an edge, a corner, bright or dark isolated points, *etc*. These detected points are useful for a subsequent search of correspondences between similar images. Some of the most popular algorithms for features detection, extraction and tracking are Canny [41], Harris [42], KLT [43], SIFT [44], SURF [45], and MSER [46].

Markerless stereo camera systems are widely used in many real applications including indoor and outdoor robotics. They provide accurate depth estimates on well-textured scenes, but often fail when the surface of the object is low-textured or textureless. In this case, it is necessary to project a known static high contrast light on it highlighting points, features, non-visible structures, *etc*. and creating an artificial texture. Then, the reflected light is captured using a stereo camera system and a matching algorithm associates the homologous points to obtain the 3D information [47]. *Ensenso* has developed several series of compact sensors based on this technique [48].

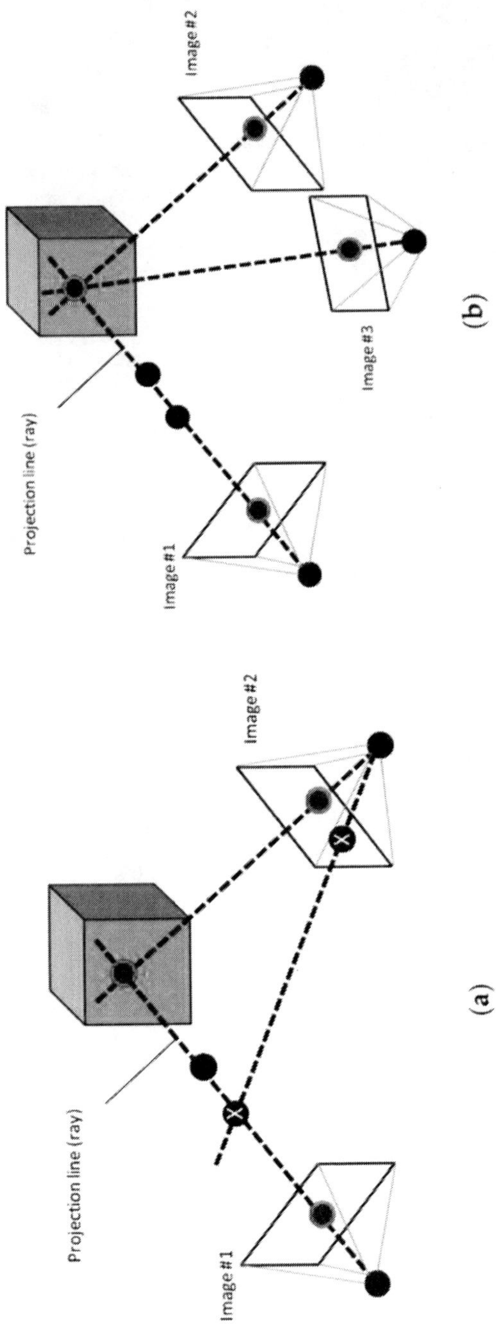

Figure 3. From 2D to 3D. (**a**) Homologous points; (**b**) Intersection of the projection lines.

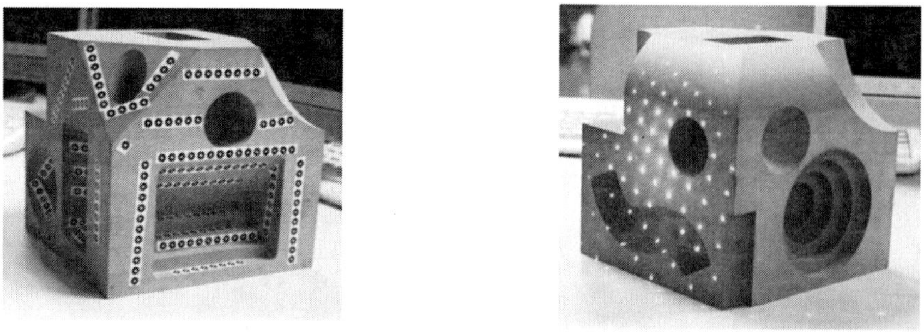

(a) (b)

Figure 4. Physical marks used in marker-based stereo vision. (**a**) Stickers; (**b**) Laser points.

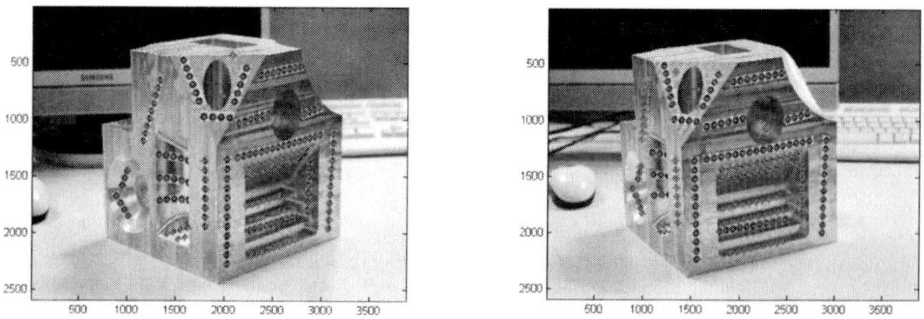

Figure 5. Detection of marks in several images.

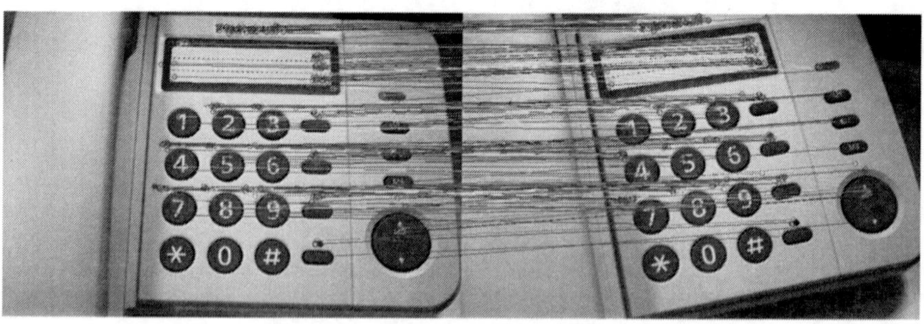

Figure 6. Feature tracking algorithms.

The projected texture is usually pulsed infrared light which is not affected by external light sources. It can take many forms including crosses, circles, squares, dot-matrices, multiple lines and random dot matrices. Finding the optimal texture, that is, the one which provides the best correspondence between features of the images, is a complicated problem, influenced by characteristics of the projector, the pattern, and the stereo cameras [49,50].

2.2. Time of Flight

Active vision techniques obtain the 3D information projecting a visible or infrared pattern on the object as shown inFigure 7. A time of flight (ToF) camera is a range camera that uses light pulses. The illumination is switched on for a very short time. The resulting light pulse is projected on the scene illuminating it and being reflected by the objects. The camera lens captures the reflected light onto the sensor plane. Depending on the distance, the incoming light experiences a delay which can be calculated as shown in Equation (5), where t_D is the delay, D is the distance to the object and c is the speed of light. The pulse width of the illumination determines the maximum range the camera can handle, thus the illumination unit is a critical part of the system. Only with some special LEDs or lasers it is possible to generate such short pulses.

$$t_D = 2 \cdot \frac{D}{c} \tag{5}$$

One of the most common sensors has been developed by *MESA Imaging* [51]. Although ToF sensors open new possibilities and applications as they are quite compact and lightweight, and allow real-time distance acquisition, the quality of raw data is quite noisy and prone to several types of disturbances. They involve major specific challenges: (1) Low resolution compared with other techniques; (2) Systematic distance error; (3) Intensity-related distance error, as the distance is influenced by the incident light; (4) Depth inhomogeneity mainly at object boundaries; (5) Motion artifacts leading to erroneous distance values; (6) Multiple reflections; and (7) Other general aspects of active systems [52].

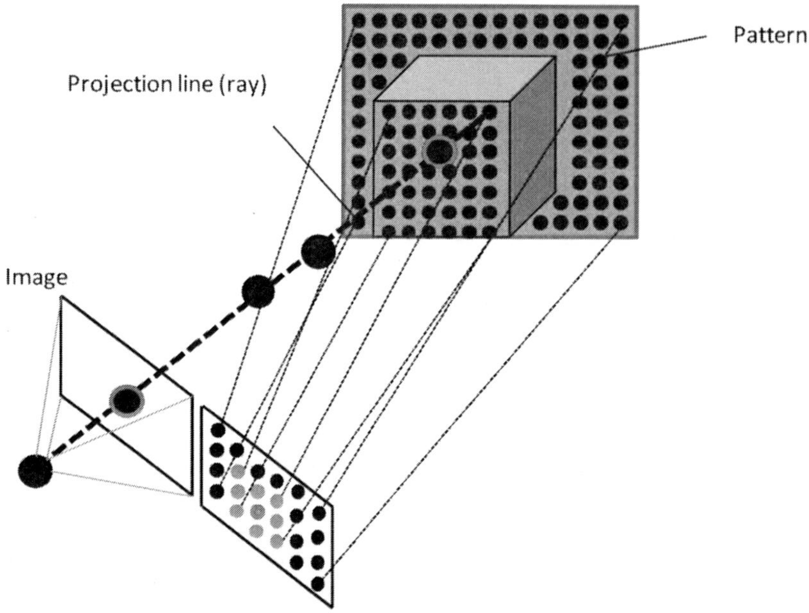

Figure 7. Projecting a pattern on the object.

2.3. Structured Light

Structured light equipment is composed of a light source (the light projector) and one or two information receptors (the cameras). Among all the structured light techniques, there are two main groups [53]: time-multiplexing techniques, which are based on projecting a sequence of binary or grey-scaled patterns, and one-shot techniques, which project a unique pattern. The advantage of time-multiplexing techniques is that, as the number of patterns is not restricted, a large resolution,*i.e.*, number of correspondences, can be achieved. However, their main constraint is that the object, the projector and the camera must all remain static during the projection of the patterns. In one-shot techniques a moving camera or projector can be considered. In order to concentrate the codification scheme in a unique pattern, each encoded point or line is uniquely identified by a local neighbourhood around it [54].

Generally, the projected light is white light which is easily generated and is not dangerous for people unlike laser. This light is modified by grids to create lines or bands with lights and shadows like a zebra (Figure 8) which are recorded by the camera. Depth is obtained from the deviations using a technique similar to triangulation which consists on calculating the intersection between planes and lines [55].

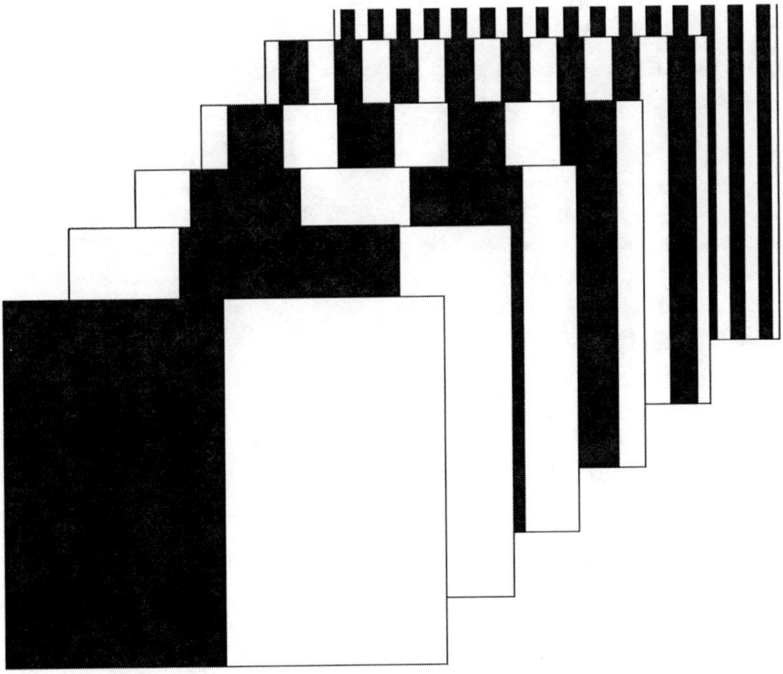

Figure 8. Structured light typical patterns.

Non-contact 3D digitizing scanners derived from structured light projection are increasingly more accurate, fastest and affordable [56]. Recently, new scanners have been launched based on blue light instead of white. As Figure 9 shows, they use a structured blue LED light module and a stereo scanner to generate the 3D point cloud. The LED module produces high contrast patterns allowing a high resolution scanning of the scenario. It is not affected by external light sources and it is safety for people. Sensors as the *HDI 109* and *HDI 120* from *LMI Technologies* can achieve an accuracy of 34 μm and 60 μm, respectively [57].

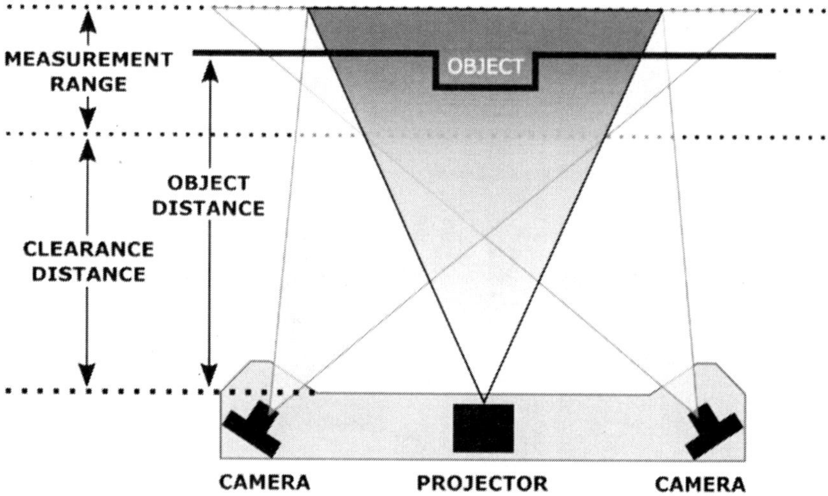

Figure 9. Blue LED sensor components.

2.4. Light Coding

Recently a whole new type of sensor technology called light coding has become available for purchase at only a small fraction of the price of other 3D range finders. Light coding uses an entirely different approach where the light source is constantly turned on, greatly reducing the need for precision timing of the measurements. It can be considered an evolution of structured light.

A laser source emits invisible light (approximately at the infrared wavelength) which passes through a filter and is scattered into a semi-random but constant pattern of small dots which is shown in Figure 10. The reflected pattern is then detected by an infrared camera and analyzed. From knowledge on the emitted light pattern, lens distortion, and distance between emitter and receiver, the distance to each dot can be estimated measuring the deformations in shape and size of the projected points [58]. The technique has been developed by the company *PrimeSense* and its most commonly extended sensor is *Microsoft Kinect.*

Light coding offers depth data at a significantly low cost, which is a great innovation not only for robotics. However, it has some limitations as these cameras do not provide a dense depth map. The delivered depth images contain holes corresponding to the zones where the sensor has problems, whether due to the material of the objects (reflection, transparency, light absorption, *etc.*) or their position (out of range, with occlusions, *etc.*). The depth map is only valid for objects that are in the range of 1–3 m in order to reduce the effect of noise and low resolution [59]. In addition to this, as it is based on an IR projector with an IR camera, and as the sun emits in the IR spectrum, sunlight negatively affects it.

Figure 10. Projected pattern in Light coding.

2.5. Laser Triangulation

In laser triangulation, the point, the camera and the laser emitter form a triangle (Figure 11). The distance between the camera and the laser emitter is known, and because of the angle of the laser emitter corner is also known, the angle of the camera corner can be determined by looking at the location of the laser dot in the camera's field of view. These three pieces of information fully determine the shape and the size of the triangle and give the location of the laser dot corner of the triangle, which is in fact the 3D point. The accuracy depends on the resolution of the CCD sensor, the quality of the lenses, the point size (spot), the laser beam quality, the surface state of the piece and other optical factors [60].

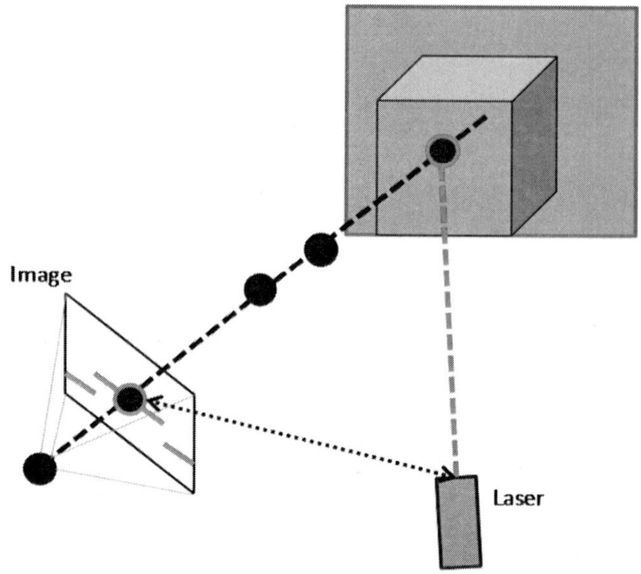

Figure 11. Laser triangulation.

Laser non-contact techniques have changed considerably in recent years. Although initially sensors gave isolated points, the technology has quickly spread to 2D sensors, measuring across a dotted line and collecting multiple points in a single frame. If the piece is moving under the sensor (or *vice versa*), the 3D model of the surface can be generated. This means that, unlike the previously presented techniques where a 3D point cloud can be obtained with a single capture, in this case it is necessary to move the piece or the sensor. In other words, it is necessary to scan the piece. As a drawback, depending on the laser power, laser sensors can be dangerous for people. They are not eye-safe.

3. ROBOT GUIDANCE IN INDUSTRIAL ENVIRONMENTS

Robot guidance using machine vision techniques is a challenging problem as it consists on providing eyes to a machine which is able to move with high repeatability but low accuracy [18] in complex industrial environments with other moving objects or even human workers. This modern technology opens up wholly new possibilities although it also creates new and fairly complex challenges in safety design [61]. Textureless surfaces, lighting conditions, occlusions, undetermined or moving objects, among others, are critical issues which the vision system has to deal with. As shown, 3D point cloud acquisition for robot pose estimation, robot guidance or any other purpose can be achieved by applying many different sensors and techniques. Which one is best suited for each particular application really depends on the needs and requirements [57]. The spatial coordinates of a large number of points can be obtained almost instantaneously or in a few seconds, but they require further treatment. Point clouds must be processed using specific algorithms to identify the geometric elements of the parts to be detected, measured or positioned. Subsequently filtering operations, structuring or interactive segmentation of the point clouds must be carried out [62]. The quality and the robustness of the final application are determined by both processes: the point cloud acquisition and the subsequent treatment.

In this section several approaches of robot guidance using different machine vision techniques are reviewed. As it will be shown, applications are oriented to scene-related tasks for environment reconstruction, including people detection, or to object-related tasks for robot pose estimation and object reconstruction for manipulation or inspection. Figure 12 provides the most common terms of robots that will be mentioned throughout the text.

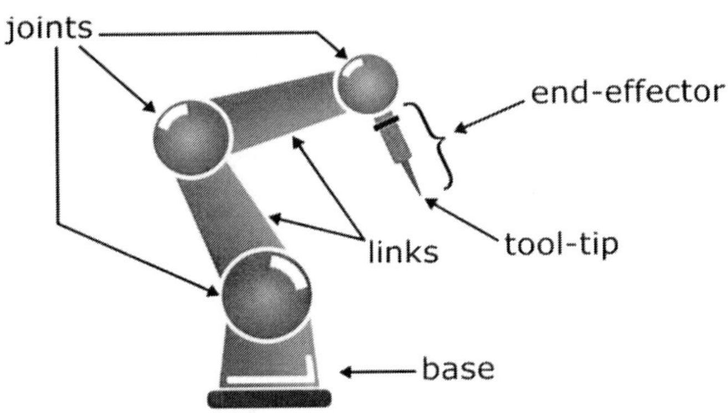

Figure 12. Robot terms.

3.1. Stereo Vision and Photogrammetry

Industrial photogrammetry covers different practical challenges in terms of specified accuracy, measurement speed, automation, process integration, cost-performance ratio, sensor integration and analysis. Main solutions are object-related in the fields of the measurement of discrete points, deformations and motions, 6 DOF (degrees of freedom) parameters, contours and surfaces [63]. Off-line photogrammetry systems can be found at automotive manufacturing (for car body deformation measurement, control of supplier parts, adjustment of tooling and rigs, *etc.*), the aerospace industry (for measurement and adjustment of mounting rigs, alignment between parts, *etc.*), wind energy systems (for deformation measurements and production control), and engineering and construction (for measurement of water dams, tanks, plant facilities, *etc.*). They offer high precise and accurate measurements (the absolute accuracy of length measurements is generally about 0.05 mm for a 2 m object [64]). On the other hand, on-line systems provide 3D information to control a connected process. Some examples include tactile probing (where a hand-held probing device is tracked in 3D space in order to provide the coordinates of the probing tip), robot calibration (where the robot tool center point is observed in order to determine its spatial trajectory), and sensor navigation (where a measurement device, such as a laser profile sensor, is tracked in 6 DOF in order to reconstruct the captured profiles). The accuracy of on-line systems is in the order of 0.2–0.5 mm over a range of 2 m [65], usually less than that of off-line systems. Nowadays, industrial photogrammetric systems are mostly used for off-line measurement of static 3D points in space. Moving from off-line to on-line systems is mainly a matter of speeding up image processing. Image acquisition, transfer, target identification and measurement usually take by far the largest part of the processing time.

There are several approaches in the literature to determine the position and orientation of a robot's end-effector with high accuracy during arbitrary robot motions based on combined and pure photogrammetric solutions. Laser tracking systems combine laser interferometry and photogrammetry [66,67]. As Figure 13 shows, the end-effector of the robot (the probe) is equipped with a number of LED reference targets suitable for camera imaging, as well as a retro-reflector suitable for laser tracking, all with calibrated local coordinates. The 6-DOF pose of the probe is measured by space resection through a camera that is integrated into the laser tracker. Distance information is provided by interferometric laser ranging while the camera measures angular information of the probe [68]. Laser trackers are also used to identify the geometric and dynamic parameters of the robot in order to improve the accuracy of the model, increasing thus the accuracy of the robot [69]. Qu [70] presents a laser tracker application to reduce the relative pose error of the robot of an aircraft assembly drilling process to less than 0.2 mm.

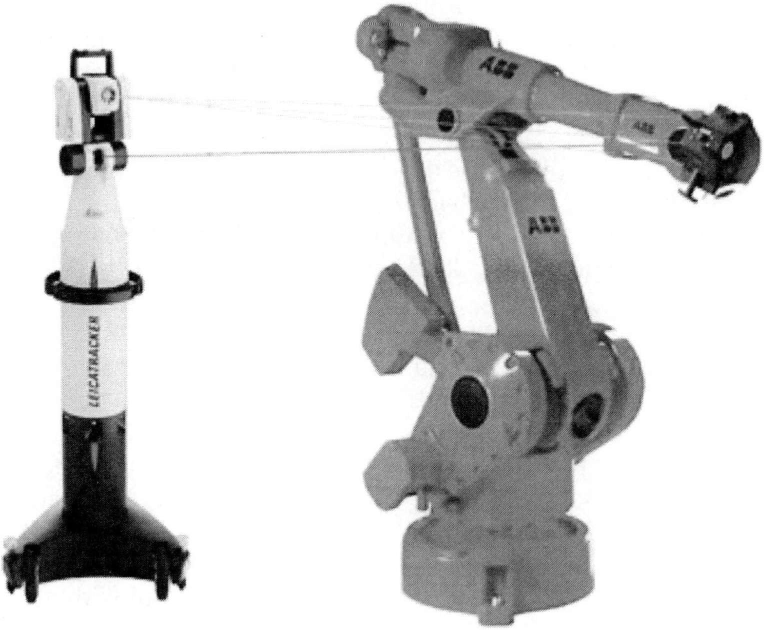

Figure 13. Laser tracker.

In pure photogrammetric solutions, there are three different approaches [18]: (1) Forward intersection, where two or more fixed cameras that are observing target points which are mounted on the end-effector (moving targets); (2) Resection, where alternatively one or more cameras can be mounted on the end-effector observing fixed targets; and (3) Bundle adjustment, which is a combination of both. At a first sight, resection arrangement may seem to be inferior compared to the forward intersection method, because a pose measurement for all possible robot poses requires targets to be placed around the entire workspace. However, most handling tasks require a robot to be accurate only in certain locations, thus the accuracy is not needed in the entire workspace.

Main documented applications are for 6-DOF measurements, robot calibration, object tracking, and robot navigation. Several simultaneously operating solid-state cameras and photogrammetric hardware and software for robot guidance tasks are used in [71]. In this work two different applications were chosen to demonstrate the accuracy, flexibility and speed of the photogrammetric system: 3D object positioning is utilized in the measurement of car body points for accurate seam-sealing robot operation, and a robotized propeller grinding cell uses profile and thickness measuring data to control the grinding process. Hefele [18] shows an off-line photogrammetric robot calibration using a high resolution camera and targets mounted to the robot end-effector. The positioning accuracy of the robot is better than 3 mm in the experiments. First results towards an on-line photogrammetric robot tracking system are also presented in [18], reducing image processing and using intelligent cameras. The bundle adjustment indicates target coordinate RMS values of 0.06 mm in depth. Some improvements were added later in [72].

When accuracy requirements are moderate, [19] presents a digital photogrammetric system for industrial robot calibration tasks. Standard deviations of 0.05–0.25 mm in the three coordinate directions could be obtained over a robot work range of $1.7 \times 1.5 \times 1.0$ m^3. In this sense, [20] describes the development of a photogrammetric 6-DOF measurement system mounted on the end-effector of an industrial robot. The functionality of the system has been demonstrated for drilling and assembly operations showing that the scheme is feasible and assesses the capability of such a system to operate within realistic tolerances. The photogrammetric system shown in Figure 14 is proposed in [73] to improve the pose accuracy of industrial robots. Experimental results show that the position error of the robot manipulator is less than 1 mm after being calibrated by the photogrammetric system. Amdal [74] gives a description of an on-line system designed for close range applications. The system has the ability to perform 3D point measurements with one single camera in combination with a measurement tool equipped with photogrammetric targets, which are precalibrated in the local tool coordinate system. Accuracy results obtained from simulation studies and measurement tests are reported. For a camera-to-object distance of 2.5 m, the accuracy was found to be 0.01 mm.

Consequently, photogrammetry is certainly able to determine robot pose accurately [75] although these measurements require special and expensive equipment and processing huge amounts of image data. Because of these reasons, nowadays photogrammetry is mainly limited for calibration, which is performed only once during the setup of the robot at the factory, instead of a continuous tracking of the pose. Recent and future developments are concentrated on higher dynamic applications, integration of systems into production chains, multi-sensor solutions and lower costs.

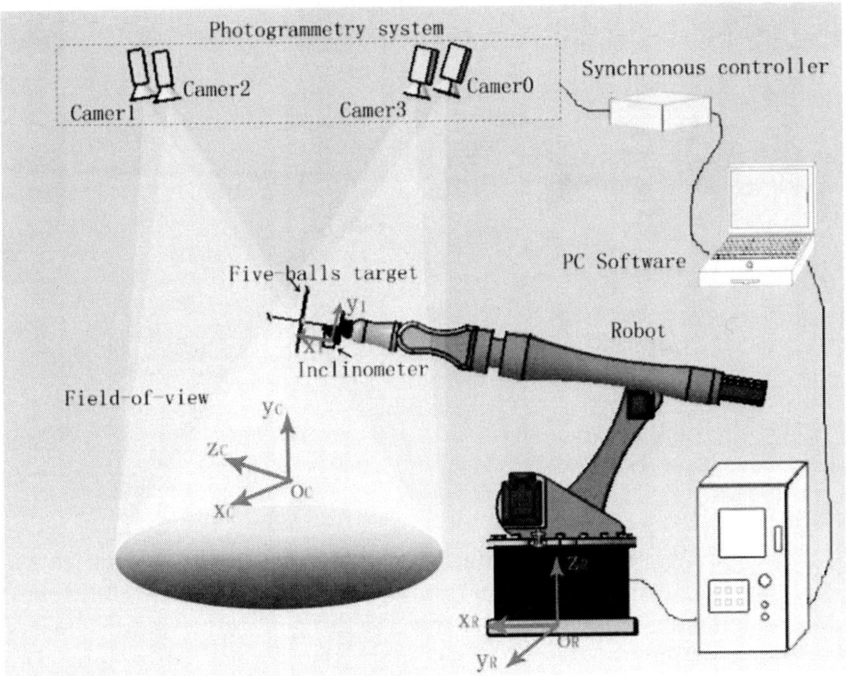

Figure 14. Multiple-sensor combination measuring system [73].

Projected texture stereo vision technique is mainly used in bin picking applications [76,77]. The task of picking random and unsorted objects from a container or a storage bin presents a number of different challenges. A fast and reliable identification of one or several objects is required in terms of shape, size, position and alignment (Figure 15). This information must be obtained and passed on to the robot controller, which is essential to the *ad hoc* generation of collision-free robot paths. This is the starting point for the use of robots in handling processes.

Figure 15. Bin picking [77].

Sturm [78] presents an approach for detecting, tracking, and learning 3D articulation models for doors and drawers using projected texture stereo vision system. The robot can use the generative models learned for the articulated objects to estimate their mechanism type, their current configuration, and to predict their opening trajectory.

3.2. Time of Flight

ToF sensors have several advantages for the development of robotic applications as they are quite compact and lightweight, and allow real-time 3D acquisition with high frame rate. They are used in scene-related tasks, generally involving mobile robots and large displacements, and in object-related tasks, involving instead robotic arms or humanoid-like robots and small depths. However, they involve some challenges as the quality of raw data is quite noisy. To overcome this limitation, some authors apply calibration methods to rectify the depth images in order to obtain better results. Others complement ToF camera information with color cameras to create a 3D point cloud with real features, with grayscale cameras for redundant stereo or with laser scanners.

In the field of scene-related task, ToF camera capabilities in terms of basic obstacle avoidance and local path-planning are evaluated in [79] and compared to the performance of a standard laser scanner. May [80] presents a new approach for on-line adaptation of different camera parameters to environment dynamics. These adaptations enable the usage reliably in real world (changing) environments and for different robotic specific tasks. In [81,82] it is proposed the use of surface normals to improve 3D maps for badly conditioned plane detection. Others, such as [83,84], cope with ToF noisy point clouds using the Iterative Closest Point algorithm to find the relation between two point clouds. Arbeiter [85] performed an environment reconstruction for a mobile robot combining a ToF camera with two color camera, which is the input for a modified fast-SLAM algorithm. This algorithm is capable of rendering environment maps. Kuhnert and Netramai [86,87] combined a ToF sensor and a stereo system for environment reconstruction.

For object-related tasks, ToF cameras have also been successfully used for object and surface reconstruction, where the range of distances is smaller. Depending on the field of view of the camera, multiple 3D point clouds need to be acquired and combined. In fact, the most common setup usually includes a ToF camera mounted on the end-effector of a robotic arm to do the captures. Point cloud registration is more critical in object modeling than in scene modeling. Even if the hand-eye system is precisely calibrated, the displacement given by the robot is usually not enough and the transformation between different point clouds has to be calculated. Some examples of object modeling and object reconstruction can be found in [88,89,90,91]. For object manipulation, unknown and unsorted objects have to be identified or categorized in order to be grasped. Generally, it is not necessary to completely reconstruct the object. Some examples are described in [92,93,94].

Finally, for human-machine interaction, ToF does not require any special background and it is a non-invasive technique, contrary to the widely extended use of special gloves, artificial marks, special attached devices, *etc.* Thus, it is commonly used in human activity recognition than other vision techniques as [95] points out. This work reviews the state of the art in the field of ToF cameras, their advantages, their limitations, and their main applications for scene-related tasks, object-related tasks, and tasks involving humans.

3.3. Structured Light

Positioning a robot with stereo vision depends on features visible from several points of view. Structured light provides artificial visual features independent of the scene, easing considerably the correspondence problem. The main inconvenience for robot guidance is the size of the sensors as they include a projector, which makes them difficult to be attached to the end-effector of a robot. Figure 16 presents a solution where only one camera is attached to the end-effector (eye-in-hand) and a static projector is installed illuminating the working pieces [96].

Figure 16. Robot positioning using structured light [96].

The achieved accuracy is 3 mm, which is enough for this concrete application. This setup also solves a problem related to the breaking of the hot lamp filament of the project due to vibrations if it is moved around. On the other side, an eye-in-hand setup avoids occlusions while it can perceive more details during robot approaching to the scene. The selection of the adequate pattern is also the main focus of most authors.

Pagès [54] proposed a coded structured light approach as a reliable and fast way to solve the correspondence problem in another eye-in-hand solution with the projector aside the robot manipulator. In this case, a coded light pattern is projected providing robust visual features independently of the object appearance for robot positioning. Experiments have demonstrated that positioning the robot with respect to planar object provides good results even in presence of occlusions. Results when using non-planar objects show that the camera motion is noisier, slower and less monotonic.

Le Moigne [97] describes some of the important operational considerations and image processing tasks required to utilize a non-scanning structured-light range sensor in path planning for robot mobility. Particular emphasis is placed on issues related to operating in ambient lighting, smoothing of range texture, grid pattern selection, albedo normalization, grid extraction, and coarse registration of images to the projected grid. The created range map can be converted to a topography map for planning short-range paths through the environment while avoiding obstacles.

The new approach of structured blue light is not very extended yet in industrial robotic applications, but it is already being used for part identification and localization in [11], where a mobile and collaborative robot has been developed for aerospace manufacturing industries. Once the robot has reached the working station, it takes the camera, acquires images to get a point cloud (Figure 17) and compares it with a CAD databank, in order to identify the part and its pose. The robot also corrects its own pose to start with the assigned task (apply sealant or do a quality inspection). In this case, the point cloud is highly accurate. However, as the sensor working distance is too short, the robot has to be very close to the part and the scanned area is small. For small parts this is not a problem, but for long ones it requires an accurate CAD matching algorithm in order to avoid deviations in the robot trajectory.

3.4. Light Coding

Nowadays this technique is commonly used in videogames for people tracking. Besides, it is been introduced in more and more industrial applications including robotics although an extra effort is necessary to achieve accuracy for robot pose estimation, and safety requirements for workspace monitoring in human-robot collaboration. It offers visual and depth data at a significantly low cost and, while it is a great innovation for robotics, it has some limitations. Algorithms use depth information for object recognition, but as the sensor produces a noisy point cloud, it is required to improve such information. One possible option is the combination of light coding sensors with HD cameras to obtain high resolution dense point cloud which can be used for robot guidance or pose correction. Experimental results reported in [98] show that this approach can significantly enhance the resolution of the point cloud on both indoor and outdoor scenes. The point cloud is at least ten times denser than the initial one only with the light coding sensor.

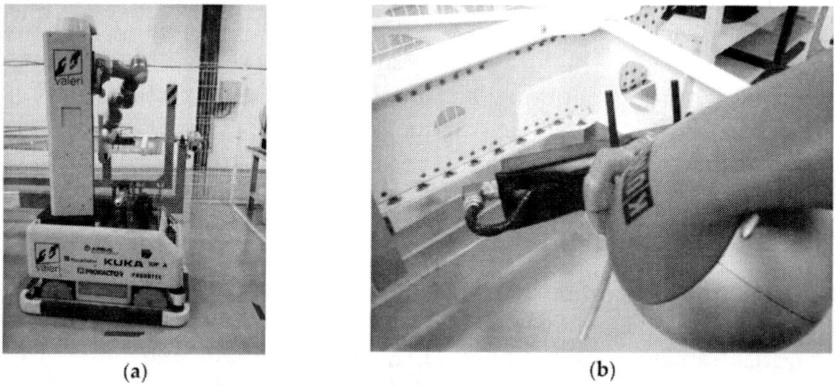

Figure 17. Mobile robot using a blue light sensor for part localization. (**a**) Mobile robot; (**b**) Sensor operating.

To significantly improve the robustness of people detection on mobile robots, light coding cameras have been combined with thermal sensors and mounted on the top of a mobile platform in [99], since humans have a distinctive thermal profile compared to non-living objects. This approach also combines classifiers created using supervised learning. Experimental results of this work have shown that the false positive rate (exclusively achieved using only the light coding sensor) is drastically reduced. As a drawback, some phantom detections near heat sources, such as industrial machines or radiators, may appear. Light coding sensors are also combined with safety certificated 3D zone monitoring cameras in [61]. Wang [100] combined virtual 3D models of robots with the information from the sensor (images of operators) for monitoring and collision detection (Figure 18). 3D models, which are used to represent a structured shop-floor environment and linked to real motion sensors, are driven to mimic the behavior of the real environment. Light coding sensors add unstructured foreign objects, including mobile operators, which are not present in the 3D models.

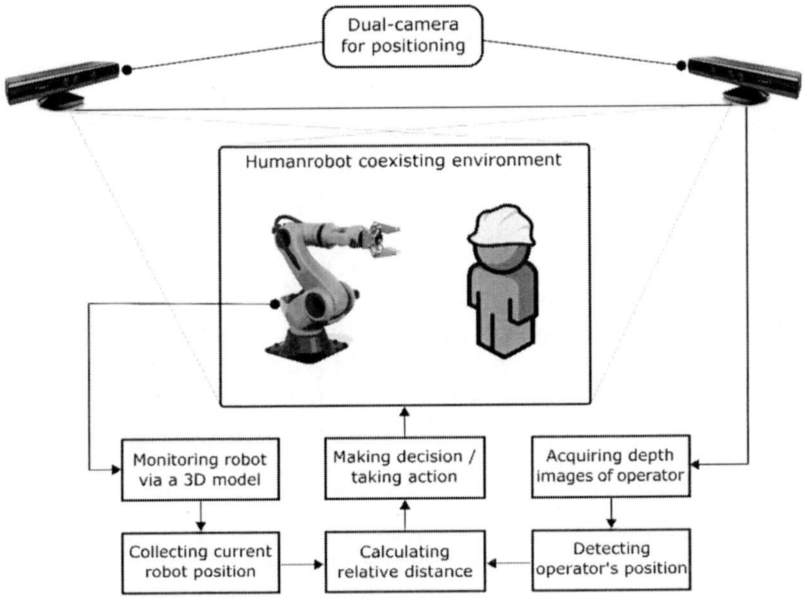

Figure 18. Combining 3D models of robots with information from sensors [100].

One common problem of light coding sensors is that they do not provide a dense depth map. The delivered depth images contain holes corresponding to the zones where the sensor has problems, whether due to the material of the objects (reflection, transparency, light absorption) or their position (out of range, with occlusions).

3.5. Laser Triangulation

This technique has been used in bin picking applications to pick up pieces, where it is necessary to recognize the piece and its pose. As it is necessary to scan the piece for 3D reconstruction, pieces are over a conveyor belt in [101] with a static camera and a static laser or camera and laser are integrated in robot tool for reconstruction and measurement as in [102]. Experimental evaluations of different line extraction algorithms on laser scans for mobile robots in indoor environments are presented in [103,104]. The comparison is carried out in terms of complexity, correctness and precision.

An implementation of a flexible, sensory-controlled robotic welding system is presented in [105]. Conventional, non-adaptive, robot welding systems can only be used when the workpieces are highly repeatable and well fixtured. A steerable cone of laser light and machine vision are used for sensing of the weld joint location and determining the detailed 3D weld joint surface geometry ahead of the welding torch. Robust vision-processing schemes for the detection and recognition of laser stripe features in noisy images are developed and implemented using a pipelined processing architecture. Approaches are proposed and implemented to incorporate the visually determined offsets in robot path planning and to control the welding process parameters. Another example of weld tracking is presented in [106]. This work offers a low-cost system that guarantees satisfactory tracking results even when the welding gap geometry varies strongly.

In [107] a sensor is created by coupling a camera and a laser stripe-. Positioning robotics tasks can be performed with good results, robustness and stability. Nevertheless, there are some constraints such as some restrictions in the laser stripe projection on to the scene. It is necessary to choose the most favorable location of the laser stripe during the calibration to achieve a robotics task under conditions of optimum stability. Pears [108] described a wide field of view range sensor for short range mobile robots maneuvers with an accuracy of 0.15% at l m, 1.3% at 2 m, and 3% at 2.5 m, and an average projected power of 0.9 mW, which is eye-safe. Generally, in robotics applications, it is necessary to take into account safety issues as human workers may be present. Depending on the laser power the sensor can result inappropriate for humans because of safety reasons.

Other works about robot navigation using laser scanners are described in [109,110,111]. In [109] the problems of self-localization of a mobile robot and map building in an *a priori* unknown indoor environment are addressed. In [110] a method for tracking the pose of a mobile robot using a laser scanner is presented. A new scheme for map building is proposed in [111]. This work describes localization techniques for a mobile robot equipped with a laser rangefinder using line segments as the basic element to build the map. According to the results, line segments provide considerable geometric information about the scene and can be used for accurate and fast localization.

4. DISCUSSION

Depending on the final goal of the application and the type of robot, different considerations and factors need to be taken into account in order to select the most adequate vision technique:

- *Accuracy* of point cloud alignment and *resolution*. They are mainly determined by hardware (sensor) and software (extraction, registration, segmentation, comparison, *etc.*), and in consistence to the size of the object and the application purpose.

- *Range of the sensor*. The working distance will be determined by the accessibility of robot, size of sensor and environment configurations

- *Light weight*. If the sensor is onboard or mounted in the end-effector, the robot has limited max load weight to ensure its full dynamics.

- *Safety issues*. The robot might work closely with human workers, thus sensors should avoid dangerous high-power laser to minimize any risk of accidents.

- *Processing time*. Processing time might be crucial to determine if a system is suitable for a certain application, especially regarding moving robots with safety constraints, *i.e.*, availability to detect and avoid collisions with humans or obstacles. Some techniques require that object and camera remain static for the capture, thus they are not applicable for moving scenarios.

- *Scanning environment*. Lighting conditions, vibrations, camera movements, *etc.* can disturb the quality of the 3D point cloud in some techniques. It is necessary to avoid these interferences.

- *Hardware and software integration* with other systems. The camera will be automatically controlled by the own robot central control unit or by an external source. *Ad hoc* developments are oriented towards the integration and, nowadays, most of current commercial vision systems are also prepared to be connected to a robot and controlled by external software using SDKs or libraries.

- *Budget*. Outside of technical issues, for a real implementation, budget should also be considered. A trade-off between cost and performance is necessary as most of the previous characteristics can be achieved or improved incrementing the invested amount of money.

A comparison of vision techniques is presented in Table 2 in terms of accuracy, range, weight, safety, processing time, and scanning environmental influences (Env. influences). Some quantitative information is provided according to the referenced specific application. Stereo vision, structured light, and laser triangulation can provide acceptable accuracy under certain conditions for most applications. Except structured white light, active vision techniques need to be closer to the object as they have a short working distance. Nowadays, there are light weight commercial sensors available to be mounted on a robot. Structured white light sensors are in general the biggest. All techniques are not dangerous for people, with the exception of some high power lasers that are not eye-safe. In terms of processing time, photogrammetry requires processing a large amount of images, and structured light techniques require that object and camera remain static during the acquisition process. Time of flight and structured blue LED light are not influenced by environmental lighting conditions.

Table 3 compares advantages and disadvantages of the reviewed techniques for robot guidance. Photogrammetry is mainly used in static applications because of its accuracy, but physical marks, such as stickers or laser points, are necessary (marker-based) and it is highly influenced by brightness and lights in industrial environments. Marks can be avoided using feature trackers (markerless), but the density of the point cloud would be low if surfaces are textureless. In fact, low-textured or textureless surfaces are also an inconvenience for stereo vision techniques with conventional 2D cameras and it is necessary to project a high contrast light creating an artificial texture to highlight points, features, *etc.* (projected texture stereo vision). Other 3D active vision techniques, such as light coding and time of flight, have low theoretical accuracy and are not valid for certain applications where the point cloud is compared with a CAD model for accurate part localization, because flat surfaces are represented with rather significant curvature. They can be used for part identification or for people and object tracking considering these accuracy issues. Laser techniques are commonly used in scanning applications where the capture is not a single snapshot, but can be dangerous for people as some laser classes (high power) are not eye-safe. Finally, structured light provides accuracy, although sometimes is influenced by ambient light and has problems to create the 3D model for surfaces of certain colors. Its main disadvantage is that most commercial sensors are quite big to be carried by a robot. Actually, research and development efforts are concentrated on miniaturizing sensors or on separating the projector and the sensor so that only one is onboard the robot. In this sense, the new evolution of this technique called structured blue LED light provides accuracy with a small sensor.

There are thousands of industrial applications but most of them are confidential for companies and are not documented or widely described in scientific papers, thus they could not be included in this survey. Table 4 summarizes the references of vision techniques for robotics reviewed in this work grouped by scene-related and object-related tasks. According to the survey, main stereo vision applications in robotics are in the field of object-related tasks for robot pose estimation and robot calibration as they may require marks, camera and object must remain static and an important amount of information needs to be processed. Time of flight, which does not require that object and camera remain static, is mainly used for environment and object reconstruction, navigation, obstacle avoidance and indeed people detection. In fact, the main application of light coding is people detection, although it is not certificated for industrial environments. Laser-based sensors are widely used especially for navigation, but also for object-related tasks.

Some other comparative reviews of machine vision techniques for robotic applications can be found in the literature. Wilson [27] reviews 3D vision techniques and solutions in a journal article with commercial purposes providing a list of applications and manufacturers. Sets of questions and advises are presented in [57] in order to help the reader to choose the right 3D vision technique for his/her project. Some of these questions are relative to the size and the surface of the target object, to the accuracy requirements, to the final destination of the obtained 3D data, or to the budget. This classification is quite similar to the one proposed by the authors of this work in Table 2.

Foix [95] focuses on ToF cameras, describing advantages, limitations and applications. It includes 68 references grouped in scene-related, object-related and human-related. Visual human-machine interaction is deeply studied as ToF cameras can be used for gesture recognition. Focusing on software, [113] reviews vision-based control algorithms for robot manipulators and [114] analyzes stereo matching algorithms used in robotics in terms of speed, accuracy, coverage, time consumption, and disparity range. Implementations of stereo matching algorithms in hardware for real-time applications are also discussed.

Table 2. Comparison of vision techniques in terms of accuracy, range, weight, safety, processing time, and environmental influences.

	Accuracy	Range	Weight	Safety	Processing Time	Environmental Influences
Stereo Vision and Photogrammetry	✓ (50 µm [64])	✓	✓	✓	X (image processing)	X (brightness)
Projected Texture Stereo Vision	✓ (0.1 mm [48])	X (0.25–3 m [48])	✓	✓	X (image processing)	X (brightness)
Time of Flight	X (10 mm [51])	X (0.8–8 m [16])	✓	✓	✓	✓
Structured White Light	✓ (0.127 mm [112])	✓	X (projector [96])	✓	X (remain static)	X (light, brightness)
Structured Blue LED Light	✓ (34 µm [57])	X (157–480 mm [57])	✓	✓	X (remain static)	✓
Light Coding	X (10 mm [58])	X (1–3 m [59])	✓	✓	✓	X (sun)
Laser Triangulation	✓	✓	✓	X (laser power)	✓	X (brightness)

Table 3. Advantages and disadvantages.

	Advantages	Disadvantages
Stereo Vision and Photogrammetry	Commonly used. Accuracy.	Influenced by environment. Physical marks are necessary. The density of the point cloud can be low. Object and camera must be static for the capture.
Projected Texture Stereo Vision	Physical marks are not required.	Influenced by environment. Object and camera must be static for the capture.
Time of Flight	Independent of ambient light. Not necessary that object and camera remain static for the capture.	Low theoretical accuracy.
Structured White Light	Accuracy.	Sometimes influenced by ambient light. Problems to create the 3D model for surfaces of certain colors. Expensive. Sensors can be quite large. Object and camera must be static for the capture.
Structured Blue LED Light	Accuracy. Small sensor.	Short working distance. Object and camera must be static for the capture. Expensive.
Light Coding	Inexpensive. Not necessary that object and camera remain static for the capture.	Low accuracy. Uncertified at industrial level.
Laser Triangulation	Commonly used. Inexpensive (depending on the laser, the accuracy).	Dangerous for people depending on laser power. Usually short working distance. Line scanner.

Table 4. Common applications in robotics.

	Scene-Related		Object-Related		
	People detection	Environment reconstruction / navigation	Object reconstruction / inspection	Bin picking / object manipulation	Robot pose / calibration
Stereo Vision and Photogrammetry			[74]		[18–20,67–73]
Projected Texture Stereo Vision				[76–78]	
Time of Flight	[95]	[79–87]	[88–91]	[92–94]	
Structured Light					[11,54,96]
Light Coding	[61,98–100]				
Laser Triangulation		[103–111]	[102]	[101]	[107]

Robots need flexibility and accuracy to carry out more complex and diverse tasks, such as collision avoidance with static and moving objects during navigation, collaborative work with humans, fine positioning, inspection, *etc.* In all the reviewed applications, each vision system has its single purpose. There has not been found one single vision system able to perform several tasks. Multiple vision systems are used (one for each individual purpose) instead of one single multi-tasking vision system. This is because requirements of each task are quite different and each technique has its scope and is more adequate than others.

5. CONCLUSIONS

In this survey, 3D vision solutions used in robotics have been organized, classified and reviewed. The purpose was to provide a compilation of the state of the art and the existing techniques so that future researchers and developers have a background information. Vision techniques for robot guidance have been analysed in terms of accuracy, range, weight, safety, processing time, and scanning environmental influences. Main advantages and main drawbacks have been also presented for each of them. Choosing which type of 3D vision system to use is highly dependent on the parts that need to be located or measured. While laser range finders using time of flight methods can be used to locate distant objects, stereo imaging systems may be better suited to imaging high-contrast objects. Where such objects are highly specular or textureless, it may be more useful to employ projected texture techniques. In addition to this, robot and industrial environments conditions also need to be considered. Each application and each type of robot need a specific vision solution. There is no universal vision technique to perform several tasks. Future woks may focus on multi-tasking or multi-purpose vision systems and their integration with other sensor types and systems.

Robots have become a core element of Industry 4.0 and flexibility can be incorporated to them by vision systems and other sensor technologies in order to achieve the requirements and functionalities of the new applications. New tasks are becoming more or more complex and it is necessary to improve the accuracy and to work collaborative with humans, which means making decisions in real-time and triggering actions. For these goals, visual feedback is the key issue, and this is in fact what vision systems provide to robots. Thus, 3D machine vision is the future for robotics. The idea of considering robot technology as an integral part of production is not new but nevertheless it is a challenge. Whether robots will be able to or should perform all the production steps in future is perhaps less a question of time than of money.

ACKNOWLEDGMENTS

The work was supported by European Union H2020 Programme under grant agreement No. 637107, SYMBIO-TIC.

AUTHOR CONTRIBUTIONS

All authors contributed extensively to the work presented in this paper and wrote the manuscript. Luis Pérez reviewed the state-of-the-art and wrote the initial version of the paper analyzing the vision techniques and their applications for robot guidance. Íñigo Rodríguez and Nuria Rodríguez participated with Luis in the analysis of the vision techniques. Rubén Usamentiaga and Daniel F. García provided suggestions and corrections during the preparation of the submitted paper and the review process.

CONFLICTS OF INTEREST

The authors declare no conflict of interest.

REFERENCES

1. Deane, P.M. The First Industrial Revolution; Cambridge University Press: Cambridge, UK, 1979.

2. Kanji, G.K. Total quality management: the second industrial revolution. Total Qual. Manag. Bus. Excell. 1990, 1, 3–12.

3. Rifkin, J. The third industrial revolution. Eng. Technol. 2008, 3, 26–27.

4. Kagermann, H.; Wahlster, W.; Helbig, J. Recommendations for Implementing the Strategic Initiative Industrie 4.0: Final Report of the Industrie 4.0 Working Group; Forschungsunion: Berlin, Germany, 2013.

5. Koeppe, R. New industrial robotics: human and robot collaboration for the factory. In Proceedings of the 2014 European Conference on Leading Enabling Technologies for Societal Challenges (LET'S 2014), Bologna, Italy, 29 September–1 October 2014.

6. European Commission. Factories of the Future in H2020. Available online: http://ec.europa.eu/research/industrial_technologies/factories-of-the-future_en.html (accessed on 5 October 2015).

7. European Factories of the Future Research Association. Factories of the Future: Multi Annual Roadmap for the Contractual PPP under Horizon 2020; Publications office of the European Union: Brussels, Belgium, 2013.

8. European Commission and Robotics. Available online: http://ec.europa.eu/programmes/horizon2020/en/h2020-section/robotics (accessed on 11 October 2015).

9. TAPAS Project. Available online: http://www.tapas-project.eu (accessed on 11 October 2015).

10. Bogh, S.; Schou, C.; Rühr, T.; Kogan, Y.; Dömel, A.; Brucke, M.; Eberst, C.; Tornese, R.; Sprunk, C.; Tipaldi, G.D.; Hennessy, T. Integration and assessment of multiple mobile manipulators in a real-world industrial production facility. In Proceedings of the 45th International Symposium on Robotics (ISR 2014), Munich, Germany, 2–4 June 2014; pp. 1–8.

11. VALERI Project. Available online: http://www.valeri-project.eu (accessed on 11 October 2015).

12. Zhou, K.; Ebenhofer, G.; Eitzinger, C.; Zimmermann, U.; Walter, C.; Saenz, J.; Pérez, L.; Fernández, M.A.; Navarro, J. Mobile manipulator is coming to aerospace manufacturing industry. In Proceedings of the 2014 IEEE International Symposium on Robotic and Sensors

Environments (ROSE 2014), Timisoara, Romania, 16–18 October 2014; pp. 94–99.

13. SYMBIO-TIC Project. Available online: http://www.symbio-tic.eu (accessed on 11 October 2015).

14. Labudzki, R.; Legutko, S. Applications of Machine Vision. Manuf. Ind. Eng. 2011, 2, 27–29.

15. Wöhler, C. 3D Computer Vision: Efficient Methods and Applications; Springer: Dortmund, Germany, 2009.

16. Alenyà, G.; Foix, S.; Torras, C. ToF cameras for active vision in robotics. Sens. Actuators A Phys. 2014, 218, 10–22.

17. Zhang, J.Y.; Zhao, C.; Zhang, D.W. Pose accuracy analysis of robot manipulators based on kinematics. Adv. Mater. Res.2011, 201, 1867–1872.

18. Hefele, J.; Brenner, C. Robot pose correction using photogrammetric tracking. In Proceedings of Intelligent Systems and Smart Manufacturing; International Society for Optics and Photonics, Boston, MA, USA, 12 February 2001; pp. 170–178.

19. Maas, H.G. Dynamic photogrammetric calibration of industrial robots. In Proceedings of Camera and System Calibration, San Diego, CA, USA, 27 July 1997.

20. Clarke, T.; Wang, X. The control of a robot end-effector using photogrammetry. Int. Arch. Photogramm. Remote Sens.2000, 33, 137–142.

21. Salvi, J.; Armangué, X.; Batlle, J. A comparative review of camera calibrating methods with accuracy evaluation.Pattern Recognit. 2002, 35, 1617–1635.

22. Faugeras, O. Three-dimensional Computer Vision: A Geometric Viewpoint; MIT Press: Massachusetts, MA, USA, 1993.

23. Usamentiaga, R.; Molleda, J.; García, D.F. Structured-light sensor using two laser stripes for 3D reconstruction without vibrations. Sensors 2014, 14, 20041–20063.

24. Sturm, P.; Ramalingam, S.; Tardif, J.P.; Gasparini, S.; Barreto, J. Camera models and fundamental concepts used in geometric computer vision. Found. Trends Comput. Gr. Vis. 2011, 6, 1–183.

25. Hanning, T. High Precision Camera Calibration; Springer: Wiesbaden, Germany, 2011.

26. Usamentiaga, R.; Molleda, J.; García, D.F.; Pérez, L.; Vecino, G. Real-time line scan extraction from infrared images using the wedge method in industrial environments. J. Electron. Imaging 2010, 19, 043017.

27. Wilson, A. Choosing a 3D Vision System for Automated Robotics Applications. Vis. Syst. Des. 2014, 19. Available online: http://www.vision-systems.com/articles/print/volume-19/issue-11/features/choosing-a-3d-vision-system-for-automated-robotics-applications.html (accessed on 11 December 2014).

28. Ramos, B.; Santos, E. Comparative study of different digitization techniques and their accuracy. Comput.-Aided Des.2011, 43, 188–206.

29. Yilmaz, H.M.; Yakar, M.; Gilec, S.A.; Dulgerler, O.N. Importance of digital close-range photogrammetry in documentation of cultural heritage. J. Cult. Herit. 2007, 8, 428–433.

30. Werner, T.; Zisserman, A. New techniques for automated architecture reconstruction from photographs. In Proceedings of the Seventh European Conference on Computer Vision (ECCV 2002), Copenhagen, Denmark, 28–31 May 2002; pp. 541–555.

31. Werner, T.; Zisserman, A. Model selection for automated architectural reconstruction from multiple views. In Proceedings of the Thirteenth British Machine Vision Conference (BMVC 2002), Cardiff, UK, 2–5 September 2002; pp. 53–62.

32. Werner, T.; Schaffalitzky, F.; Zisserman, A. Automated architecture reconstruction from close-range photogrammetry.Int. Arch. Photogramm. Remote Sens. Spat. Inf. Sci. 2002, 34, 352–359.

33. Lane, S.N.; James, T.D.; Crowell, M.D. Application of digital photogrammetry to complex topography for geomorphological research. Photogramm. Rec. 2000, 16, 793–821.

34. Fonstad, M.A.; Dietrich, J.T.; Corville, B.C.; Jensen, J.L.; Carbonneau, P.E. Topographic structure from motion: A new development in photogrammetric measurement. Earth Surf. Process. Landf. 2013, 38, 421–430.

35. Dueholm, K.S.; Garde, A.A.; Pedersen, A.K. Preparation of accurate geological and structural maps, cross-sections or block diagrams from colour slides, using multi-model photogrammetry. J. Struct. Geol. 1993, 15, 933–937.

36. Eisenbeiss, H.; Lambers, K.; Sauerbier, M.; Li, Z. Photogrammetric documentation of an archaeological site using and autonomous model helicopter. Int. Arch. Photogramm. Remote Sens. Spat. Inf. Sci. 2005, 36, 238–243.

37. Granshaw, S.I. Bundle adjustment methods in engineering photogrammetry. Photogramm. Rec. 1980, 10, 181–207.

38. Fraser, C.S.; Brown, D.C. Industrial photogrammetry: New developments and recent applications. Photogramm. Rec.1986, 12, 197–217.

39. Goldan, M.; Kroon, R. As-built products modelling and reverse engineering in shipbuilding through combined digital photogrammetry and CAD/CAM technology. J. Sh. Prod. 2003, 19, 98–104.

40. Luhmann, T.; Robson, S.; Kyle, S.; Harley, I. Close Range Photogrammetry. Principles, techniques and applications; Whittles Publishing: Caithness, UK, 2006.

41. Canny, J. A computational approach to edge detection. IEEE Trans. Pattern Anal. Mach. Intell. 1986, 8, 679–698.

42. Harris, C.; Stephens, M. A combined corner and edge detector. In Proceedings of the Alvey vision Conference, Manchester, UK, 2 September 1998.

43. Lucas, B.D.; Kanade, T. An iterative image registration technique with an application to stereo vision. In Proceedings of the Seventh International Joint Conference on Artificial Intelligence (IJCAI 1981), Vancouver, BC, Canada, 24–28 August 1981; pp. 674–679.

44. Lowe, D.G. Distinctive image features from scale-invariant keypoints. Int. J. Comput. Vis. 2004, 60, 91–110.

45. Bay, H.; Ess, A.; Tuytelaars, T.; Van Gool, L. Speeded-up robust features (SURF). Comput. Vis. Image Underst. 2008, 110, 346–359.

46. Kimmel, R.; Zhang, C.; Bronstein, A.; Bronstein, M. Are MSER features really interesting? IEEE Trans. Pattern Anal. Mach. Intell. 2011, 33, 2316–2320.

47. IDS Whitepapers. Available online: https://en.ids-imaging.com/whitepaper.html (accessed on 30 July 2015).

48. Ensenso—Stereo 3D Cameras. Available online: http://www.ensenso.com (accessed on 13 December 2015).

49. Lim, J. Optimized projection pattern supplementing stereo systems. In Proceedings of the 2009 IEEE International Conference on Robotics and Automation (ICRA 2009), Kobe, Japan, 12–17 May 2009; pp. 2823–2829.

50. Konolige, K. Projected texture stereo. In Proceedings of the 2010 IEEE International Conference on Robotics and Automation (ICRA 2010), Anchorage, KY, USA, 3–7 May 2010; pp. 148–155.

51. Time of Flight-Heptagon. Available online: http://hptg.com/technology/time-of-flight/ (accessed on 13 December 2015).

52. Kolb, A.; Barth, E.; Koch, R.; Larsen, R. Time-of-flight sensors in computer graphics (state-of-the-art report). In Proceedings of Eurographics 2009-State of the Art Reports, Munich, Germany, 30 March–2 April 2009.

53. Chen, F.; Brown, G.; Song, M. Overview of three dimensional shape measurement using optical methods. Opt. Eng.2000, 39, 10–22.

54. Pagès, J.; Collewet, C.; Chaumette, F.; Salvi, J. A camera-projector system for robot positioning by visual servoing. In Proceedings of the 2006 Conference on Computer Vision and Pattern Recognition Workshop (CVPRW 2006), New York, NY, USA, 17–22 June 2006.

55. Salvi, J. An Approach to Coded Structured Light to Obtain Three Dimensional Information. Ph.D. Thesis, University of Gerona, Gerona, Spain, 1997.

56. Bernal, C.; Agustina, B.; Marín, M.M.; Camacho, A.M. Performance evaluation of optical scanner based on blue led structured light. Proc. Eng. 2013, 63, 591–598.

57. LMI Technologies. Available online: http://lmi3d.com/products (accessed on 30 October 2015).

58. Viager, M. Analysis of Kinect for Mobile Robots; Individual course report; Technical University of Denmark: Kongens Lyngby, Denmark, 2011.

59. Khoshelham, K.; Elberink, S.O. Accuracy and resolution of kinect depth data for indoor mapping applications. Sensors2012, 12, 1437–1454.

60. Mahmud, M.; Joannic, D.; Roy, M.; Isheil, A.; Fontaine, J.F. 3D part inspection path planning of a laser scanner with control on the uncertainty. Comput.-Aided Des. 2011, 43, 345–355.

61. Salmi, T.; Väätäinen, O.; Malm, T.; Montonen, J.; Marstio, I. Meeting new challenges and possibilities with modern robot safety technologies. In Enabling Manufacturing Competitiveness and Economic Sustainability; Springer International Publishing: Montreal, QC, Canada, 2014; pp. 183–188.

62. Point Cloud Library (PCL). Available online: http://pointclouds.org/documentation/tutorials/ (accessed on 29 July 2015).

63. Luhmann, T. Close range photogrammetry for industrial applications. ISPRS J. Photogramm. Remote Sens. 2010, 65, 558–569.

64. Rieke-Zapp, D.; Tecklenburg, W.; Peipe, J.; Hastedt, H.; Haig, C. Evaluation of the geometric stability and the accuracy potential of digital cameras-Comparing mechanical stabilisation versus parametrisation. ISPRS J. Photogramm. Remote Sens. 2009, 64, 248–258.

65. Broers, H.; Jansing, N. How precise is navigation for minimally invasive surgery? Int. Orthop. 2007, 31, 39–42.

66. Laser Tracker Systems—Leica Geosystems. Available online: http://www.leica-geosystems.com/en/Laser-Tracker-Systems_69045.htm (accessed on 2 November 2015).

67. Shirinzadeh, B.; Teoh, P.L.; Tian, Y.; Dalvand, M.M.; Zhong, Y.; Liaw, H.C. Laser interferometry-based guidance methodology for high precision positioning of mechanisms and robots. Robotics Computer-Integrated Manuf. 2010, 26, 74–82.

68. Vincze, M.; Prenninger, J.P.; Gander, H. A laser tracking system to measure position and orientation of robot end effectors under motion. Int. J. Robotics Res. 1994, 13, 305–314.

69. Dumas, C.; Caro, S.; Mehdi, C.; Garnier, S.; Furet, B. Joint stiffness identification of industrial serial robots. Robotica2012, 30, 649–659.

70. Qu, W.W.; Dong, H.Y.; Ke, Y.L. Pose accuracy compensation technology in robot-aided aircraft assembly drilling process. Acta Aeronaut. Astronaut. Sinica 2011, 32, 1951–1960.

71. Leikas, E. Robot guidance with a photogrammetric 3-D measuring system. Ind. Robot 1999, 26, 105–108.

72. Hefele, J.; Brenner, C. Real-time photogrammetric algorithms for robot calibration. Int. Archives Photogramm. Remote Sens. Spat. Inf. Sci. 2002, 34, 33–38.

73. Liu, B.; Zhang, F.; Qu, X. A method for improving the pose accuracy of a robot manipulator based on multi-sensor combined measurement and data fusion. Sensors. 2015, 15, 7933–7952.

74. Amdal, K. Single camera system for close range industrial photogrammetry. Int. Archives Photogramm. Remote Sens.1992, 29, 6–10.

75. Luhmann, T. Precision potential of photogrammetric 6DOF pose estimation with a single camera. ISPRS J. Photogramm. Remote Sens. 2009, 64, 275–284.

76. IDS Case Studies. Available online: https://en.ids-imaging.com/case-studies.html (accessed on 30 July 2015).

77. Carroll, J. 3D vision system assists in robotic bin picking. Vis. Syst. Des. 2014, 19. Available online: http://www.vision-systems.com/articles/2014/08/3d-vision-system-assists-in-robotic-bin-picking.html (accessed on 29 August 2014).

78. Sturm, J.; Konolige, K.; Stachniss, C.; Burgard, W. 3D pose estimation, tracking and model learning of articulated objects from dense depth video using projected texture stereo. In Proceedings of the 2010 RGB-D: Advanced Reasoning with Depth Cameras Workshop, Zaragoza, Spain, 27 June 2010.

79. Weingarten, J.W.; Gruener, G.; Siegwart, R. A state-of-the-art 3D sensor for robot navigation. In Proceedings of the 2004 IEEE/RSJ International Conference on Intelligent Robots and Systems (IROS 2004), Sendai, Japan, 28 September–2 October 2004; pp. 2155–2160.

80. May, S.; Werner, B.; Surmann, H.; Pervolz, K. 3D time-of-flight cameras for mobile robotics. In Proceedings of the 2006 IEEE/RSJ International Conference on Intelligent Robots and Systems (IROS 2006), Beijing, China, 9–15 October 2006; pp. 790–795.

81. May, S.; Droeschel, D.; Holz, D.; Wiesen, C.; Fuchs, S. 3D pose estimation and mapping with time-of-flight cameras. In Proceedings of the 2008 IEEE/RSJ International Conference on Intelligent Robots and Systems (IROS 2008), 3D Mapping Workshop, Nice, France, 22–26 September 2008.

82. Hedge, G.; Ye, C. Extraction of planar features from Swissranger SR-3000 range images by a clustering method using normalized cuts. In Proceedings of the 2009 IEEE/RSJ International Conference on Intelligent Robots and Systems (IROS 2009), St. Louis, MO, USA, 10–15 October 2009; pp. 4034–4039.

83. Ohno, K.; Nomura, T.; Tadokoro, S. Real-time robot trajectory estimation and 3D map construction using 3D camera. In Proceedings of the 2006 IEEE/RSJ International Conference on Intelligent Robots and Systems (IROS 2006), Beijing, China, 9–15 October 2006; pp. 5279–5285.

84. Stipes, J.A.; Cole, J.G.P.; Humphreys, J. 4D scan registration with the SR-3000 LIDAR. In Proceedings of the 2008 International Conference on Robotics and Automation (ICRA 2008), Pasadena, CA, USA, 19–23 May 2008; pp. 2988–2993.

85. Arbeiter, G.; Fischer, J.; Verl, A. 3-D-Environment reconstruction for mobile robots using fast-SLAM and feature extraction. In Proceedings of the Forty-first International Symposium on Robotics (ISR 2010), Munich, Germany, 7–9 June 2010.

86. Kuhnert, K.D.; Stommel, M. Fusion of stereo-camera and PMD-camera data for realtime suited precise 3D environment reconstruction. In Proceedings of the 2006 IEEE/RSJ International Conference on Intelligent Robots and Systems (IROS 2006), Beijing, China, 9–15 October 2006; pp. 4780–4785.

87. Netramai, C.; Oleksandr, M.; Joochim, C.; Roth, H. Motion estimation of a mobile robot using different types of 3D sensors. In Proceedings of the Fourth International Conference on Autonomic and Autonomous Systems (ICAS 2008), Gosier, France, 16–21 March 2008; pp. 148–153.

88. Dellen, B.; Alenyà, G.; Foix, S.; Torras, C. 3D object reconstruction from swissranger sensors data using a spring-mass model. In Proceedings of the Fourth International Conference on Computer Vision Theory Applications, Lisbon, Portugal, 5–8 February 2009; pp. 368–372.

89. Foix, S.; Alenyà, G.; Andrade-Cetto, J.; Torras, C. Object modelling using a ToF camera under an uncertainty reduction approach. In Proceedings of the 2010 IEEE International Conference on Robotics Automation (ICRA 2010), Anchorage, KY, USA, 3–7 May 2010; pp. 1306–1312.

90. Haddadin, S.; Suppa, M.; Fuchs, S.; Bodenmüller, T.; Albu-Schäffer, A.; Hirzinger, G. Towards the robotic co-worker.Robotics Res. 2011, 70, 261–282.

91. Fuchs, S.; May, S. Calibration and registration for precise surface reconstruction with time of flight cameras. Int. J. Intell. Syst. Technol. Appl. 2008, 5, 274–284.

92. Kuehnle, J.U.; Xue, Z.; Stotz, M.; Zoellner, J.M.; Verl, A.; Dillmann, R. Grasping in depth maps of time-of-flight cameras. In Proceedings of the 2008 IEEE International Workshop on Robotic and Sensors Environments (ROSE 2008), Ottawa, ON, Canada, 17–18 October 2008; pp. 132–137.

93. Saxena, A.; Wong, L.; Ng, A.Y. Learning grasp strategies with partial shape information. In Proceedings of the Twenty-third AAAI Conference on Artificial Intelligence, Chicago, IL, USA, 13–17 July 2008; pp. 1491–1494.

94. Maldonado, A.; Klank, U.; Beetz, M. Robotic grasping of unmodeled objects using time-of-flight range data and finger torque information. In Proceedings of the 2010 IEEE/RSJ International Conference on Intelligent Robots and Systems (IROS 2010), Taipei, Taiwan, 18–22 October 2010; pp. 2586–2591.

95. Foix, S.; Alenyà, G.; Torras, C. Exploitation of Time-of-Flight (ToF) Cameras; Technical Report; CSIC-UPC: Barcelona, Spain; December; 2010.

96. Claes, K.; Bruyninckx, H. Robot positioning using structured light patterns suitable for self calibration and 3D tracking. In Proceedings of the Thirteenth International Conference on Advanced Robotics, Daegu, Korea (South), 22–25 August 2007.

97. Le Moigne, J.J.; Waxman, A.M. Structured light patterns for robot mobility. J. Robotics Autom. 1988, 4, 541–548.

98. Patra, S.; Bhowmick, B.; Banerjee, S.; Kalra, P. High resolution point cloud generation from kinect and HD cameras using graph cut. In Proceedings of the 2012 International Joint Conference on Computer Vision, Imaging and Computer Graphics Theory and Applications (VISAPP 2012), Rome, Italy, 24–26 February 2012.

99. Susperregi, L.; Sierra, B.; Castrillón, M.; Lorenzo, J.; Martínez-Otzeta, J.M.; Lazkano, E. On the use of a low-cost thermal sensor to improve kinect people detection in a mobile robot. Sensors. 2013, 13, 14687–14713.

100. Wang, L.; Schmidt, B.; Nee, A.Y.C. Vision-guided active collision avoidance for human-robot collaborations. Manuf. Lett. 2013, 1, 5–8.

101. FlexSort Project. Available online: http://www.prodintec.es/prodintec/g_noticias?accion=detalleNoticia&id=159(accessed on 15 November 2015).

102. Brosed, F.J.; Santolaria, J.; Aguilar, J.J.; Guillomía, D. Laser triangulation sensor and six axes anthropomorphic robot manipulator modelling for the measurement of complex geometry products. Robot. Comput.-Integr. Manuf. 2012, 2, 660–671.

103. Nguyen, V.; Martinelli, A.; Tomatis, N.; Siegwart, R. A comparison of line extraction algorithms using 2D laser rangefinder for indoor

mobile robotics. In Proceedings of the 2005 IEEE/RSJ International Conference on Intelligent Robots and Systems (IROS 2005), Edmonton, AB, Canada, 2–6 August 2005; pp. 1929–1934.

104. Borges, G.A.; Aldon, M.J. line extraction in 2D range images for mobile robotics. J. Intell. Robotic Syst. 2004, 40, 267–297.

105. Agapakis, J.E.; Katz, J.M.; Friedman, J.M.; Epstein, G.N. Vision-aided robotic welding: An approach and a flexible implementation. Int. J. Robotics Res. 1990, 9, 17–34.

106. Fernández, A.; Acevedo, R.G.; Alvarez, E.A.; López, A.C.; García, D.F.; Usamentiaga, R.; Sánchez, J. Low-cost system for weld tracking based on artificial vision. IEEE Trans. Ind. Appl. 2011, 47, 1159–1167.

107. Khadraoui, D.; Motyl, G.; Martinet, P.; Gallice, J.; Chaumette, F. Visual servoing in robotics scheme using a camera/laser-stripe sensor. In Proceedings of the 1996 IEEE International Conference on Robotics and Automation (ICRA 1996), Minneapolis, MN, USA, 22–28 April 1996; pp. 743–750.

108. Pears, N.; Probert, P. An optical range sensor for mobile robot guidance. In Proceedings of the 1993 IEEE International Conference on Robotics and Automation (ICRA 1993), Atlanta, GA, USA, 2–6 May 1993; pp. 659–664.

109. Einsele, T. Real-time self-localization in unknown indoor environments using a panorama laser range finder. In Proceedings of the 1997 IEEE/RSJ International Conference on Intelligent Robots and Systems (IROS 1997), Grenoble, France, 11 September 1997; pp. 697–702.

110. Jensfelt, P.; Christensen, H. Laser based position acquisition and tracking in an indoor environment. In Proceedings of the 1998 International Symposium on Robotics and Automation (ISRA 1998), Leuven, Belgium, 20 May 1998.

111. Zhang, L.; Ghosh, B.K. Line segment based map building and localization using 2D laser rangefinder. In Proceedings of the 2000 IEEE International Conference on Robotics and Automation (ICRA 2000), San Francisco, CA, USA, 24–28 April 2000; pp. 2538–2543.

112. Gühring, J. Dense 3D surface acquisition by structured light using off-the-shelf components. In Proceedings of Videometrics and Optical Methods for 3D Shape Measurement, San Jose, CA, USA, 20 January 2001. SPIE: 2001.

113. Hashimoto, K. A Review on vision-based control of robot manipulators. Adv. Robotics 2003, 17, 969–991.

114. Lazaros, N.; Sirakoulis, G.C.; Gasteratos, A. review of stereo vision algorithms: from software to hardware. Int. J. Optomechatronics 2008, 2, 435–462.

2

A COMPUTER VISION APPROACH FOR AUTOMATED ANALYSIS AND CLASSIFICATION OF MICROSTRUCTURAL IMAGE DATA

Brian L. DeCost , Elizabeth A. Holm

HIGHLIGHTS

- A computer vision approach is used to compute microstructural fingerprints.
- Using these fingerprints, microstructures can be classified with >80% accuracy.
- Microstructural fingerprints form the basis for a visual image search engine.

ABSTRACT

The 'bag of visual features' image representation was applied to create generic microstructural signatures that can be used to automatically find relationships in large and diverse microstructural image data sets. Using this representation, a support vector machine (SVM) was trained to classify microstructures into one of seven groups with greater than 80% accuracy over 5-fold cross validation. In addition, the bag of visual features was implemented as the basis for a visual search engine that determines the best matches for a query image in a database of microstructures. These novel applications demonstrate the potential and the limitations of computer vision concepts in microstructural science.

KEYWORDS

Microstructure; Computer vision; Machine learning; Image data; Feature extraction

1. INTRODUCTION

Over the past century, materials scientists have made great progress in acquiring, analyzing, and comparing microstructural images [1], [2], [3], [4], [5], [6], [7], [8], [9], [10],[11], [12], [13], [14], [15], [16], [17], [18], [19], [20], [21] and [22]. Much of the effort has been directed toward deep understanding of particular materials systems or classes of microstructures—and rightly so. When the catalog of possible microstructural features is known or easily enumerated, digital image analysis techniques can take advantage of these well-defined features to segment, characterize, and compare microstructures with high precision. The current paradigm in microstructure analytics is a focus on extracting structure–properties relationships through image descriptors that explicitly describe the shape and appearance of the pertinent microstructural features. A classic example is the characterization of phase volume fraction in two-phase systems. Recent progress has focused on quantifying the phase morphology of fully segmented two-phase systems using higher order point statistics [2]; moment invariant shape descriptors [23] and [24]; and, more recently, sets of shape descriptors and shape correlation functions that are tailored to particular microstructure systems through a machine learning approach [22].

However, when the feature set or particular features of interest are not known *a priori* or when microstructures differ in significant or unknown ways, these methods become intractable, inaccurate, or fail completely. For example, image segmentation is the process of assigning each pixel a label designating the microstructural feature to which it belongs (e.g. grain or phase membership). When the catalog of features is not known, the segmentation scheme may not be able to differentiate between a void, a precipitate, and a polishing scratch, for example. Because of this, the choice of an optimal segmentation scheme is highly contingent upon prior knowledge of the material system being analyzed, and for many materials systems no adequate segmentation scheme is known. This limits general applicability of microstructure analysis techniques that operate on segmented images. Likewise, although n-point correlation functions are theoretically able to exactly represent a microstructure, in practice the computational cost increases exponentially with each additional pixel state; performing even 2-point correlation analysis on images with 256 grayscale values is prohibitive. Therefore, these methods are typically applied only to a pre-selected set of micrographs, chosen by a human expert[2], [3], [6], [25], [26] and [22].

In contrast, our goal is to develop a new general method to find useful characteristics and relationships within and between micrographs without any assumptions about what features may be present. Research in the field of computer vision, particularly in image texture recognition applications, has laid the groundwork for this approach. Image texture recognition refers to the task of quantifying the spatial distribution of image intensity in order to identify distinct regions [27]. Some applications include automatic segmentation of satellite imagery [28], automatic differentiation between macroscopic surfaces of various materials (such as wood, sandpaper, and cotton) [29], and diagnostic analysis in medical imaging [30]. Commonly used image texture features include Gabor filter banks[31], wavelet transforms [32], characteristic image patches [33], and local image descriptors [34]. An approach based on these well-established computer vision methods can capitalize on the explosion in digital microstructure data over the past two decades to survey the breadth of available microstructures efficiently and without significant human intervention [35], [36], [37], [38], [39] and [40].

This model of aggregating and systematizing large, diverse data sets is the basis for data science efforts in a variety of fields [41], [42], [43] and [44]. We are inspired to apply these concepts to microstructural image data by the Never Ending Image Learner (NEIL), which is a computer program that has been analyzing images and text on the web in an attempt to learn visual concepts and common sense relationships between them in a semi-unsupervised manner [45]. Examples of such relationships include "Sparrow is a kind of/looks similar to Bird" or "Horse can be found in Pasture". The creators of NEIL describe their approach as a form of 'macro-vision': extracting statistical patterns and relationships from large collections of images. This is in contrast to 'micro-vision', the more traditional computer vision task of extracting information from images on an individual basis. We envision a similar set of tools to enable general studies of the concept of microstructure, within and across materials systems, in contrast to the traditional materials science sense of studying the microstructural features of particular materials systems.

Our primary contribution in this work is to apply established computer vision methods to a diverse collection of microstructure data to develop quantitative microstructure descriptors and methods for defining objective classes of microstructures. The resulting microstructure descriptors can be computed in real-time, and can capture the meaningful details and defining characteristics of microstructural images without explicit fine-tuning from human experts. This constitutes a novel paradigm for microstructure analytics, which complements the current research emphasis on quantitative characterization and design of particular microstructural systems. We hypothesize that this approach to microstructure data will be flexible enough to span a diverse set of materials systems and quantitatively robust enough to enable automatic search and accurate classification of large collections of microstructural image data.

2. MICROSTRUCTURE REPRESENTATION

In this exploratory study, we apply the bag of visual features image representation commonly used in the object and scene recognition literature [34], [46] and [47]. This approach is inspired by the bag of words representation for document classification, which models a class of documents as a probability distribution of word occurrences over the set of words in a vocabulary (the English language, for example) [48] and [49]. Likewise, the bag of visual features representation models a class of images as a probability distribution over a set of visually distinctive features, or 'visual words'. This image representation can be quickly computed for arbitrary and unsegmented images, yielding a quantitative microstructure representation that requires no *a priori* knowledge of which microstructural features are the most relevant for characterization. The resulting general microstructural representation is well suited for use with a variety of machine learning approaches.

The typical bag of visual features pipeline is split into stages: detection and characterization of local image features [50], [51] and [52], extraction of a visual dictionary (typically through cluster analysis on a subset of detected features), and construction of the bag of visual features representations [46] and [47], which can be further analyzed using a variety of machine learning approaches. The fast-moving field of computer vision offers a wide array of techniques for accomplishing each step in this pipeline, and in practice the performance of any given technique may depend heavily on the application domain. At this early stage of our inquiry, we have chosen a set of techniques with a proven track record of good performance in a variety of applications, keeping in mind that good general microstructure descriptors should be robust against affine image transformations such as changes in scale and orientation. Due to space constraints, we do not attempt to give a comprehensive treatment of the specific computer vision and machine learning techniques that we make use of, which are extensively detailed in the literature.[1]

2.1. Detect keypoint features

To localize distinctive microstructural features that will be useful for characterization, we employ the commonly used Harris-Laplace and Difference of Gaussian (DoG) interest point (or keypoint) operators. Both of these interest point operators detect a sparse set of image regions that contain complex image gradient structure. We used VLFeat, a popular open source computer vision library, to compute these interest point operators [54]. The DoG operator localizes blob-like interest points by approximating the image Laplacian at multiple scales using the difference between two Gaussian-smoothed versions of the same image; the scale is set by the variance of the two Gaussians [51]. The Harris-Laplace operator uses the Harris cornerness metric (a combination of determinant and trace of the image intensity Hessian matrix) to detect corner-like interest points, and determines their characteristic scale using the extrema of the multiscale image Laplacian[50]. The resulting set of interest regions that exhibit large image intensity changes in multiple directions, with a characteristic scale that approximately matches the scale of the local image structure [55]. These two interest point operators detect complementary sets of image features [55]. Fig. 1 illustrates the types of keypoints that are localized by these detectors in a pearlitic cast iron microstructure (micrograph 354 from [56]). The size of each circle is corresponds to the characteristic scale of the keypoint feature it represents. Here, the keypoints include large black graphite nodules, the edges of the nodules, pearlitic patches, and so on. These correspond well to the features a materials scientist would likely identify as characteristic of this structure. However, note that keypoint selection is performed on a strictly visual basis, and no physical meaning is construed from them.

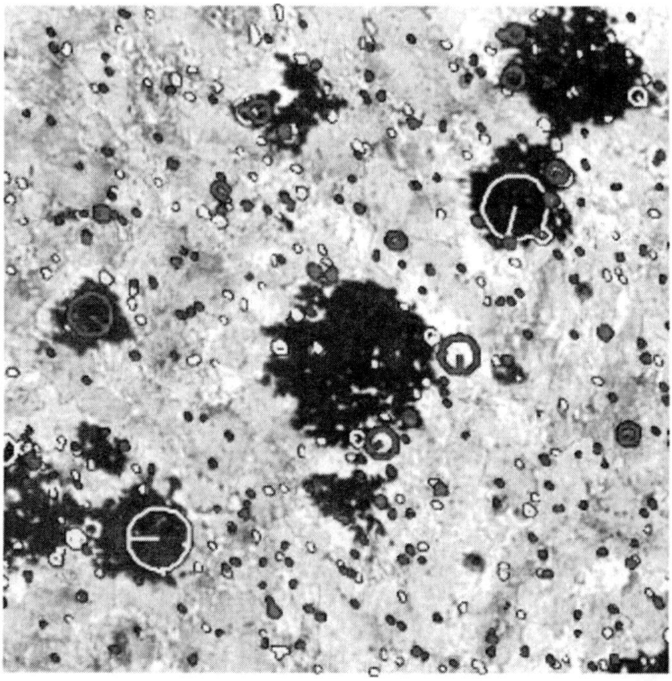

Figure. 1. Micrograph of pearlitic cast iron [56] showing keypoints (circles) randomly selected from the 4754 keypoints identified by the Harris-Laplace detector (yellow) and the 8510 keypoints identified by the Difference of Gaussians detector (red). The size of the circle corresponds to the keypoint scale, and the orientation is given by the compass mark. (For interpretation of the references to color in this figure legend, the reader is referred to the web version of this article.)

2.2. Characterize local image features

Many computer vision approaches represent the visual structure of keypoint features through a pattern or distribution of local image gradient values. In this work we use the Scale-Invariant Feature Transform (SIFT) [51] and [52] as implemented by VLFeat[54]. SIFT is a commonly used keypoint descriptor that offers rotational invariance by using a reference frame that is normalized with respect to the characteristic scale of each individual keypoint feature. Note that the characteristic scale of each keypoint feature is computed during the keypoint detection step. The SIFT descriptor models local visual structure as a histogram of oriented image intensity gradient values in a 4×4 grid of spatial bins, each with 8 bins for the image gradient orientation, as shown in Fig. 2. This collection of image gradient histograms is compactly represented by a 128-dimensional vector, which can conveniently serve as input to a variety of machine learning algorithms.

Figure. 2. Graphical depiction of the SIFT descriptor corresponding to the central black nodule (circle). Average intensity gradients (arrows) are calculated for each box in a 4×4 grid of bins surrounding the feature. Each bin contains 8 sub-bins for the gradient orientation.

2.3. Extract a visual dictionary

The bag of visual features approach treats an image as a collection of local image gradient patterns, each of which is represented by a high-dimensional vector that characterizes the local visual appearance of a keypoint feature. This high-dimensional feature space is quantized into a visual vocabulary to allow for fast matching and application of information retrieval techniques. A visual vocabulary is obtained by performing cluster analysis on a random subset of keypoint descriptors extracted from a representative training set of images. We used *k*-means clustering [57] and [58] with 100 clusters to quantize the SIFT descriptors extracted from the full training set for all of the current experiments. The cluster centers represent the visual words that make up the vocabulary. The optimal choice of *k*, the number of clusters, can be highly to the size and visual content of the image dataset. Although several means of selecting a value for *k*exist, there is no consensus over which method is 'correct' [59]. In computer vision applications, generally larger codebooks yield higher performance, and the value for this parameter is often simply tuned in an Edisonian fashion by interrogating the cross-validation performance of a classifier system trained with varying values of *k*, though care must be taken to avoid overfitting [47]. Because we have a relatively small classification dataset, we make no attempt to optimize *k* here, but recognize this as an area for future investigation. The result for our current classification dataset is the visual dictionary of 100 features shown in Fig. 3. It is apparent that this dictionary contains features corresponding to dark circles, textured regions, dark lines, line junctions, and feature edges, as well as other less obvious visual words.

A single visual dictionary is extracted from a set of images containing the full range of microstructural variation pertinent to the task at hand. Thus, for a study of related materials systems (i.e. alloys), examples of each materials system of interest should be included in the training set used to construct the visual dictionary. For a general study of all materials systems (i.e. the archives of a materials science journal), a representative sample of all the microstructural images appearing in the dataset should be used to construct the visual dictionary.

2.4. Construct microstructural fingerprints

The bag of visual features representation for an image is a normalized histogram measuring the frequency of each visual word in the image. Each keypoint feature counts as an instance of the visual word corresponding to the closest cluster center in the visual dictionary, as illustrated in Fig. 4. Thus, the image histogram is a 'fingerprint' of the microstructure that generated it. We compare image histograms using the χ^2 distance, which is a metric for quantifying the difference between two histograms that performs well for image texture recognition applications [60]. For two m -bin histograms $X=(x_1,\ldots,x_m)$ and $Y=(y_1,\ldots,y_m)$ the χ^2 distance is:

$$D(X,Y)=\frac{1}{2}\sum_{i=1}^{m}\frac{(x_i-y_i)^2}{x_i+y_i} \tag{1}$$

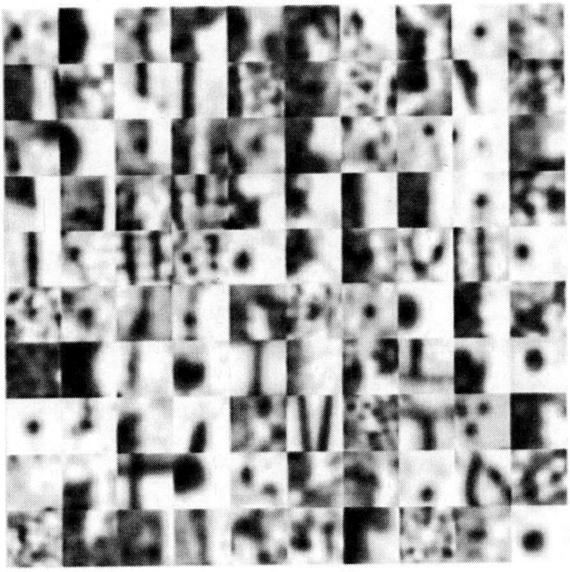

Figure. 3. Representative image patches corresponding to the 100-word visual dictionary extracted from our 7-category classification dataset with k-means clustering.

Just as in fingerprint matching, the smaller the difference between image histograms (therefore the more features in common), the more similar two microstructures are presumed to be. Naturally, below a certain threshold, two similar microstructures could have indistinguishable bag of features histograms. Note that the microstructure representation we use here does not capture spatial correlations between microstructural features in any way.

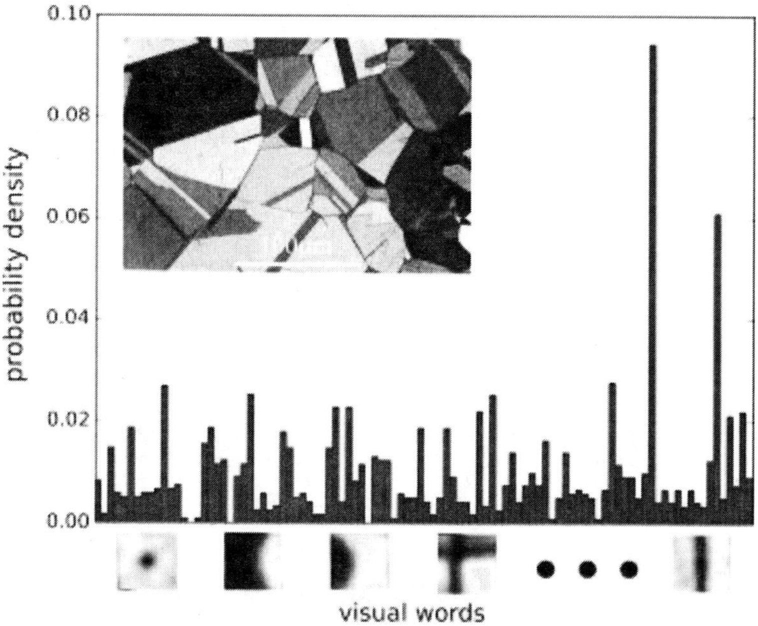

Figure. 4. The bag of microstructural words histogram for the highly twinned microstructure (inset, micrograph 430 from [56]). Each bin along the horizontal axis corresponds to a visual word, as schematically indicated. This histogram is the microstructural fingerprint of the image.

3. RESULTS AND DISCUSSION

Microstructures vary widely across different materials systems and processing history, and there is currently no easy way to automatically sort and classify them. We have performed a small classification experiment to demonstrate the utility (and evaluate the effectiveness) of the bag of visual features representation as a general microstructure descriptor. We also used the bag of visual features representation to rank the images in a microstructure database on the basis of microstructural similarity. We used separate visual dictionaries for each application: In the classification experiment, the visual dictionary was extracted from the training set of microstructures. In the microstructure similarity experiment, the visual dictionary was extracted using the entire microstructure database as the source of keypoint features.

3.1. Microstructure classification

Using an internet search engine, we manually collected and labeled a small dataset consisting of 105 micrographs belonging to the seven distinct classes of microstructure shown in Fig. 5: brass, ductile cast iron, gray cast iron, hypoeutectoid steel, malleable cast iron, superalloy, and annealing twins. We demonstrate the utility of the bag of words microstructure representation by using it to train a support vector machine (SVM)[61] and [62] classifier using the χ^2 kernel [60]. This classifier can automatically discriminate between these seven different microstructure classes.

The SVM is a machine learning classifier that is commonly used in computer vision applications. We used the one-vs-all scheme for multi-class SVM classification [63]: for each image class, one SVM classifier is trained to distinguish that class from all other classes. To predict the class of a previously unseen test image, the class prediction by each classifier is computed given the bag of words representation of the test image, and the test image is assigned according to the prediction with the highest confidence. We used scikit-learn, a popular machine learning library, for SVM classification [64].

We performed our classification experiment using a stratified 5-fold cross-validation scheme, a method for using all available data for training without sacrificing unbiased measurements of accuracy [59]. We partition the complete dataset into five *folds*, each consisting of 21 images (three images per microstructure class). For each of the five folds, we train a classifier system on a training set consisting of the remaining four folds. We measure the performance of this classifier system using a validation set that consists of the fold that was excluded from the current training set. Thus each of the 105 images in the dataset is used for training the classifier four times, and appears in a validation set exactly once. The overall accuracy estimate is the average accuracy out of the five cross-validation folds.

Our classifier system achieves a 5-fold cross-validation accuracy of 83% with standard deviation 3%. The confusion matrix in Fig. 6 graphically shows the classification performance with respect to each individual class: The vertical axis corresponds to the true class of each validation image, and the horizontal axis corresponds to the class predicted by the SVM classifier. Thus correct classifications lie along the diagonal of the confusion matrix. For example, three of the micrographs with annealing twins were misclassified as gray cast iron, while two micrographs of superalloy were misclassified as the annealing twin class. The misclassification between annealing twins and gray cast iron is interesting because of the preponderance of straight line features in both classes of microstructure. In contrast, every brass image was correctly classified, and only one micrograph (a gray cast iron) was misclassified as brass.

Due to our limited dataset size, we have made no efforts to tune model hyper-parameters such as the number of visual words or the SVM regularization parameter, which would require an additional cross-validation loop. This is primarily to avoid overfitting to the relatively small dataset, which would result in overestimation of the generalization performance of our classifier system. Nonetheless, these results demonstrate the potential for machine vision approaches to microstructural classification. Even using untuned model parameters and a small training set, the system achieves impressively accurate classification performance without human intervention, compared with a random-guessing accuracy of about 14%. This is somewhat lower than the performance of state of the art texture recognition systems evaluated on commonly used image texture datasets. For many datasets, the state of the art texture recognition performance is in the high 90% range [29]. However, these datasets are larger and carefully collected. We expect that with further optimization of our method, future quantitative microstructure studies can achieve similar performance. Additionally, even our current performance results are sufficient to support data mining on historical archives of microstructural images. In fact, this method is the only current candidate to search and/or classify sets of arbitrary, unsegmented micrographs.

3.2. Microstructural similarity ranking

The bag of visual features microstructure representation also unlocks the potential for novel microstructural data mining approaches. One example is a visual search engine for exploring a microstructure database. We demonstrate this concept by visually indexing 772 microstructure images from the Cambridge DoITPoMS micrograph library [56], again using the χ^2 kernel [60] to compare microstructure signatures. Fig. 7 shows the closest four matches in the database for five example queries. Bear in mind that this database is meant for teaching applications, and is thus relatively sparse: many materials systems are represented by just two or three examples. The first row shows a brass query microstructure which returns four visually similar brass microstructures. The second row shows an alumina–graphite composite microstructure that matches closely with another magnesium oxide–graphite composite, and then two steel microstructures that appear to have similar visual texture, and finally a gun metal bronze—a very different material system that contains some visually similar globular features. The third row shows a dendritic steel microstructure that returns four more steel and cast iron microstructures that share visual features with the query, but the overall scales between the images differ substantially. The fourth row shows a series of ductile iron micrographs with prominent spheroidal graphite inclusions. The fourth-closest match found is a hypoeutectoid steel, which has similar visual texture. The fifth row shows a close view of dendritic cast iron, which returns much broader views of similar dendritic cast irons and TRIP steels. Again, although this system has not yet been optimized, these results are encouraging. Given a query image, the search engine returns microstructures that are objectively related to it, and often the relationship is subjectively obvious as well.

3.3. Applications

The bag of visual features representation is a general microstructure descriptor that presumes nothing about the material system or microstructural features of interest. Instead, the computer system learns a set of discriminative microstructural features from the data itself. The underlying feature descriptors are robust to changes in scale, orientation, and overall illumination or imaging conditions. These qualities are critical for automatically comparing images of disparate microstructural classes at a variety of magnifications or physical scales, in an arbitrary body of microstructural data. Once a visual dictionary has been learned from a training set of microstructural images, the bag of visual features representations can be quickly computed; SIFT and related computer vision techniques are computationally efficient enough for real-time video analysis applications [65], [66] and [67].

Figure. 5. Example microstructures for the seven microstructure classes used in the classification test. (a) Brass/bronze, (b) ductile cast iron, (c) gray cast iron, (d) hypoeutectoid steel, (e) malleable cast iron, (f) superalloy and (g) all 15 annealing twin images.

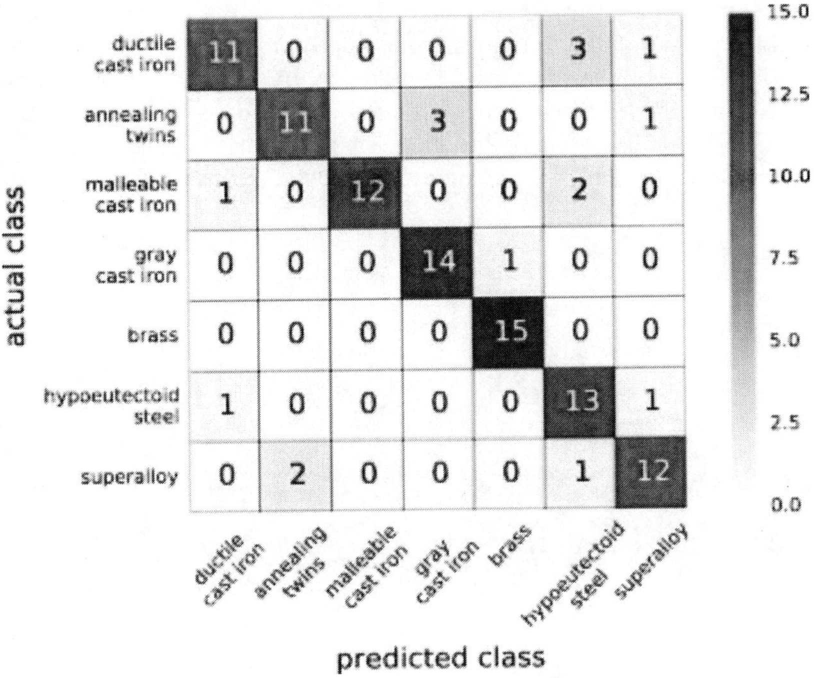

Figure. 6. Confusion matrix showing performance of the microstructural classification scheme. For micrographs in a particular actual class, the rows tally the predicted class assignments by the microstructure classifier. The upper-left to lower-right diagonal entries give the number of accurate classifications for each actual class.

Applying the bag of visual features representation to microstructure images enables a variety of outcomes based on machine learning, which could provide new ways for materials scientists to study relationships between broad classes of microstructures and materials. Indeed, a general quantitative microstructure representation could allow materials scientists to define objective classes of microstructure. Microstructural classification and search methods could be used to organize, search, and mine microstructural databases in order to unlock the wealth of information stored in academic, industrial, and journal archives [39]. Furthermore, the bag of visual words representation could extend quantitative microstructure–properties investigations to microstructural systems which are not readily segmented. If microstructural images are linked to metadata such as processing conditions and material properties, machine learning methods could be used to extract microstructure–processing–properties relationships, a key element of creating materials by design [68] and [69]. Finally, quickly computed quantitative microstructure representations combined with automated metallography could enable online microstructure monitoring for applications in industrial process control systems. In each case, the key element is automated and quantitative characterization of microstructural images, efficiently and without human intervention.

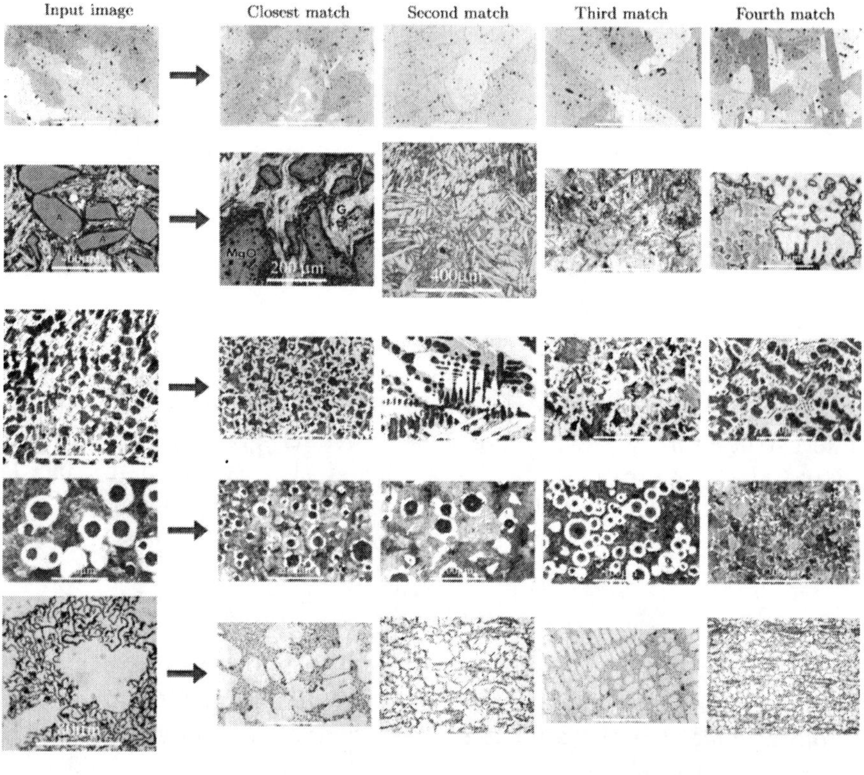

Figure. 7. Results of the visual microstructure search of the DoITPoMS micrograph library [56] for five query images (left column). The right four columns show the top four matches for each query image.

3.4. Limitations

Though the bag of visual features microstructure representation is an efficiently computed quantitative microstructure descriptor, it is ultimately an approximate measure of the visual structure of a micrograph rather than an objective measure of the physical structure of the analyte material. Thus any microstructure relationships extracted using this approach are likely to be empirical in nature, and correlative rather than causative. Furthermore, our current approach is strongly rooted in representing microstructural images as visual textures or scenes. This model is not appropriate for understanding micrographs that are not representative of their class, particularly closeups of individual features or high resolution transmission electron micrographs. These kinds of micrographs are problematic in general for all statistical characterization methods, because they contain a scan area that is smaller than the representative volume element (RVE) at the pertinent length scale. However, the bag of visual features histogram could be used as a convergence metric to help determine the RVE size for future microstructure studies.

Microstructural images may contain considerable data that are not included in the bag of visual words representation. For example, while color is often used to indicate crystallography, composition, phase, etc., the feature descriptors utilized here operate on intensity gradients only and ignore absolute color. Likewise, although the scale-invariant nature of the bag of visual features makes it robust with respect to analyzing images at different physical scales or magnification (and even to evaluating microstructures where no scale information is available), the physical scale of microstructural features may be important both for comparing microstructures and for correlating with physical properties. Finally, the bag of visual features representation makes no attempt to assess spatial relationships between microstructural features, such as proximity, directionality, or clustering. Clearly, incorporating these important and influential microstructural aspects into the image representation is an opportunity for future work.

On a broader scale, many computer vision systems are most effective when applied to web-scale data: for example, the NEIL project has analyzed more than two million images gathered from the internet [45]. A large dataset both improves fidelity and enables additional analyses, such as multi-label classification (i.e. a dendritic structure may also be a metal alloy). Though materials scientists and metallurgists have been collecting micrographs for over 100 years, compared to web-scale image data the full set of microstructure data is quite small. While much of this data set exists in digital form, it is fragmented across various academic and industrial archives. Open microstructure databases are a critical need for the advancement of microstructural data mining, both to provide a large enough dataset for meaningful algorithmic development and validation, and to foster a healthy microstructure informatics community.

4. CONCLUSIONS

The problem of structuring and managing large microstructural databases in a way that enables the synthesis of microstructural knowledge is very much an open one [35], [36],[37], [38], [39] and [40]. We show that the bag of visual features image representation can be used to compute microstructural fingerprints that capture the defining features of individual microstructures. By comparing the histograms of visual features, a support vector machine (SVM) can classify microstructures into groups automatically and with high accuracy, even using relatively small training data sets. In addition, the feature histogram can provide the basis for a visual search engine that finds the best matches for a query image in a database of microstructures. Ultimately, this automatic and objective computer vision system offers a new approach to archiving, analyzing, and utilizing microstructural data.

ACKNOWLEDGMENTS

This work was supported in part by the National Science Foundation under grant DMR-1307138. B.L.D. would also like to acknowledge the support of the John and Claire Bertucci Graduate Fellowship Foundation. We would also like to thank Professor Abhinav Gupta and Xinlei Chen of the Carnegie Mellon University School of Computer Science for stimulating conversation, advice, and inspiration through their work on the NEIL project.

REFERENCES

1. David W. Rosen, Namin Jeong, Yan Wang, Comput.-Aided Des. 45 (7) (2013) 1068–1078.

2. S.R. Kalidindi, D.T. Fullwood, JOM 59 (9) (2007) 26–31.

3. Surya R. Kalidindi, Stephen R. Niezgoda, Ayman A. Salem, JOM 63 (4) (2011) 34–41.

4. S.R. Niezgoda, D.T. Fullwood, S.R. Kalidindi, Acta Mater. 56 (18) (2008) 5285–5292.

5. G. Saheli, H. Garmestani, B.L. Adams, J. Comput.-Aided Mater. Des. 11 (2–3) (2004) 103–115.

6. Stephen R. Niezgoda, Anand K. Kanjarla, Surya R. Kalidindi, Integrating Mater. Manuf. Innovat. 2 (1) (2013) 1–27.

7. Ossama B. Abouelatta, J. Am. Sci. 9 (6) (2013).

8. D.T. Fullwood, S.R. Kalidindi, S.R. Niezgoda, A. Fast, N. Hampson, Mater. Sci. Eng.: A 494 (1) (2008) 68–72.

9. Thiago M. Nunes, Victor Hugo C. De Albuquerque, Joao P. Papa, Cleiton C. Silva, Paulo G. Normando, Elineudo P. Moura, Joao Manuel R.S. Tavares, Expert Syst. Appl. 40 (8) (2013) 3096–3105.

10. Cyril Stanley Smith, A History of Metallography-the Development of Ideas on the Structure of Metals before 1890, The University of Chicago Press, 1960.

11. Umesh Adiga, Murali Gorantla, James Scott, Daniel Banks, Yoon-Suk Choi, Building 3d microstructure database using an advanced metallographic serial sectioning technique and robust 3d segmentation tools, in: Proceedings of the 2nd World Congress on Integrated Computational Materials Engineering (ICME), John Wiley & Sons, 2013, p. 243.

12. Mary Comer, Charles A. Bouman, Marc De Graef, Jeff P Simmons, JOM J. Miner., Met. Mater. Soc. 63 (7) (2011) 55–57.

13. E. Gulsoy, M. Degraef, Microscopy Microanal. 15 (S2) (2009) 606–607.

14. W.B. Lievers, A.K. Pilkey, Mater. Sci. Eng.: A 381 (1) (2004) 134–142.

15. Aleks Y.M. Ontman, Gary J. Shiflet, Metall. Mater. Trans. A 41 (9) (2010) 2236–2247.

16. Pattan Prakash, V.D. Mytri, P.S. Hiremath, Microscopy Microanal. 17 (06) (2011) 896–902.

17. Veeraraghavan Sundararaghavan, Nicholas Zabaras, Computat. Mater. Sci. 32 (2) (2005) 223–239.

18. George F. Vander Voort, Metallography – Past, Present, and Future: 75th Anniversary Volume, vol. 11, Astm International, 1993.

19. Jarrell Waggoner, Youjie Zhou, Jeff Simmons, Marc De Graef, Song Wang, IEEE Trans. Image Process. 22 (12) (2013) 5282–5293.

20. Cyril Stanley Smith, Trans. Metall. Soc. AIME 175 (1948) 15–51.

21. J. Warren, L. Freidersdorf, in: Materials Science and Technology: MS&T'14. TMS, October 2014.

22. Hongyi Xu, Ruoqian Liu, Alok Choudhary, Wei Chen, J. Mech. Des. 137 (5) (2015). 051403-1–051403-10.

23. J.P. MacSleyne, J.P. Simmons, M. De Graef, Acta Mater. 56 (3) (2008) 427–437.

24. J.P. MacSleyne, J.P. Simmons, M. De Graef, Modell. Simul. Mater. Sci. Eng. 16 (4) (2008) 045008.

25. Stephen R. Niezgoda, Surya R. Kalidindi, Xiaohua Hu, Gordana A. Cingara, David S. Wilkinson, Mukesh Jain, Peidong Wu, Raja K. Mishra, M. Arafin, J. Szpunar, Mater. Continua 14 (2) (2010) 79–98.

26. M.A. Tschopp, M.A. Groeber, R. Fahringer, J.P. Simmons, A.H. Rosenberger, C. Woodward, Modell. Simul. Mater. Sci. Eng. 18 (2) (2010) 025014.

27. Robert M. Haralick, Karthikeyan Shanmugam, Its' Hak Dinstein, IEEE Trans. Syst., Man Cybernet. SMC-3 (6) (1973) 610–621.

28. A.P. Carleer, Olivier Debeir, Eléonore Wolff, Photogramm. Eng. Remote Sens. 71 (11) (2005) 1285–1294.

29. Barbara Caputo, Eric Hayman, Mario Fritz, Jan-Olof Eklundh, Image Vision Comput. 28 (1) (2010) 150–163.

30. Tim F. Cootes, Christopher J. Taylor, in: Medical Imaging 2001, International Society for Optics and Photonics, 2001, pp. 236–248.

31. S. Livens, P. Scheunders, G. Van de Wouwer, D. Van Dyck, Sixth International Conference on Image Processing and Its Applications, vol. 2, IET, 1997, pp. 581–585.

32. Michael Unser, IEEE Trans. Image Process. 4 (11) (1995) 1549–1560.

33. Manik Varma, Andrew Zisserman, IEEE Trans. Pattern Anal. Mach. Intell. 31 (11) (2009) 2032–2047.

34. [34] Svetlana Lazebnik, Cordelia Schmid, Jean Ponce, IEEE Trans. Pattern Anal. Mach. Intell. 27 (8) (2005) 1265–1278.

35. National Research Council, Big Data in Materials Research and Development: Summary of a Workshop, The National Academies Press, Washington, DC, 2014.

36. J. Warren, R.F. Boisvert, Workshop Report: Building the Materials Innovation Infrastructure: Data and Standards, Technical Report NISTIR 7898, National Institute of Standards and Technology, November 2012.

37. Ad-hoc Interagency Group on Advanced Materials, Materials Genome Initiative for Global Competitiveness, National Science and Technology Council OSTP, July 2011, pp. 1–18.

38. National Research Council Committee on Integrated Computational Materials Engineering, Integrated Computational Materials Engineering: A Transformational Discipline for Improved Competitiveness and National Security, The National Academies Press, Washington, DC, 2008.

39. Subcommittee on the Materials Genome Initiative. Materials Genome Initiative Strategic Plan, Technical Report NISTIR 7898, National Institute of Standards and Technology, Washington, DC, USA, December 2014.

40. P. Bajcsy, Y. Khalidi, H. Peng, K.D. Borne, in: Big Data Science: BigData'14. TMS, October 2014.

41. Doug Howe, Maria Costanzo, Petra Fey, Takashi Gojobori, Linda Hannick, Winston Hide, David P. Hill, Renate Kania, Mary Schaeffer, Susan St. Pierre, Nature 455 (7209) (2008) 47–50.

42. Kieran Jay Edwards, Mohamed Medhat Gaber, Astronomy and Big Data, vol. 6, Springer, New York, 2014.

43. Geoff Brumfiel, Nature 469 (20) (2011) 282–283.

44. A. Kassner, R.E. Thornhill, Am. J. Neuroradiol. 31 (5) (2010) 809–816.

45. Xinlei Chen, Abhinav Shrivastava, Abhinav Gupta, Neil: extracting visual knowledge from web data, in: 2013 IEEE International Conference on Computer Vision (ICCV), IEEE, 2013, pp. 1409–1416.

46. Gabriella Csurka, Christopher Dance, Lixin Fan, Jutta Willamowski, Cédric Bray, Workshop on Statistical Learning in Computer Vision, vol. 1, ECCV, 2004, pp. 1–2.

47. Eric Nowak, Frédéric Jurie, Bill Triggs, in: Computer Vision – ECCV 2006, Springer, 2006, pp. 490–503.

48. Hans Peter Luhn, IBM J. Res. Dev. 2 (2) (1958) 159–165.

49. Gerard Salton, Michael J. McGill, Introduction to Modern Information Retrieval, McGraw-Hill, Inc., 1986.

50. Krystian Mikolajczyk, Cordelia Schmid, Proceedings. Eighth IEEE International Conference on Computer Vision, 2001. ICCV 2001, vol. 1, IEEE, 2001, pp. 525–531.

51. David G. Lowe, The Proceedings of the Seventh IEEE International Conference on Computer Vision, vol. 2, IEEE, 1999, pp. 1150–1157.

52. David G. Lowe, Int. J. Comput. Vision 60 (2) (2004) 91–110.

53. Richard Szeliski, Computer Vision: Algorithms and Applications, Springer, 2010.

54. Andrea Vedaldi, Brian Fulkerson, in: Proceedings of the International Conference on Multimedia, ACM, 2010, pp. 1469–1472.

55. Krystian Mikolajczyk, Cordelia Schmid, Int. J. Comput. Vision 60 (1) (2004) 63–86.

56. Z.H. Barber, J.A. Leake, T.W. Clyne, J. Mater. Educ. 29 (1/2) (2007) 7.

57. Stuart Lloyd, IEEE Trans. Inform. Theory 28 (2) (1982) 129–137.

58. David Arthur, Sergei Vassilvitskii, in: Proceedings of the Eighteenth Annual ACM-SIAM Symposium on Discrete Algorithms, Society for Industrial and Applied Mathematics, 2007, pp. 1027–1035.

59. Trevor Hastie, Robert Tibshirani, Jerome Friedman, T. Hastie, J. Friedman, R. Tibshirani, The Elements of Statistical lLearning, vol. 2, Springer, 2009.

60. Jianguo Zhang, Marcin Marszałek, Svetlana Lazebnik, Cordelia Schmid, Int. J. Comput. Vision 73 (2) (2007) 213–238.

61. Corinna Cortes, Vladimir Vapnik, Mach. Learn. 20 (3) (1995) 273–297.

62. Bernhard Schölkopf, Alexander J. Smola, Learning with Kernels: Support Vector Machines, Regularization, Optimization, and Beyond, MIT Press, 2002.

63. Chih-Wei Hsu, Chih-Jen Lin, IEEE Trans. Neural Networks 13 (2) (2002) 415–425.

64. Fabian Pedregosa, Gaël Varoquaux, Alexandre Gramfort, Vincent Michel, Bertrand Thirion, Olivier Grisel, Mathieu Blondel, Peter Prettenhofer, Ron Weiss, Vincent Dubourg, J. Mach. Learn. Res. 12 (2011) 2825–2830.

65. Herbert Bay, Andreas Ess, Tinne Tuytelaars, Luc Van Gool, Comput. Vision Image Underst. 110 (3) (2008) 346–359.

66. Sudipta N. Sinha, Jan-Michael Frahm, Marc Pollefeys, Yakup Genc, in: EDGE, Workshop on Edge Computing Using New Commodity Architectures, vol. 278, 2006, p. 4321.

67. Kristen Grauman, Trevor Darrell, The pyramid match kernel: discriminative classification with sets of image features, Tenth IEEE International Conference on Computer Vision, 2005. ICCV 2005, vol. 2, IEEE, 2005, pp. 1458–1465.

68. Gregory B. Olson, Science 277 (5330) (1997) 1237–1242.

69. Gregory B. Olson, Science 288 (5468) (2000) 993–998.

3

HUMAN DETECTION FROM A MOBILE ROBOT USING FUSION OF LASER AND VISION INFORMATION

Efstathios P. Fotiadis *, Mario Garzón and Antonio Barrientos

Centro de Automática y Robótica, UPM-CSIC. Calle José Gutiérrez Abascal, 2. Madrid 28006, Spain

ABSTRACT

This paper presents a human detection system that can be employed on board a mobile platform for use in autonomous surveillance of large outdoor infrastructures. The prediction is based on the fusion of two detection modules, one for the laser and another for the vision data. In the laser module, a novel feature set that better encapsulates variations due to noise, distance and human pose is proposed. This enhances the generalization of the system, while at the same time, increasing the outdoor performance in comparison with current methods. The vision module uses the combination of the histogram of oriented gradients descriptor and the linear support vector machine classifier. Current approaches use a fixed-size projection to define regions of interest on the image data using the range information from the laser range finder. When applied to small size unmanned ground vehicles, these techniques suffer from misalignment, due to platform vibrations and terrain irregularities. This is effectively addressed in this work by using a novel adaptive projection technique, which is based on a probabilistic formulation of the classifier performance. Finally, a probability calibration step is introduced in order to optimally fuse the information from both modules. Experiments in real world environments demonstrate the robustness of the proposed method.

KEYWORDS

human detection; unmanned ground vehicle; outdoors surveillance; sensor fusion; laser range finder; monocular vision

1. INTRODUCTION

The surveillance of critical infrastructure is heavily based on the detection and evaluation of human presence. Current systems usually employ a variety of strategically placed sensors and rely on human supervision. However, these systems suffer, due to the overwhelming amount of data, which are difficult to follow, and, moreover, from repetition that leads to mental and visual fatigue. In order to alleviate these problems, various methods for the automatic detection of suspicious actions have been proposed [1].

In large outdoor infrastructures, the magnitude of the area under inspection renders the task implausible to fulfill with static sensors alone. A distributed mobile robot system could help towards such a direction. Using autonomous navigation, robots can follow predetermined or random paths along the perimeter or in between the buildings of the infrastructure. In case of intrusion, detection algorithms can trigger an alarm or provoke further action. Moreover, the detection of the intruder allows his or her tracking and following, while keeping security personnel informed. In order to complete this task, the robotic platform needs to be equipped with an effective human detection module.

Detecting humans from a moving platform raises many difficulties. Outdoor environments are very noisy, and sensors can be affected by weather conditions, changes in illumination, movement or terrain irregularities, among many other factors. Constrains on the on board computational power together with the need of real time processing make the problem ever more demanding. Therefore, a robust and computationally-efficient set of algorithms is required.

This work presents a robust method for human detection on board an unmanned ground vehicle (UGV). The method is based on an information fusion scheme that uses a laser range finder and image data. Both sensors have their own advantages and drawbacks. Using them in a complementary way increases the overall performance compared to employing each one individually.

The laser data provide useful information about range and the geometrical characteristics of the surrounding objects. The segmentation of laser points into clusters and using a set of features to classify whether they belong to a human or not has been proposed [2]. Although this method has been proven efficient indoors, it is designed for human leg detection and uses distance-based features. An extension of this work is proposed here, intended to be used outdoors and with the premise of obtaining only one cluster per person. The distance-based features capture scene-specific information, and although very discriminative, they harm the generalization capability of the algorithm. In other words, the classifier learns the scene dependent features well, and it fails to deliver competent performance on different scenarios. Furthermore, the laser sensor is very prone to outdoor noise, and the features are dependent on the human pose. In order to better handle the information variations due to distance, human pose and sensor noise, a novel feature set has been proposed. It not only performs better outdoors, but at the same time, significantly improves the generalization of the system, making it capable of performing well in scenes that it was not trained to cope with.

Despite their usefulness, the information contained in the laser data is limited. Since the number of points returned is relatively low, the detection based solely on laser data may be unreliable. The camera vision signal is generally more informative and provides object texture and shape, which makes it ideal for human recognition [3]. Since no localization is provided, the whole image must be thoroughly processed, something that slows down the detection task significantly. The range information from the laser can be very helpful in localizing separate objects in the environment [4]. By exploiting the localization information of the laser, the computational time needed by the vision system can be reduced. Due to the geometrical setup, this localization can be well defined only on the horizontal axis. Surface abnormalities, steep inclinations, inherent vibrations or rapid acceleration of the UGV can introduce noise in the estimation. All these factors make the definition and projection of a correct region of interest (ROI) a non-trivial task [5]. In this work, this is addressed by a novel adaptive projection technique that uses *a priori* information about the classifier to construct a probabilistic detection model.

Fusion of the probabilistic outcome of the two sensor modules enables the extraction of non-redundant information. This is achieved by incorporating them in a probabilistic fusion framework that can be useful in difficult situations, such as occlusions, when one sensor alone cannot provide a correct detection [6]. In order to optimally combine the two outcomes and reduce the correlation between them, an off-line classifier calibration process is introduced.

The main contributions of the work presented here can be summarized by the following points:

- Laser detection: An extended feature set targeted for large outdoors environments, based solely on structural information, is proposed. The information variations due to distance, the human pose and sensor noise are encapsulated through feature normalization, providing better generalization.

- Vision detection: The problem of vertically localizing a projection from the laser to the image plane is addressed. A novel adaptive region of interest (ROI) projection technique helps compensate for misalignment, caused by otherwise uncontrolled factors, which often leads to false predictions.

- Information fusion: The redundancy and the correlation between the two classifiers is reduced by first calibrating them. The output probability of the fusion scheme is thus more optimal.

Our approach adapts and builds upon well established techniques in the human detection field. The techniques proposed have been assessed in detail, so as to provide a competent tradeoff between performance, scalability and execution speed time, when it is used on board a robotic mobile platform.

The paper is organized as follows. In the next section, previous work related to ours is briefly discussed. In Section 3, an overview of the proposed method is described. Detailed descriptions of the laser and vision detection modules are found in Sections 4 and 5, respectively. The information fusion methodologies are presented in Section 6. Then, Section 7 explains the experiments held in order to validate the method. Finally, Section 8 shows the results of the experiments, followed by our conclusions.

2. RELATED WORK

During the few last years, applications of human detection have been proven attainable. Intelligent systems have improved the surveillance and safety of public places [1]. More recently, commercial cars have been equipped with active pedestrian detection and avoidance systems [7,8]. Similarly, such systems are being deployed in service robots [9].

Nevertheless, human detection is not an easy task. A lot of different methodologies using various sensor modalities have been proposed. The most commonly used sensor is a camera in a multitude of setups, such as monocular or stereo vision, sensitive to either the visible or the infrared light spectrum. The fact that computer vision can provide a rich three-dimensional signal, while remaining relatively inexpensive and easy to deploy, has led to the advancement of many different approaches in human detection in this field [3,10].

A plethora of these algorithms uses a *sliding window* approach. Dalal and Triggs [11] proposed a method for human detection that is based on this approach, with very good detection results at a comparatively efficient speed. The detection window is subdivided into cells, and for each one, a histogram of oriented gradients (HoG) is accordingly computed. The final detection is performed by a linear support vector machine (SVM) classifier. *Shape-based* methods use template matching algorithms to detect the appearance of human silhouettes on the image [12]. Another distinct approach is *part-based representations*. In this case, instead of exhaustively searching the image, this technique tries to learn and identify human parts and their relative positions [13]. A variation of the HoG descriptor is used in the vision module of this work (see Section 5.1).

Although significant advances have been introduced, vision-based systems suffer mainly from high computational requirements. Additionally, when real time applications are developed for systems like a small UGV, they are constrained to lower resolutions, due to the limited processing power and low payload capacity. As a consequence, the detection range is also limited. This work uses the laser range readings to reduce the search space and to comply with the real-time requirements of an autonomous surveillance UGV.

Laser range finders have been extensively used on autonomous ground vehicles for multiple tasks, such as object recognition and avoidance, or simultaneous localization and mapping (SLAM). The fact that human parts—especially legs—display distinct geometric characteristics in laser range data has been exploited for the detection and tracking of humans. These techniques generally rely on the segmentation of the two dimensional signal into separate *clusters* [14]. Consequently, for each cluster, various geometric and statistical characteristics are extracted. The identification can be made by either manually selecting fitting thresholds [15] or through machine learning [2]. Nevertheless, the information of the laser data is not enough to provide a set of highly discriminative features. Tracking of the moving object is commonly used in order to improve the performance. Human motion or gait models combined with tracking algorithms provide the necessary formulation for this task [4,16]. Another approach is based on occupancy grids, where the space is divided in cells, and the probability of each cell being occupied is computed based on information from current and previous laser scans [17]. Apparently, both tracking and occupancy grid methods are susceptible to occasions where humans remain stationary.

The work of Arras *et al.* [2] has been shown to be effective indoors. Using their method as a basis, this work proposes an extension aimed at being used in more diverse outdoor environments. The problem with feature-based methods arises from the use of characteristics dependent on the particular surroundings, such as the distance from the laser or the distance between objects. Although highly discriminative, these features tend to be scene-specific and to provide very poor generalization, a disadvantage that becomes more apparent in outdoor scenes that have greater variability. Furthermore, outdoors, the laser sensor is very susceptible to noise. Another finding is that the features are also dependent on the relative pose of the objects. In order to alleviate these phenomena, a novel feature set that captures the aforementioned dependencies is proposed in this work. The use of normalization techniques helps the classifier to adapt itself and discard intrinsic correlations, providing better overall outdoor performance. At the same time, it significantly increases the robustness of new scenes, which is critical in applications concerning large outdoor infrastructures.

Simultaneous use of both laser and computer vision has been used to provide a more reliable prediction, both in terms of detection accuracy and speed [18]. Applications of such bimodal detection systems have been introduced in mobile service robots [9] and automated braking systems for vehicles [19]. In various works, the range data from the laser are used in combination with geometric models of the surroundings to confine the search on the image data into areas of high interest [19,20]. The localization, provided by the laser data, assists in deducing ROIs that are subsequently processed and classified by the vision module. This approach helps to dramatically increase the execution speed, while at the same time, decreasing false alarms, because the detection is bounded to relevant areas.

However, the latter approach is limited in the sense that it does not take into account the laser discriminative information that could, in combination with the vision detection, provide more reliable results. With fusion techniques, information from both sources is evaluated; thus, partial incompleteness of the human appearance in one source can be addressed using the other. This is especially helpful in *hard* situations, when occlusions happen, due to the interaction between dynamic and static elements of the environment.

Fusion methods are generally divided into two categories, depending on which level the fusion is being done. In feature level fusion, the features for each laser cluster and vision region are computed separately and are then concatenated to a single vector used by a subsequent classification scheme [21,22]. In high or detector-level fusion, the data provided by each sensor lead to two separate classification results, and the combination of the results is done in a final fusion step. As before, laser data are used to reduce the vision module search space. Prior assumptions about human height and the geometric characteristics of the environment are used to define a projection ROI [6,23–26]. Other approaches are based solely on the geometric constraints of the system and the scene to construct a relevant space hypothesis [9,27,28].

Many of the methods that have been presented make use of fixed-size window projection. In this case, the vision module is highly susceptible to projection errors that occur when the platform is moving. Although the horizontal boundaries of the apparent cluster are easily defined by laser data, there are a lot of misplaced projections produced by factors, such as the acceleration of the platform, ground irregularities and steep slopes. In such cases, the assumption that the ground is level and the robot is neither rolling nor pitching does not stand true [25]. This becomes more important when a descriptor, like HoG, which is sensitive to the relative position of the human on the detection window, is used [23]. Furthermore, while these shortcomings are found on big mobile platforms, such as a car, a small-sized UGV is significantly more sensitive to them, due to its smaller form. In order to overcome this, ground plane extraction using a 3D laser scanner has been proposed with the objective of finding an accurate estimate of the platforms pitch and roll [23]. In this work, an adaptive projection scheme is proposed to address this problem; it is a simpler solution, which does not require the use of complex sensors or algorithms. The size of the projection window is increased to compensate for the misalignment, and the resulting ROI is thoroughly searched for human presence. The final prediction outcome is based on a probabilistic formulation that incorporates *a priori* knowledge about the classifier's performance. The result is a more versatile detection system that is capable of correctly detecting hard situations, even when the person is not on the same level with the UGV. At the same time, the computational cost is held low by restricting the search to a meaningful scale-space only.

Laser and camera fusion systems produce the final prediction probability using the score outcomes from the two modules. The accurate conversion of the classifier outcome to a probability distribution is therefore essential. Classifiers, like adaptive boosting (AdaBoost) and SVM, are commonly used in detection, but their outcome consists of uncalibrated scores [29]. When cascades are used, the sum of the weak classifier weights can be used to provide an estimate [9,23,25]. The logistic function has also been used to normalize the outcomes [26]. Here, this problem is addressed by calibrating the classifiers using a well-known method, thus generating more precise probability distributions [30].

3. METHODOLOGY OVERVIEW

This system is aimed to be used on board a UGV performing surveillance operations around a critical infrastructure. The main goal is to achieve the best detection performance possible while maintaining real time processing.

The UGV is equipped with a laser range finder and a camera sensor. In order to be able to use the range data of the laser together with the image from the camera, first, the sensors need to be calibrated, both intrinsically and extrinsically. This calibration process provides the translation and rotation vectors, which are needed for converting a point in the laser scan to a corresponding pixel in the image, as is described in Section 7.1.

The data readings from the two sensors are synchronized and then individually processed. Both modules, laser and vision, are comprised of two parts: a feature extraction algorithm and the subsequent pattern recognition process. Initially, the laser data are segmented into clusters, and a set of geometrical and statistical features is computed for each one. Afterwards, a Real AdaBoost classifier produces a probability estimate of whether it belongs to a person or not. Furthermore, these clusters are projected to the camera image for further processing in the vision module. For each projection, a corresponding ROI in the image is assessed using an adaptive window approach that utilizes a HoG descriptor and an SVM classifier. The probability outcome of both modules is subsequently merged into a single likelihood using fusion information techniques. Since the angular range of the laser range finder is much greater than that of the camera, some clusters do not have corresponding projections on the image. Nevertheless, those clusters are processed only from the laser module. A schematic overview of the method can be found in Figure 1.

4. LASER DETECTION MODULE

The laser detection module has a dual function. On the one hand, it provides the first estimation of human presence, which is later used in the fusion scheme. On the other hand, the range values from the sensor are used for localizing the apparent structures in the image plane, thus reducing the search space significantly

Data are acquired from the device as an ordered sequence of n points, $P = \{p_1, p_2, \ldots, p_n\}$. Each point is represented in Cartesian coordinates, $p_i = (x_l, z_l)$, derived from the polar coordinates, ϕ, ρ, of each range reading ($x_l = \rho \sin \phi$, $z_l = \rho \cos \phi$). In order to be consistent with the calibration, the laser readings are considered to belong in the plane where $y_l = 0$.

4.1. Prepossessing and Segmentation

Individual points provide little to none structural information. Before any further processing is made, it is very crucial to obtain clusters representing distinct surrounding objects. Since the data points are sequential, a one-dimensional gradient filter mask [−, 1] can be applied to produce a vector of differences, Δ. Values greater than a given threshold, T_Δ, define the borders of the clusters. This method is widely known as jumping distance segmentation. When big differences exist in readings between two consecutive laser points, it is very common to have a shadow effect, which means that the readings are erroneously somewhere between the two points. Methods based on Euclidean distance are greatly affected by this phenomenon. An appropriate adaptive filtering is applied beforehand in order to alleviate this effect. This is a relatively simple and fast algorithm; for an overview of segmentation methods and threshold estimation techniques, see [14].

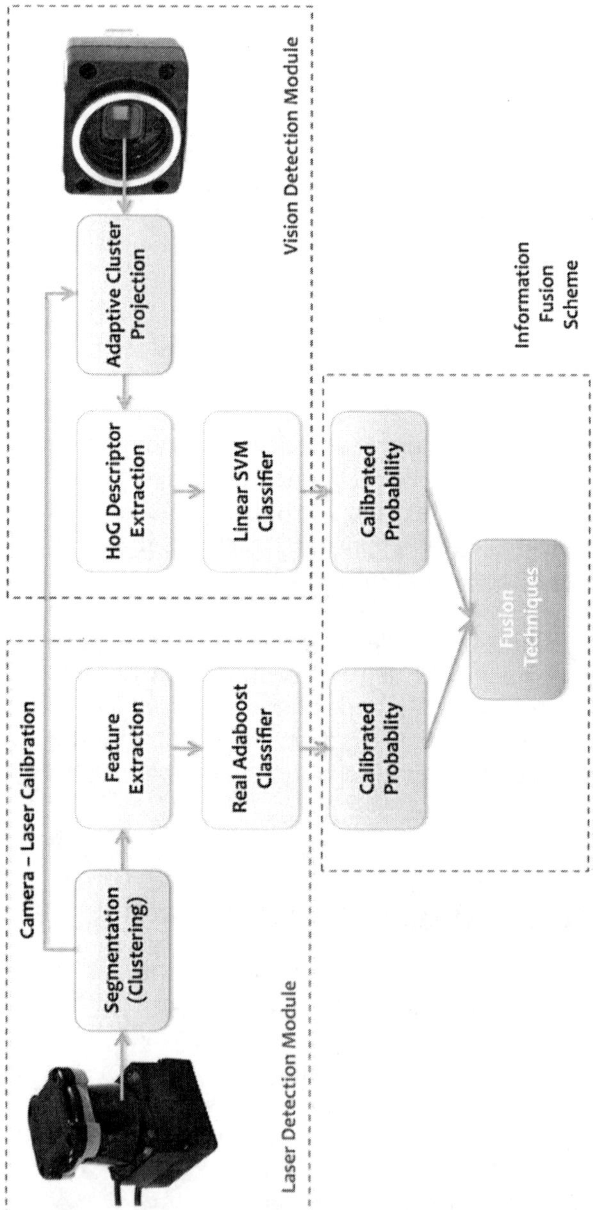

Figure 1. Schematic diagram of the proposed method.

This type of segmentation was originally conceived to work in indoor environments and normally leads to two distinct clusters, one for each leg. In our application, it is important to obtain a single cluster for each human in order to correctly project a region of interest in the image plane. This is partially achieved by placing the laser at upper leg height. However, as has already been discussed, this cannot be trusted, due to pitch variations of the UGV. Furthermore, outdoor conditions are much more versatile and affected by noise, which usually causes oversegmentation. Thus, a second cluster aggregation step is employed. When the euclidean distance between two distinct clusters is less than T_Δ, they are united to form a new composite one. The value of T_Δ is the same as before. Very small remaining clusters that consist of less than three points are discarded as noise. In Figure 2, the segmentation of the laser data and their respective projection on the camera frame is shown.

Figure 2. Projection of laser segmented clusters to the image plane using the calibration parameters. In the left image, the shaded area indicates the field of view of the camera. The color and number of each cluster are the same in both views.

4.2. Feature Extraction

After the segmentation has been completed, the next step is to extract a set of characteristics for each cluster. The feature extraction can be considered as a function where the input is the set of points of the cluster in *two-dimensional* Cartesian coordinates and the output is a vector in *n-dimensional* space, $f: \mathbb{R}^2 \rightarrow \mathbb{R}^n$. In [2], Arras *et al.* propose a scheme for indoor human detection from laser data that is considered a work of reference in the field [6,23]. They use a combination of geometrical, statistical and distance-dependent features. Some of them are obtained by the cluster points themselves and others by their relationship with the surroundings, such as the distance from the sensor, the distance between clusters and the speed of the cluster. Those features do not conform to the aforementioned mathematical description, because the distance between objects cannot be inferred using the points of a sole cluster.

The aforementioned features have been built for describing human legs in indoor environments. The proposed extension is developed in order to produce a more appropriate feature set for the outdoor environment with the additional constraint of having only one cluster for each person. Since outdoors surroundings tend to be more complex, using features that are context specific, such as the distance between objects, harms the generalization of the detector. Furthermore, in outdoor areas, the distance between the laser and the targets can be large, so that far away objects may be represented by only a few points. The number of points of a human cluster is also dependent on other uncontrolled factors, such as the lighting conditions, the platform movement and the objects relative pose with respect to the laser. In order to study the variations on the feature values with respect to the aforementioned factors, normalization methods are employed. The distance from the camera and the number of laser points are used as normalization factors. The initial feature basis containing the distance-independent components that have been used in this work can be found in Table 1. From the initial feature basis, a final vector with 63 components is acquired as follows:

- The initial 13 features from the feature basis of Table 1.
- The initial 13 features divided by the distance from the origin.
- The initial 13 features multiplied by the distance from the origin.
- Features 2 to 13 divided by the number of points.
- Features 2 to 13 features multiplied by the number of points.

No distance-dependent feature is explicitly included in the final set. Using this novel extended feature set, the classifier employed in the subsequent step can learn and compensate for distance, noise and human pose-dependent variations, ultimately providing better generalization.

Table 1. List of the laser feature basis.

1. Number of points	8. Boundary length
2. Standard deviation from centroid	9. Boundary regularity
3. Mean average deviation from median	10. Mean curvature
4. Width	11. Mean angular difference
5. Linearity	12. Kurtosis
6. Circularity	13. Aspect ratio
7. Radius	

Three feature sets were considered for comparison reasons: the feature basis of Table 1, the feature basis with distance features added and the proposed 63-dimensional feature set. In Table 2a and 2b, a performance comparison between the three sets is presented, and the results are further discussed in Section 8.

Table 2. Three feature sets are compared. The feature basis is described in Table 1. DIST denotes the addition of distance features to the feature basis. The proposed feature set is described in Section 4.2. The laser data sets from Table 3 were used.

	Static			Moving		
	Basis	**Basis + DIST**	**Proposed**	**Basis**	**Basis + DIST**	**Proposed**
Precision	95.25%	98.89%	97.86%	86.67%	91.26%	89.75%
Recall	88.60%	98.67%	96.96%	84.66%	90.14%	88.57%
Specificity	99.75%	99.94%	99.88%	98.27%	98.86%	98.66%

(a) Gymnasium experiments.

	Moving		
	Basis	**Basis + DIST**	**Proposed**
Precision	76.84%	76.83%	78.97%
Recall	59.93%	63.36%	66.11%
Specificity	97.97%	97.83%	98.00%

(b) Outdoor experiments.

4.3. Classification

The identification of the cluster is performed by an AdaBoost (*i.e.*, adaptive boosting) classifier. In boosting, a set of discriminative *weak* classifiers are combined to construct a final *strong* classifier [31]. Individual classifiers are called weak because the only requirement is to perform better than random guessing. Due to their simplicity, they are computationally inexpensive. Generally, AdaBoost techniques tend towards margin maximization between the classes. Overfitting of the data is very improbable in practice, and the classifier provides good generalization. There are various different schemes of the AdaBoost algorithm; an overview can be found in the work of Friedman *et al.* [32].

The training input consists of labeled data, (s_i, l_i), $i = 1 \ldots N$, where N is the number of samples. Each sample consists of an$n$-dimensional descriptor, $s_i \in \mathbb{R}^n$, and an annotation label, $l_i \in \{+1,-1\}$, denoting a positive or a negative example. In our case, the descriptor is a 63-dimensional feature vector, while the label signifies if the sample belongs to a human or not. In each iteration, the algorithm trains a weak classifier, which produces a weak hypothesis, $h_t(s_i) : \mathbb{R}^n \rightarrow \mathbb{R}$, over the weighted distribution, D_t, of the training samples. Subsequently, the weight distribution is recalculated, taking into account the error of the previous step. With this method, the weight of the wrongly classified examples is increased, forcing the next classifier to focus more on those *hard* cases. The final strong classifier, $H(s_i)$, is produced by the weighted sum of the T best weak hypotheses. An outline of this procedure can be found in Algorithm 1.

In their implementation, Arras *et al.* used a modified version of the Discrete AdaBoost algorithm with stumps as weak classifiers. This variation of AdaBoost uses a weak hypothesis with a response restrained to a discrete outcome, essentially two classes, $h_t(s_i) : \mathbb{R}^n \rightarrow \{-1, +1\}$. In our implementation, the Real Adaboost version has been used. It is reported to be less immune to noise and generalizes better in practice than its Discrete counterpart [31,32]. Furthermore, our data set is significantly larger than that of Arras *et al.*, and our experiments showed that using stumps results in a classifier that is too weak and that underfits the data. Therefore, our choice for a weak classifier is a two-split decision tree. Finally, our proposed feature set yields better results when more classifiers are used, so empirically, T was set to 20. These changes provide considerable performance improvements and better generalization at a very low speed cost (see Section 8).

Algorithm 1 Outline of Real AdaBoost.

Input: Training data samples, $(s_i, l_i), i = 1, 2, \ldots, N; s_i \in \mathbb{R}^n, l_i \in \{+1, -1\}$

Initialization: Set uniform sample weights, $w_1(i) = \frac{1}{N}$.

Iteration: For $t = 1, 2, \ldots, T$, repeat the following steps:

1. Train the weak classifier to obtain a class probability estimate, $P(l = 1|s) \in [0, 1]$, using the weighted samples.
2. Set $h_t(s) = \frac{1}{2} \log \frac{P(l=1|s)}{P(l=-1|s)}$.
3. Update the sample weights: $w_i^{(t+1)} = w_i^{(t)} \exp\left(-y_i h_t(s_i)\right), i = 1, 2, \ldots, N$.
4. Normalize the weight distribution: $w_i^{(t+1)} = \frac{w_i^{(t+1)}}{\sum_{i=1}^{N} w_i^{(t+1)}}$.

Output: The final strong classifier, $H(s) = sign\left(\sum_{t=1}^{T} h_t(s)\right)$

The low cost comes also from another advantage of AdaBoost classifiers. After the training procedure has been completed, the classification is based on a smaller subset of the complete feature vector. Since this knowledge is *a priori* available, the feature extraction algorithm can be accordingly adjusted to only compute the appropriate features, thus leading to faster execution time.

5. VISION DETECTION MODULE

The vision detection module serves as a second opinion observer that helps to improve the overall detection performance of the system. The detection is based on the established method of the histogram of oriented gradients. A novel adaptive projection method has been developed in order to obtain an accurate ROI from the image.

5.1. Histogram of Oriented Gradients

Edge orientation histograms have been extensively used in the computer vision field for object detection. Lowe's *Scale Invariant Feature Transformation (SIFT)* combines gradient orientation information with local spatial histogramming in a sparse grid [33]. The *histogram of oriented gradients* descriptor, proposed by Dalal and Triggs, uses a dense overlapping grid along with local contrast normalization and has been proven very effective for human detection in images [11].

Though HoG entails a lot of details and parameters, a brief description of the algorithm is provided here. The parameters used in our work have been reported to provide the best results and are considered as *standard* in recent implementations. The descriptor is evaluated over a fixed-size sliding window of 128 × 64 pixels. First, the magnitude and orientation for each pixel of the image is computed. The window is divided into smaller regions called *cells.* For each cell, a nine-bin local histogram over the gradient orientations is composed with the magnitude of the gradients serving as a weighted vote. Contrast normalization of local responses is applied over larger spatial regions in order to overcome illumination variations, called *blocks.* The block dimensions are 2×2 cells, and the grid is overlapping, so each cell finally contributes in more than one block. Before being fed to the SVM classifier, the features are concatenated into a 3,780 dimension vector. The partition of a region into blocks and cells and the corresponding oriented histograms can been seen in Figure 3.

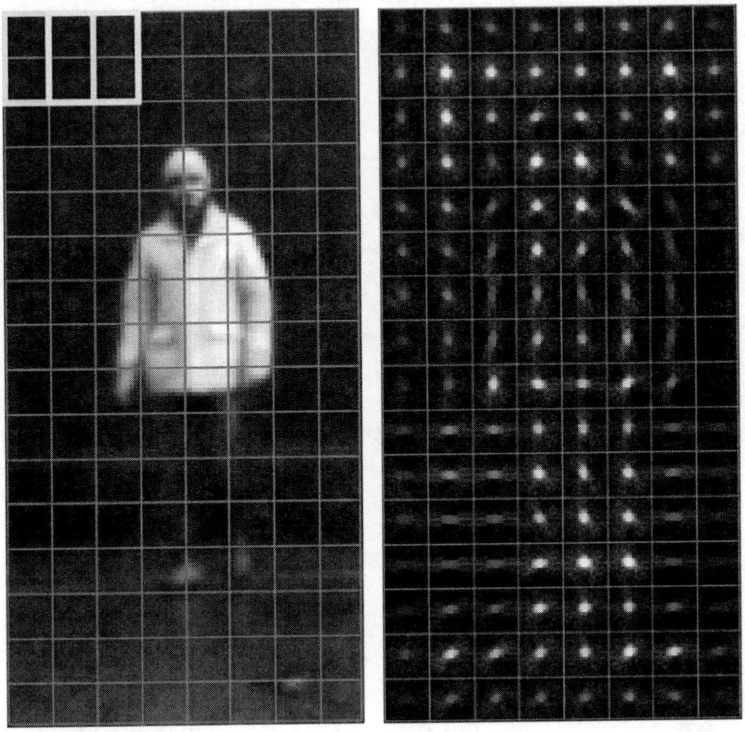

(a) (b)

Figure 3. (a) The histogram of oriented gradients (HoG) descriptor is computed over image cells (in red) and 2 × 2 overlapping blocks of cells (green and cyan); **(b)**visualization of the HoG descriptor computed for the same image

5.2. SVM Classifier

The evaluation of the HoG descriptors is performed by a linear support vector machine classifier. SVM is a machine learning algorithm, proposed by Cortes and Vapnik [34], that has been extensively used in pattern recognition applications. The linear SVM method conceptually follows and extends the idea that input vectors, $s_i \in \mathbb{R}^n$, can be effectively separated by a hyper plane, $w^T w + b > 0$, lying on the same n-dimensional space. It mainly focuses on finding the hyper plane that achieves the maximum separation between the two classes. For that, it is also known as a maximal margin classifier. By using kernels, such as polynomials or Radial Basis Functions, the data can be mapped into higher dimensions, $f(s_i) : \mathbb{R}^n \rightarrow \mathbb{R}^m$, $m > n$. This allows further insight into higher order feature spaces. Finally, since the method is less susceptible to outliers, it has been proven to be very effective on non-separable classes.

5.3. Adaptive ROI Projection

The laser module performs the segmentation of the laser data into separate clusters, described in Section 4.1. Each individual cluster is, afterwards, projected into the image plane using the parameters obtained by the laser—camera extrinsic calibration, as explained in Section 7.1 and shown in Figure 2. Considering that the field of view of the camera is much smaller than the angular range of the laser range finder, it is apparent that only a portion of the clusters can be accordingly projected.

From the optical theory, the distance of an object with known dimensions can be calculated from its projection on the sensor. If the procedure is inverted, it is possible to obtain the height in pixels of an object, when its distance and dimensions are known, as described by Equation (1).

$$ROI\ Height(pixel) = \frac{Object\ Height(m) \times Frame\ Height(pixel) \times Focal\ Length(m)}{Distance(m) \times Sensor\ Height(m)} \tag{1}$$

In Equation (1), ROI height is the wanted height of the projection window in pixels, object height is the corresponding height in the physical world, the frame height is the sensor's pixel resolution in the corresponding axis, focal length is the intrinsic lens parameter, distance is the distance of the cluster's centroid from the camera and sensor height is the camera's physical sensor dimension. The range information from the laser and the extrinsic calibration provide the distance of the object's centroid from the camera. An approximation of the object dimensions can be acquired by taking into account the medium human height and also by using some detailed information on how the HoG descriptor classifier is trained.

The dimensions of the training images are 128 × 64 pixels, and according to the creators, there is a sixteen pixel margin around the person [11]. This means that the human figure occupies 75% of the image height. In Section 7.3, INRIAand MIThuman databases are described in more detail. According to recent statistics, medium human height is estimated to be 175 ± 15 *cm* [35]. The projection window dimensions can be estimated by adding the margin used for the training data set and taking into account the variations around mediums. These estimations range from 2.0 × 1.0 *m* to 3.0 × 1.5 *m*. It is worth noting that, since HoG is computed over a region of constant dimensions, the maximum effective distance is linearly related to the projected window size. This can be illustratively seen in Figure 4a.

It is evident that strictly defining the ROI size leads to some misclassifications, due to human height variations. Furthermore, the laser data can only confine the extremes of each object horizontally. The vertical boundaries can be estimated by taking into account the distance of the object and the height of the laser sensor with respect to the ground. Unfortunately, this hypothesis only stands true for even surfaces and while the UGV is static. When the platform is moving, pitch changes are very probable to occur, due to inherent vibrations, acceleration or deceleration. Furthermore, terrain irregularities, steep inclination and other uncontrolled factors may produce the same effect.

A novel method of adaptive projection has been used in order to restrict these effects. Instead of using a fixed-size window, a pyramid of meaningful sizes is constructed and thoroughly searched for possible human presence. Additionally, the use of an enlarged projection window increases the operational range of the vision module, thus producing overall more reliable results.

Initially, a 3.0 × 1.5 *m* ROI is extracted from the image, according to the distance of the cluster. Next, the HoG descriptors are computed with a sliding window of dimensions 128 × 64 over an overlapping grid with a step of eight pixels in each direction. A visualization of the overlapping sliding window can be seen in Figure 4b. As previously mentioned, there is no use in probing regions of size less than 2.0 × 1.0 *m*. Therefore, in this first step, if the sliding window corresponds to a size smaller than this threshold, the original region is scaled down in pixels accordingly. This significantly speeds up the process by eliminating searches in a space of irrelevant size. Afterwards, the extracted region is scaled down by a predetermined factor, and the procedure continues iteratively until the sliding window reaches the final scale of 3.0 × 1.5 *m*. Finally, the pyramid of the descriptors is evaluated by the previously trained SVM classifier.

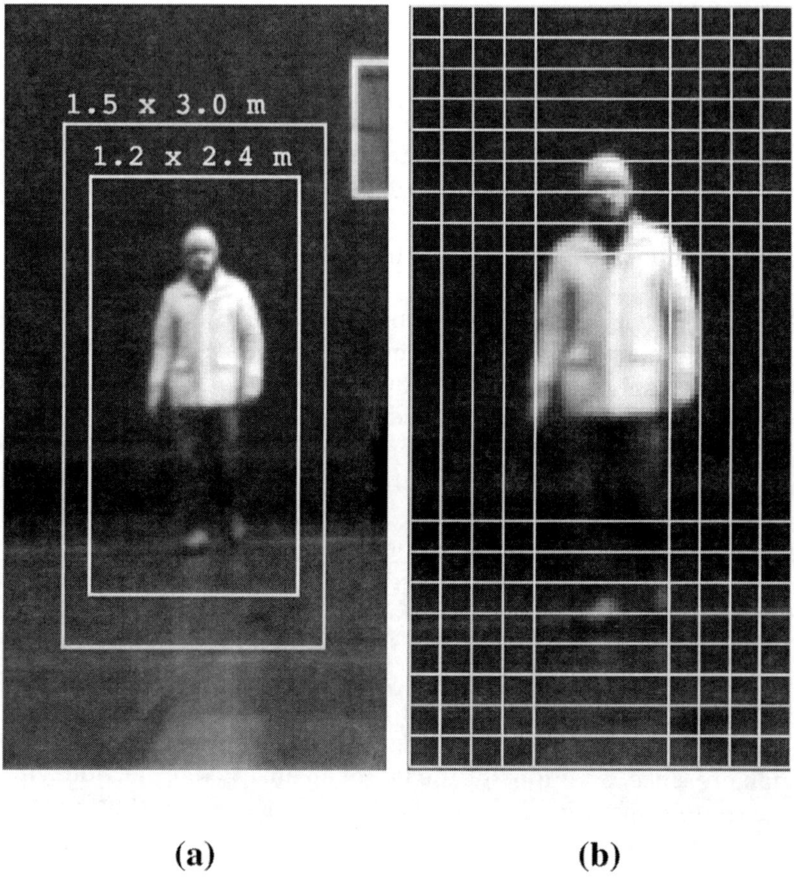

Figure 4. (a) Projection of the same cluster for different corresponding sizes. The cyan rectangle is used in the fixed case, and the larger green window is used in the proposed adaptive method. **(b)** In the adaptive method, the region of interest (ROI) is scanned by an overlapping sliding window over multiple scales. In this figure, the maximum scale of the pyramid is depicted and the sliding window is of the size 2.0 × 1.0 meters.

The evaluation over a large number of sliding windows, typically contained in a region, will likely contain some false predictions. Methods, like non-maximum suppression and mean shift, have been proposed in order to cluster multiple detections when no prior knowledge is available [36]. In order to take into account the extra information available from the range data, a new way to discriminate between positive and negative examples is proposed. As previously mentioned, the classifier used has a high rejection rate, which produces only a few false alarms. Therefore the space-scale pyramidal search can be approached from a statistical perspective as a *Bernoulli process* with a product space given by $P = \{p, 1 - p\}^{\mathbb{N}}$, where $p$is the possibility of success and N, the number of trials. Consequently, the evaluation of each sliding window corresponds to a *Bernoulli trial.* The probability of *success rate* can be approximated by the true negative rate of the SVM classifier on a representative test set. From the above results, the probability of having k true negative predictions out of n trials is given by the following equation:

$$P(X = k) = \binom{n}{k} p^k (1 - p)^{n-k} \tag{2}$$

In Equation (2), n is known, so it is possible to deduct the number of trials, k_{thr}, so that $P(X > k_{thr}) \leq 1 - T_P$. In practice, the value of the probability threshold, T_P, is not very important, provided it is sufficiently small to reject random false alarms. If the number of trials classified as belonging to the positive class is greater than k_{thr}, then the output of the algorithm is positive.

Since a multitude of sub-windows is evaluated for each cluster, there is an increase in the computational cost of the algorithm. Nevertheless, this increase is not significant enough to create a bottleneck and, thus, does not limit the real time functionality of the method. An outline of the method is shown in Algorithm 2.

6. INFORMATION FUSION SCHEME

In the fusion module, the output prediction is improved by combining information from the two different sources in a meaningful way. The process of correlating data between the two sensors is addressed with the adaptive ROI projection described in Section 5.3. This preliminary fusion step ensures the correspondence between the outcome of the sensors, permitting further exploitation of their relationship.

Algorithm 2 Outline of adaptive projection window method.

Input: A 3.0 *by* 1.5 m image region $I \in \mathbb{R}^{2N \times N}$ and $T_P \ll 1$ probability threshold, where N is the width of I in pixels.

Initialization: If the filter sliding window, S, of 128×64 pixels corresponds to less than 2.0 *by* 1.0 m, then, accordingly, scale down I.

Procedure:

while S corresponding dimension $\leq$ 3.0 *by* 1.5m **do**
    $n = 0$; ▷ number of total pyramid windows
    for $i = 1$; until S traverses all I vertically; $i \leftarrow i + 8$ **do**
        for $j = 1$; until S traverses all I horizontally; $j \leftarrow j + 8$ **do**
            $H_n \leftarrow$ HoG descriptor of $S(I_{i,j})$
            $C_n, P_n \leftarrow$ class and probability output of linear SVM classifier for input H_n
            $n \leftarrow n + 1$
        end for
    end for
    Scale down I by a constant scaling factor, F.
end while
Find k for which $P(X > k) = \binom{n}{k} p^k (1-p)^{n-k} \leq 1 - T_P$
if $sum(C_n == +1) > k$ **then**
    $C_{out} \leftarrow +1$
    $P_{out} \leftarrow max(P_n)$
else
    $C_{out} \leftarrow -1$
    $P_{out} \leftarrow min(P_n)$
end if

Output: The output class, C_{out}, and probability, P_{out}

The decentralized fusion scheme employed in this study uses probability estimations derived from each detection module. Initially, the outputs of each individual detector have to be mapped to a calibrated probability distribution. After that, three different approaches of probabilistic fusion are assessed to obtain a final estimation of certainty.

6.1. Calibrated Probabilities

The fusion scheme is focused on providing increased accuracy by integrating the two distinct detection methodologies described previously. Since the techniques are based on probabilistic estimates, the accuracy of those estimates is very important.

Classifiers, like SVM and AdaBoost, tend to maximize the margin between the two classes, and their calculated scores are shifted away from the typical range of probability values. This bias creates a distorted probability distribution. A method, *f*, for transforming the classifier score, *x*, to posterior probability is necessary in order to overcome this inconsistency:

$$x \in (-\infty, \infty) \xrightarrow{f} P(y = 1|x) \in (0, 1)$$

Considering support vector machines, Platt [29] proposed that this could be accomplished by passing the output of the classifier through a parametric sigmoid function:

$$P(y = 1|x) = \frac{1}{1 + \exp(Ax + b)} \quad (3)$$

The parameters of the sigmoid are fitted post-training, using maximum likelihood estimation on a calibration set (x_i, y_i), as shown in Equation (4). Gradient descent is used for the minimization process.

$$\underset{A,b}{\text{argmin}} \left\{ -\sum_i y_i log(p_i) + (1 - y_i) log(1 - p_i) \right\} \quad (4)$$

Where

$$p_i = \frac{1}{1 + \exp(Ax_i + b)}$$

The statistical interpretation of AdaBoost dictates that calibrated probabilities can be obtained by logistic correction. In this case, the theoretically proven parameters of the sigmoid are $A = -2$ and $b = 0$ [32]. This method works in the case of decision stumps, but when decision trees with more splits are used, the calibration tends to be poor. Similarly to SVM, Platt's scaling method has been experimentally tested with AdaBoost and other large margin classifiers, providing good calibration results [30].

6.2. Fusion Techniques

A probabilistic framework is incorporated to combine the outputs of the classifiers. The outputs inferred from the sensor data, z, are considered as conditional probabilities that depend on the underlying state, x, of the object under examination. Their likelihood is denoted as $\Lambda_i(x_j) = P(z_i|x_j)$, where i is the label of the sensor, $z_i \in \{z_l \equiv \text{laser}, z_c \equiv \text{camera}\}$, and $j$corresponds to the states, $x_j \in \{x_1 \equiv \text{person}, x_2 \equiv \text{not person}\}$. When an observation is made, the sensor reading is considered fixed, and i is known; thus, the likelihood function, $\Lambda_i(x_j)$, is considered a distribution in x_j.

A reasonable hypothesis is to assume the same confidence for both sensors, so the same weight is assigned to them in every fusion technique. Their likelihood is finally combined to compute the posterior probability, which corresponds to the presence of a person, $P(x_1|z_l \cap z_c)$. Three different formulas—maximum, average and Bayesian-average—are evaluated for the purposes of comparison. The first two are simple and straightforward. The maximum formula is expressed as:

$$Maximum(P(x_1|z_l \cap z_c)) = \max_{i=l,c}(\Lambda_i(x_1)) \tag{5}$$

while the average formula is:

$$Average(P(x_1|z_l \cap z_c)) = \frac{\sum\limits_{i=l,c}(\Lambda_i(x_1))}{2} \tag{6}$$

The third fusion technique is inspired and derived from the Bayes theorem. In this formulation, a posterior distribution,$P(x_1|z_l \cap z_c)$, can be expressed as the normalized product of the likelihoods, $\Lambda_i(x_1)$, given the presence of a person. From Bayes theorem, this can be directly written as follows:

$$P(x_1|z_l \cap z_c) = \frac{P(z_l \cap z_c|x_1)P(x_1)}{P(z_l \cap z_c)} \tag{7}$$

The joint distribution, $P(z_l \cap z_c|x_1)$, must be known for computing the posterior probability, which is generally a difficult and complex task. In practice, the information obtained by different sources, z_l and z_c, can be considered *independent* when conditioned on the real underlying state of the object. Although this condition does not always stand true, it facilitates the computation of the combined posterior probability for different values of the state. The resulting equation is known as the*independent likelihood pool* [37]. Moreover, Equation (7) depends on prior information, $P(x_j)$, representing any previous knowledge about the occurrence of the states. Under the strong assumption that individual states are described by a *uniform prior,* $\mathcal{U}(x_j)$, the final formula is devised:

$$Bayes(P(x_1|z_l \cap z_c)) = \frac{\prod_{i=l,c} \Lambda_i(x_1)}{P(z_l \cap z_c)} \tag{8}$$

where the denominator constitutes the marginal distribution, which acts as a normalizing factor, and can be defined as:

$$P(z_l \cap z_c) = \sum_{j=1}^{2} \prod_{i=l,c} \Lambda_i(x_j) \tag{9}$$

7. EXPERIMENTS

In this section, the platform used for testing our methodology is briefly described. First, the laser-camera calibration procedure is described. Then, the experiments carried out to collect the data sets are explained in detail. Furthermore, it also describes how the classifier training was made and which evaluation criteria were used.

7.1. Calibration

A correct calibration of the sensors is very important for the fusion implementation, because it serves two purposes. First, the intrinsic calibration provides the focal length (f_x, f_y) and principal point (c_x, c_y) of the camera sensors. It also provides the necessary radial and tangential parameters to compensate for inherent lens distortion (k_1, k_2, k_3, p_1, p_2). Additionally, extrinsic laser-camera calibration is used to obtain the requisite rotation and translation matrices (R, T), which allow the transformation of a point belonging to the laser plane, into the image sensor pixel coordinates.

The procedure is formulated by the pinhole camera model, which has been implemented with a numerical precision of up to sixth order coefficients. First, using the translation and rotation matrices, the points are converted from the laser frame to a frame fixed with respect to the camera. Next, the points from the camera frame are perspectively projected to the image plane. The projection to the image plane is distorted, due to imperfections of the lens. This can be compensated for by undistorting the image using the distortion coefficients provided by the intrinsic calibration. Finally, the undistorted image plane coordinates are transformed into the equivalent pixel coordinates of the sensor using the intrinsic camera parameters of focal length principal point. The procedure is depicted in Figure 5.

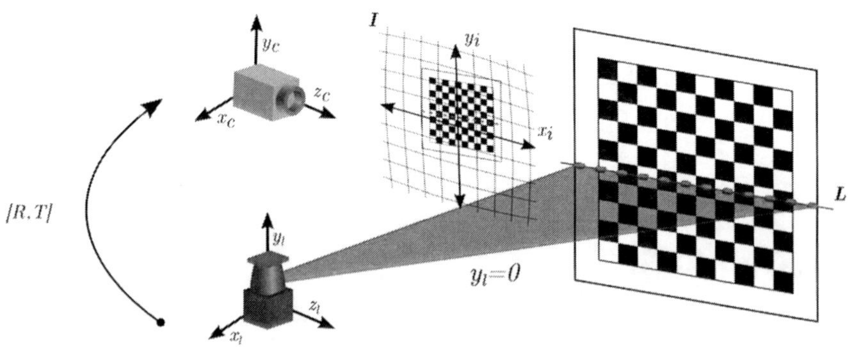

Figure 5. Two reference frames are shown, one with respect to the camera (x_c, y_c, x_c) and another with respect to the laser (x_l, y_l, x_l). The extrinsic calibration provides the matrices, *R*, *T*, containing the rotation and translation between the two frames. *I*corresponds to the 2D image plane. The laser plane, *L*, is defined by $y_l = 0$.

A reference object, such as a flat checkerboard, is used for the calibration process. In order to record the calibration data, the object is positioned at various distances and orientations with respect to the sensors. Consequently, the normal vector of the checkerboard is extracted for every image, and the matching line parameters are computed from the range data. Therefore, to minimize the discrepancy between them, Zhang and Pless [38] proposed a two-stage process. First, a linear estimation is computed in order to get a rough estimate of the *R* and *T* matrices. Then, their final values are obtained by the optimization of a quadratic error function. Further improvements in the automatic object extraction and optimization can be found in [39].

7.2. Platform

The proposed methodology was assessed using data acquired on board a *Summit XL*™ mobile robotic platform developed by *Robotnik*™. It is equipped with a range of active and passive sensors, such as an IMU, a differential GPS, a pan-tilt-zoom camera and a laser range finder, among others. The maximum speed of the platform, which can be seen in Figure 6a, is three meters per second.

(a) (b)

Figure 6. Platform and sensors used in experiments. (**a**) Summit XL mobile platform; (**b**) Hokuyo laser range finder above the Firefly camera.

In our setup, a *Hokuyo UTM-30LX-EW*™ is used. It is a laser range finder that provides a measurement range of 30 meters and an angular range of 270° degrees with 40 Hz (scans per second) acquisition frequency. All data points have a fixed angular resolution of 0.25° degrees. The data are transferred through the TCP/IPprotocol and are collected using a driver built upon the communication specification protocol of the laser (SCIP). Data points are represented by polar coordinates (ϕ,ρ).

The vision system consists of a monochrome *Firefly MV*® camera by *Point Grey*™ with a resolution of 752 × 480 pixels, a horizontal angle of view of 59° and a frame rate of 60 FPS. The camera uses the IEEE1394 (FireWire) protocol to send the data through a USB cable. The acquisition was made with a driver developed using a Linux APIfor FireWire cameras. Automatic CMOSsensor parameters were used where possible.

Before any data acquisition, the sensors were calibrated both intrinsically (camera) and extrinsically (camera-laser) with the procedure described in Section 7.1. Both sensors stamp their data with the acquisition time to enable the synchronization between scans and frames. Figure 6b shows a detailed image of the two sensors and their geometrical configuration.

7.3. Data Acquisition

The data were gathered while manually driving the platform inside the campus of the School of Industrial Engineering of the Polytechnic University of Madrid (ETSII-UPM). Three different datasets were collected in two different places. The first two sets of data were collected in the campus gymnasium, the first while the platform was held static and the second while it was moving. Although being a closed environment, the gymnasium was illuminated with dispersed natural light under cloudy conditions. In order to record the third set of data, another experiment was carried out in an outdoor area of the campus, where, usually, a lot of pedestrians pass by. Throughout this experiment, the platform was moving. Lighting conditions consisted mostly of direct sunlight with temporary cloud interference.

Inside the gym, in the static scenarios, only one person, following a predetermined route, passed in front of the robot each time. In the moving scenarios, a random number of people passed in front of the robot while it was moving. The people were walking in random paths, and in many cases, occlusions have happened, when people have crossed with each other. In one specific scenario, the people were standing still, while the robot was moving. There were no obstacles between the robot and the people walking in the gymnasium experiments. Outdoors, the experiments were held in a university campus area, and the people were walking in front of the moving robot in various directions. Some people were static and others at a level different from the robot. Furthermore, more occlusions happened when people crossed with each other or when they interacted with other surrounding elements. The robot's speed in the gymnasium was 0.25–0.50 m/s and outdoors, 0.50–0.75 m/s.

The complete set of data consists of 21,550 time-synchronized pairs of laser scans and image frames. The laser scans were segmented into clusters using the algorithm described in Section 4.1. The segmentation threshold was initially estimated using methods from [14]. These methods are more suitable for discerning between human legs. Since the creation of one cluster per person is important for the subsequent projection, the threshold was experimentally adjusted to the final value of*30 cm*. After the segmentation, a total of 485,420 laser clusters were produced, 43,040 of which belong to humans. Annotation of the clusters was done manually, aided by vision images where possible. To accelerate the annotation process, an assistive algorithm was developed. Our entire set corresponds to more than 625 seconds of real world data recordings. Altogether 28 distinct people appear in all three scenarios. A detailed description of the data sets can be found in Table 3.

Table 3. Overview of the acquired data set. Three scenarios in two different places were collected in total.

	Gymnasium		Outdoors	Total
	Static	Moving	Moving	
Scans	10,350	10,800	4,000	25,150
Total segments	191,418	191,426	102,576	485,420
Human segments	10,179	22,412	10,449	43,040
Seconds	258.75	270	100	628.75
Persons appearing	6	12	10	28

As has been noted, the vision module only takes part in the classification of a portion of the segments produced by the laser. The number and the quality characteristics of these clusters vary, depending on which projection size and method are used. In this work, two different methods are compared. The first one is the fixed projection window, and the other one is the proposed adaptive projection algorithm. Our experiments have shown that in the fixed-width case, a size of 2.4 × 1.2 m gives the best results. In the adaptive projection case, the size of 3.0 × 1.5 *m* corresponds to the maximum scale of the pyramid.

From Equation (1), the range of the fixed window is calculated between 3.33–12.5 *m*, while that of the adaptive projection is 4.17–15.63 *m*. This increased range means that the critically more distant clusters are evaluated by both detection modules, something that increases the overall detection performance and the robustness of the method. Apart from the farther reach, the projective window approach also increases the operational range from 9.17 *m* to 11.46 *m*. This is the reason why more clusters are evaluated overall by *both* modules. Since the fusion of the two outcomes generates better results, this can be considered another advantage over the fixed-size projection. The difference in the evaluated clusters is depicted in Table 4, where the fusion data sets corresponding to the adaptive projection method are significantly larger that their fixed method counterparts.

Table 4. Data sets used for fusion detection. Different ROI projection sizes lead to different data sets.

	Fixed-size ROI	Adaptive ROI
Total segments	12,686	18,504
Human segments	10,780	12,531

(a) Gymnasium experiment (moving scenario).

	Fixed-size ROI	Adaptive ROI
Total segments	27,261	30,543
Human segments	6480	6611

(b) Outdoors experiment.

7.4. Classifier Training and Calibration

Two distinct classifiers were trained and calibrated, one for each detection module. For the laser module, a Real AdaBoost classifier is used. It is made up of twenty weak classifiers, namely two-split decision trees. This setting is chosen, after several experiments, on the grounds of performance *versus* computational cost tradeoff, while trying to avoid overfitting, as well. Three different feature sets are compared. The first one is composed of the feature basis of Table 1. The second one is derived by the addition of distance-based features to the feature basis, and the third consists of the proposed 63-feature vector that is described in Section 4.2.

The stratified two-fold cross validation (holdout method) is used to produce the results. The training and test sets are derived from the complete data sets of Table 3. First, the training is done on the training set and the evaluation on the test set, followed by the reverse order. This way, each cluster on the test set is used both for training and evaluation. A separate classifier is trained and tested for each one of the three data sets.

Furthermore, the generalization properties of the method are also tested. A classifier is trained using the complete data set from the gymnasium moving scenario. It is then tested on the data from the outdoors scenario. The procedure is also done*vice versa*. This gives an insight of how well each feature set can adapt to a new environment.

For the vision module, two established, openly available databases were used. The first one is the MIT pedestrian image database, which consists of 924 pedestrian images (positive) limited to frontal and rear views [40]. The second one is the more challenging and complete INRIA person database [11]. The picture quality of the databases is very similar to the one produced by the camera used in our experiments. The rationale on using established databases over a proprietary data-set is because they cover a large number of human poses in a large variety of scenes that would be very difficult to replicate within our experiments. Using a restricted database could possible harm the generalization of the method, and since the objective of the proposed system is to be applied in a diverse environment, a more versatile approach was adopted.

The INRIA training set contains 2,416 positive images and 1,218 negative images, and the test set contains 1,126 positive and 453 negative images. Positive images from both databases are scaled to a size of 128 × 64 pixels, with the person located at the center of the image. Around the person, there is a sixteen pixel-wide margin. People appear in various poses and orientations in a broad range of backgrounds. From each non-pedestrian image of the INRIA database, a number of negative cropped images are randomly extracted, both for the training and the testing sets.

The HoG descriptors, computed for each image of the dataset, were used to train an SVM classifier. After some initial tests, it was observed that non-linear kernels show very small improvement—less than two percent—in comparison with the linear case. This improvement was accompanied by a disproportional increase in the computational cost. In their work, Dalal *et al.* [11] have drawn analogous conclusions. Furthermore, our results have not shown observable overfitting, neither in the initial cross validations tests nor with the final test set. Under the assumption that the database is uncorrelated, this can be attributed to the relatively high ratio between the input vector dimension and the training dataset size. For such reasons, the implementation used in this work is based on the linear version of the method. The only choice that had been made was the value of *C*, which modulates the importance of outliers lying beyond the support vectors. Using a relatively small value (0.01) means putting less importance on outliers and results in the training of what is commonly mentioned as a*soft* SVM classifier.

The training procedure consists of two steps. First, a preliminary linear SVM classifier is individually trained using the randomly extracted negative samples described above. Afterwards, all the negative images are exhaustively searched over the space-scale pyramid using the preliminary classifier. Every example that is falsely classified as one containing a human (false positive) is considered a *hard example*, and it is added to the negative training pool. The final SVM classifier is trained using the extended negative training set constructed in the previous step. These preliminary and final training sets along with the test set can be seen in Table 5. The final classifier is evaluated on the aforementioned test set, and the resulting confusion matrix is presented in Table 6. Note that the true negative ratio in this table serves as an approximation of the probability, *p*, in the binomial distribution expressed in Equation (2).

Table 5. Data sets used for support vector machine (SVM) classifier training.

	Preliminary Training	**Final Training**	**Testing**
Positive (Human) [INRIA,MIT]	3,340	3,340	1,126
Negative (Non-human) [INRIA]	12,800	47,229	4,530

Table 6. Confusion matrix of the final HoG-SVM classifier on the INRIA test set. The percentages in parenthesis are computed horizontally and correspond to TPR, FNR, FPR and TNR, respectively.

		Predicted Label	
		Human	Non-human
Actual	Human	1,071 (95.12%)	55 (4.88%)
	Non human	40 (0.88%)	4,490 (99.12%)

After the training of the classifiers, the probability calibration is necessary in order to obtain accurate fusion results. As explained in Section 6.1, Platt's scaling method is used for extracting the parameters, A and b, of the sigmoid in Equation (3). As a calibrating set, the test sets of each classifier are used. The results for the SVM are $A = -3.82$, $b = 0.56$ and for the AdaBoost, $A = -1.78$, $b = -0.067$, accordingly. It is worth noting that when stumps (one-split decision trees) were used in our experiments as weak classifiers for boosting, the theoretically expected values of $A = -2$, $b = 0$ were experimentally verified.

8. RESULTS

The results of a classifier are often presented in the form of confusion matrices. Unfortunately, when several data sets are used, confusion matrices become relatively difficult to compare. In order to facilitate the comparison of results, a combination of three well-known metrics that capture the classifier behavior in total are used: precision, recall and specificity. Recall is otherwise referred to as sensitivity or the true positive rate, while specificity is also known as the true negative rate.

For the visualization of the results, various modalities exist in the literature, such as the receiver operating characteristic (ROC) curves and precision-recall graphs. In our work, detection error tradeoff (DET) graphs are chosen in order to simplify performance comparison. DET plots are variants of ROC curves that provide better insight when a particular operating range is of principal interest [41]. The false positive rate between 10^{-3} and 10^{-1}, which is the most important in our case, is well articulated using this method. It thereby facilitates comparison.

8.1. Laser Module Results

First, the laser module on the complete acquired data sets, as described in Table 3, is evaluated. Three feature sets are used to train two distinct Real AdaBoost classifiers in each scenario: the basis feature set of Table 1, the basis with distance features added (Basis + DIST) and the proposed feature set.

It is observed that, regardless of the feature set used, the experiments carried out indoors give better results than those performed outdoors. Likewise, static experiments in the gym are *easier* than the moving experiments in the same scene. This can be attributed to the different complexities of the scenario and to the fact that outdoors, there is more noise in the data, due to direct sunlight illumination, terrain irregularities and other factors.

More specifically, the results show that the Basis + DIST feature set performs better in the experiments carried out inside the gymnasium, while the set proposed here is better suited for the outdoors environment. The simple basis set without the distance features has inferior performance in all experiments in comparison with the other two features sets. In the moving scenarios of the gymnasium experiment, the Basis + DIST feature set provides a 1.5% increase in recall and precision when compared to the proposed one. On the other hand, outdoors, our proposed set provides an improvement of more than 3.5% in recall and more than 2% in precision over the Basis + DIST set performance. These findings are also evident in the DET plot in Figure 7a, where it is shown that the proposed feature set provides better recall rates over the complete operating range in the outdoors experiment. At the same time, the Basis + DIST set offers an increase over the basis set of more than 10% in recall and 3.5% in precision for the gym experiment, but only a smaller increase in recall of 3.4% outdoors, affirming that distant-dependent features are less important in outdoor scenarios. Detailed metrics are shown in Table 2.

On the second experiment, the training and test sets correspond to different scenarios. In this case, the importance of using distance-independent features becomes more apparent. As observed in Figure 7b, the proposed feature set generalizes and performs better than the Basis + DIST set for the whole operating range. Specifically, when the outdoor data were used as the training set and the gymnasium data as the test set, the gain in recall is more than 10% for false positive rates less than 10^{-2}. From the same figure, it can be deduced that the normal basis set performs very similarly to the Basis + DIST set and even better in the critical operational range between 10^{-3} and 10^{-2}. This further solidifies the hypotheses that the inclusion of distance-dependent features may harm the robustness of the method.

Another interesting conclusion that can be drawn from this graph is that, when data from outdoors are used for training and data from the gymnasium are used for testing, the classifiers perform significantly better than the opposite case. This was somewhat expected, since outdoor environments are generally more diverse or *difficult*. In the gymnasium experiments, the information is more canonical and cannot embrace the additional perplexity.

Generally, the results can be explained in the sense that the indoor readings are significantly confined from the surrounding structures. In a setting like this, distance-based features can be highly discriminative. On the contrary, in large outdoor environments, the same restrictions do not usually occur, and the need for a more generalized feature set becomes apparent. Additionally, in such environments, the information available is more noisy, due to sunlight, platform vibration and other uncontrolled factors; thus, the clusters are represented by a varying number of points. The proposed feature vector is able to encompass these variations, and the classifier learns to discriminate the data better. Most importantly, using our method results in a more robust training of the classifier, helping it to perform better in diverse scenarios, even if it was trained with a different dataset. This aspect is crucial for applications in autonomous large infrastructure surveillance.

Finally, it should be noted that although the feature vector in the proposed set is much larger, the execution speed is the same or even better. This happens because in the real time applications, only the feature subset chosen by the trained AdaBoost classifier needs to be extracted instead of the whole feature set.

8.2. Fusion Results

For the fusion experiments, only the two moving scenarios were taken into account. Comparisons are considered in two domains: first, between the performance of individual sensors and the three fusion techniques—maximum, mean, Bayes—presented in Section 6.2; second, between the fixed and proposed adaptive projection methods. Data sets are shown in Table 4, and their difference is explained in Section 7.3.

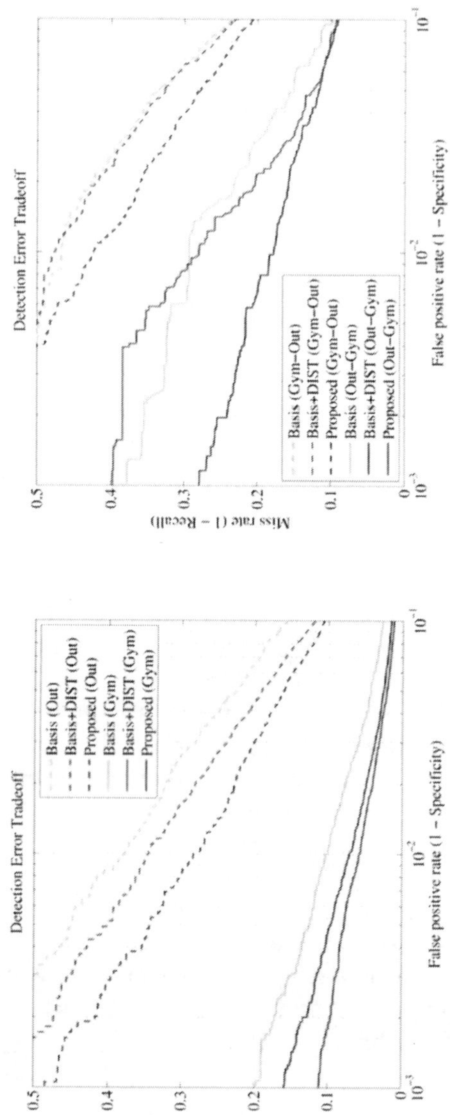

(a) Train and test on the same experiment.

(b) Cross experiment validation.

Figure 7. In both figures, the green line corresponds to the basis feature set, the red line to the basis plus the distance features and the blue line to the proposed feature set. (**a**) The training and test sets are acquired from the split up of same experimental data: solid lines indicate the gymnasium and dotted lines the outdoors data sets, respectively. (**b**) Solid lines signify that the outdoor data set is used for training and its gymnasium counterpart for testing. Dotted lines signify the reverse procedure.

Some common observations can be made from the results of both experiments in Tables 7 and 8. First of all, it should be pointed out that since the datasets for the adaptive and fixed-size projections are of different sizes, direct comparison of the results cannot be entirely conclusive. Nevertheless, the two datasets are highly correlated, because they are obtained by the same raw data. Additionally, the dataset of the adaptive method should be considered of higher complexity, not only because of its larger size, but because it includes samples lying at further distances from the sensors. This increase in maximum distance, from 12.5 *m* to 15.63 *m*, generally results in more noisy data, thus rendering the classification task more difficult.

Table 7. Comparison of the fixed (**a**) and the proposed adaptive (**b**) projection methods. The performance of using each sensor individually is also compared with three different information fusion techniques. The data sets used for these results are shown in Table 4a.

	Individual Sensors		**Information Fusion**		
	Laser	**Camera**	**Maximum**	**Mean**	**Bayes**
Precision	99.29%	99.85%	99.26%	99.82%	99.82%
Recall	92.61%	91.33%	98.15%	94.58%	94.58%
Specificity	96.28%	99.21%	95.86%	99.01%	99.01%

(**a**) Fixed-size projection.

	Individual Sensors		**Information Fusion**		
	Laser	**Camera**	**Maximum**	**Mean**	**Bayes**
Precision	98.44%	99.54%	98.44%	99.88%	99.88%
Recall	90.72%	95.68%	99.27%	95.20%	95.20%
Specificity	97.12%	99.05%	96.65%	99.76%	99.76%

(**b**) Adaptive projection.

Equivalently to the laser-only detection, the gymnasium scenario turned out to be *easier* than outdoors. What also becomes apparent is that fusion methods have better detection rates than the individual detectors in every case. More specifically, over the laser-only approach, all metrics are improved with mean and Bayesian fusion. Maximum fusion is primarily shown for comparison. However, it can be considered a reasonable choice when high recall is of great importance or when the specificity and precision of the individual classifiers is high, as observed in the gymnasium experiments.

Table 8. Comparison of the fixed (**a**) and the proposed adaptive (**b**) projection methods. The performance of using each sensor individually is also compared with three different information fusion techniques. The data sets used for these results are shown in Table 4b.

	Individual Sensors		Information Fusion		
	Laser	**Camera**	**Maximum**	**Mean**	**Bayes**
Precision	86.22%	87.17%	85.51%	99.63%	99.63%
Recall	69.43%	83.15%	91.17%	79.83%	79.83%
Specificity	96.54%	96.18%	95.18%	99.99%	99.99%

(**a**) Fixed-size projection.

	Individual Sensors		Information Fusion		
	Laser	**Camera**	**Maximum**	**Mean**	**Bayes**
Precision	85.02%	86.42%	81.55%	98.58%	98.58%
Recall	64.38%	87.52%	93.01%	82.95%	82.95%
Specificity	96.87%	96.20%	94.19%	99.67%	99.67%

(**b**) Adaptive projection.

Another finding is that the laser recall is decreased when the adaptive projection is used. This can be mainly attributed to the increased detection range, which allows more *hard* clusters to be evaluated. Less information is available for the clusters that are far away, so it is more difficult to classify them. Despite that fact, the vision module performs even better in this case, manifesting an important advantage of the adaptive approach. In both experiments, the improvement over the fixed-size method is more than 4%.

In the gymnasium experiment, the gains by fusion are moderate. The individual classifiers are already very accurate. Nevertheless, using the fixed projection, an increase of almost 2% in recall can be seen, and with the proposed method, the increase is slightly less than 4.5%. Precision and specificity improvement, over the laser results, in both cases, is more than 2.5%. It needs to be clarified that the results of mean and Bayesian fusion appear to be the same because the same threshold value has been used (0.5). Their quantitative and qualitative differences are depicted in detail in the DET curves of Figure 8. From these plots, it can be deduced that Bayesian fusion is better when the fixed projection size is used with a miss rate of 3.5% at a 10^{-2} false positive rate. With the adaptive projection, the mean rule provides the best tradeoff, with a 2.4% miss rate at the same false positive rate. Note that direct comparison with the individual sensor curves is not applicable, since the operating point can be adjusted independently for each one.

The fusion in the outdoors experiment, in general, and the adaptive projection method, in particular, demonstrate a considerable increase in metrics. As far as individual classifier performance is concerned, when the adaptive projection is used, the vision module performance increases by more than 4.3%, while the laser module recall drops by more than 5%. This is because the laser module is heavily affected by the inclusion of further, more difficult to classify, clusters. Fusion with the fixed-width projection improves recall, precision and specificity by more than 10.4%, 13.4% and 3.4%, respectively. In the adaptive projection, recall is boosted by more than 18.5%, precision by 13.5% and specificity by 3.2%. The most prominent improvement in recall is when the maximum fusion ruled is used. In this case, the increase is almost 22% for the fixed-window projection and greater than 28% for adaptive projection. Detailed results can be found in Table 8. Similarly to the gymnasium experiment, the Bayesian rule gives better tradeoff curves when the fixed-size projection is used and the mean rule in the adaptive method, as can be observed in Figure 9. Overall, the advantage of the adaptive projection is twofold: significantly improving the fusion results, while providing further detections and a larger operating range.

Since the system is designed to be used in real-time surveillance, computational efficiency is also of high importance. The results presented here were produced by offline processing of data using a prototype of the method. At the same time, a speed optimized version was developed. Although not yet fully deployed, preliminary tests show an execution rate of more than 8 Hz, depending mainly on the number of clusters and, to a lesser extent, on their distance from the camera.

The visualization of the detection algorithm in Figure 10 gives a qualitative view of the proposed methodology. They include various people crossing each other and moving along the surroundings, in both experimental scenes.

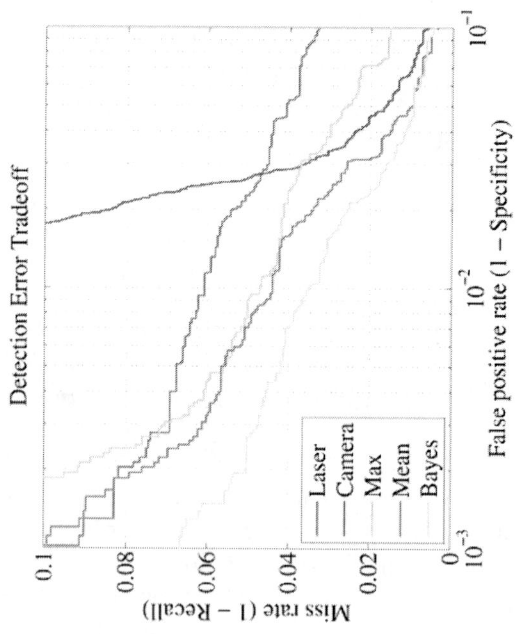

(a) Fixed-size projection.

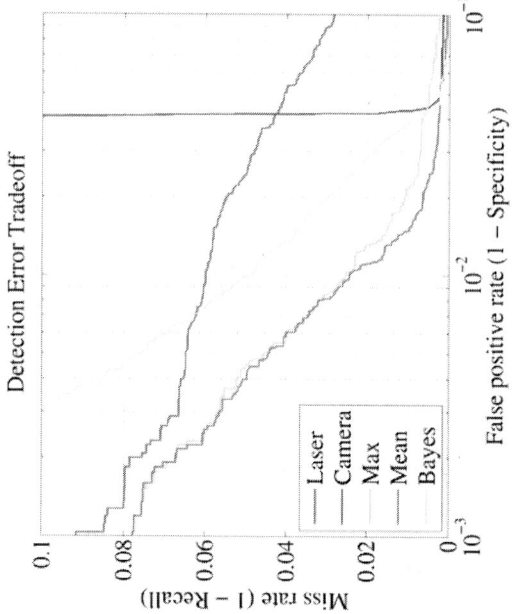

(b) Adaptive projection.

Figure 8. The curves are plotted for each sensor individually and, also, for the three fusion techniques. Fixed-size **(a)** and adaptive **(b)** projection techniques are compared.

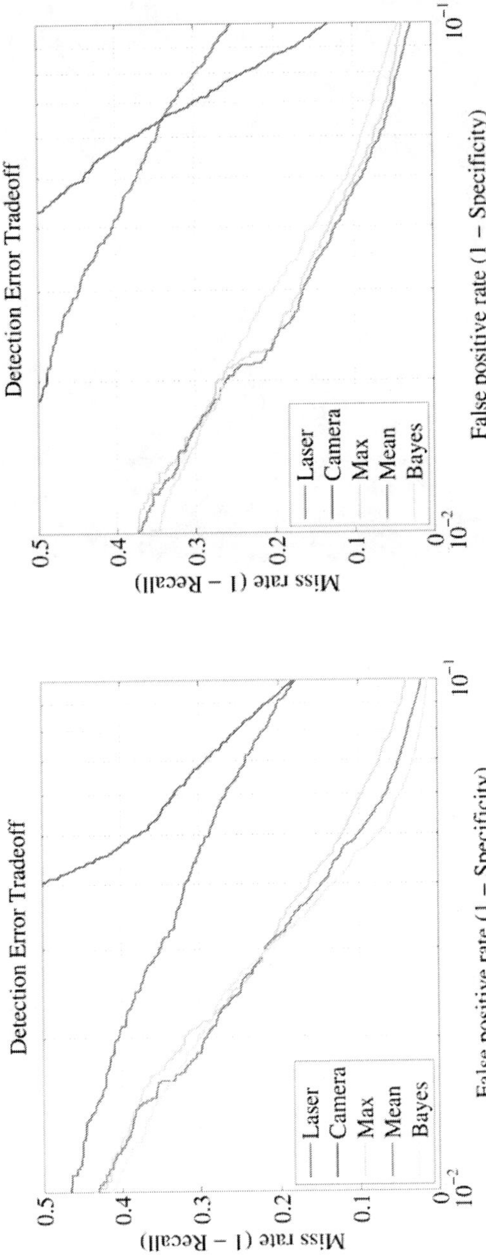

(a) Fixed-size projection.

(b) Adaptive projection.

Figure 9. The curves are plotted for each sensor individually and, also, for the three fusion techniques. Fixed-size **(a)** and adaptive **(b)** projection techniques are compared.

Figure 10. Detector images from the gymnasium **(a)**, **(b)** and outdoor experiments **(c)**,**(d)**. The boxes above each cluster give the probability of the laser and image detection modules and the mean fused probability. Cluster distance is shown at the bottom of the enclosing rectangle. **(a)** Typical scenario with multiple people, movement in various directions and occlusions. **(b)** The laser module does not detect the right person correctly. Due to correct camera classification, the person is eventually detected after fusion. **(c)** Outdoors, the laser detector performance is considerably lower. **(d)**The right person (blue rectangle) is misclassified from both sensor modules. The person in the middle is too close to the camera; in this case, the cluster is evaluated by the laser classifier only. Persons hidden by the bench on the right are not detected by the laser.

Certainly, our approach shows some shortcomings. First, the detection range is restricted by the vision sensor resolution. Fortunately, this can be resolved by utilizing another sensor. The cost in speed will not be significantly affected, due to the downscaling step at the beginning of Algorithm 2. Moreover, uneven terrain levels and rapid accelerations of the mobile platform can be addressed by the adaptive projection method only to a certain extent.

9. CONCLUSIONS

This work has demonstrated that it is feasible to accurately detect human presence from a robotic mobile platform using information from both laser and vision sensors. It is observed that meaningful fusion significantly improves the performance over single sensor detection. Furthermore, an adaptive method to address the issue of misalignment of image projection is introduced. This method was shown to outperform fixed-size projection methods, while providing longer and further detection range. For the laser detection domain, a scene independent feature set based on state-of-the-art characteristics has been created. By utilizing normalization techniques, the classifier learns feature variations. It is also observed that the proposed feature set performs and generalizes better than previous approaches. Finally, a classifier probability calibration step was introduced in order to facilitate the information fusion from the two modules. The effectiveness of our method was verified through extensive tests on real world data, which were collected from diverse experimental scenarios.

Future work will be focused on integrating the input from the fusion detector within a tracking framework for developing a human following system. Vision data could also be exploited to distinguish among different people being tracked. Moreover, extending the method for use with a distributed multi-robot system is an ongoing line of work in our research group.

ACKNOWLEDGMENTS

This work was supported by the Robotics and Cybernetics Group at Universidad Politécnica de Madrid (Spain) and funded under the projects: ROTOS—multi-robot system for outdoor infrastructures protection—sponsored by Spanish Ministry of Education and Science (DPI2010-17998), and ROBOCITY 2030, sponsored by the Community of Madrid (S-0505/DPI/000235).

CONFLICTS OF INTEREST

The authors declare no conflict of interest.

REFERENCES

1. Valera, M.; Velastin, S. Intelligent distributed surveillance systems: A review. *IEEE Proc. Vis. Image Signal Process.* **2005**,*152*, 192–204.

2. Arras, K.; Mozos, O.; Burgard, W. Using Boosted Features for the Detection of People in 2D Range Data. Proceedings of the IEEE International Conference on Robotics and Automation, Roma, Italy, 10–14 April 2007; pp. 3402–3407.

3. Dollar, P.; Wojek, C.; Schiele, B.; Perona, P. Pedestrian detection: An evaluation of the state of the art. *IEEE Trans. Patt. Anal. Mach. Intell.* **2012**, *34*, 743–761.

4. Mertz, C.; Navarro-Serment, L.E.; MacLachlan, R.; Rybski, P.; Steinfeld, A.; Supp, A.; Urmson, C.; Vandapel, N.; Hebert, M.; Thorpe, C.; *et al.* Moving object detection with laser scanners. *J. Field Robot.* **2013**, *30*, 17–43.

5. Spinello, L.; Triebel, R.; Siegwart, R. Multimodal Detection and Tracking of Pedestrians in Urban Environments with Explicit Ground Plane Extraction. Proceedings of the IEEE/RSJ International Conference on Intelligent Robots and Systems, Nice, France, 22–26 September 2008; pp. 1823–1829.

6. Premebida, C.; Ludwig, O.; Nunes, U. LIDAR and vision-based pedestrian detection system. *J. Field Robot.* **2009**, *26*, 696–711.

7. Gandhi, T.; Trivedi, M. Pedestrian protection systems: Issues, survey, and challenges. *IEEE Trans. Intell. Transp. Syst.***2007**, *8*, 413–430.

8. Geronimo, D.; Lopez, A.M.; Sappa, A.D.; Graf, T. Survey of pedestrian detection for advanced driver assistance systems. *IEEE Trans. Patt. Anal. Mach. Intell.* **2010**, *32*, 1239–1258.

9. Bellotto, N.; Hu, H. A bank of unscented kalman filters for multimodal human perception with mobile service robots.*Int. J. Soc. Robot.* **2010**, *2*, 121–136.

10. Gerónimo, D.; López, A.; Sappa, A.D. Computer Vision Approaches to Pedestrian Detection: Visible Spectrum Survey. In *Pattern Recognition and Image Analysis*; Springer: Berlin/Heidelberg, Germany, 2007; pp. 547–554.

11. Dalal, N.; Triggs, B. Histograms of Oriented Gradients for Human Detection. Proceedings of the IEEE Computer Society Conference on Computer Vision and Pattern Recognition, San Diego, CA, USA, 25 June 2005; Volume 1, pp. 886–893.

12. Gavrila, D.M.; Munder, S. Multi-cue pedestrian detection and tracking from a moving vehicle. *Int. J. Comput. Vis.* **2007**,*73*, 41–59.

13. Leibe, B.; Leonardis, A.; Schiele, B. Robust object detection with interleaved categorization and segmentation. *Int. J. Comput. Vis.* **2008**, *77*, 259–289.

14. Premebida, C.; Nunes, U. Segmentation and Geometric Primitives Extraction from 2D Laser Range Data for Mobile Robot Applications. Proceedings of the Robotica 2005—5th National Festival of Robotics Scientific Meeting, Coimbra, Portugal, 29 April–1 May 2005; pp. 17–25.

15. Xavier, J.; Pacheco, M.; Castro, D.; Ruano, A.; Nunes, U. Fast Line, Arc/Circle and Leg Detection from Laser Scan Data in a Player Driver. Proceedings of the IEEE International Conference on Robotics and Automation, Barcelona, Spain, 18–22 April 2005; pp. 3930–3935.

16. Zhao, H.; Chen, Y.; Shao, X.; Katabira, K.; Shibasaki, R. Monitoring a Populated Environment Using Single-row Laser Range Scanners from a Mobile Platform. Proceedings of the IEEE International Conference on Robotics and Automation, Roma, Italy, 3–8 May 2007; pp. 4739–4745.

17. Ozaki, M.; Kakimuma, K.; Hashimoto, M.; Takahashi, K. Laser-based pedestrian tracking in outdoor environments by multiple mobile robots. *Sensors* **2012**, *12*, 14489–14507.

18. Labayrade, R.; Royere, C.; Gruyer, D.; Aubert, D. Cooperative fusion for multi-obstacles detection with use of stereovision and laser scanner. *Auton. Robot.* **2005**, *19*, 117–140.

19. Broggi, A.; Cerri, P.; Ghidoni, S.; Grisleri, P.; Jung, H.G. A new approach to urban pedestrian detection for automatic braking. *IEEE Trans. Intell. Trans. Syst.* **2009**, *10*, 594–605.

20. Hu, H.; Qu, Z.; Li, Z.; Hu, J.; Wei, F. Fast pedestrian recognition based on multisensor fusion. *Discret. Dyn. Nat. Soc.***2012**, *2012*, 318305:1–318305:14.

21. Douillard, B.; Fox, D.; Ramos, F. Laser and Vision Based Outdoor Object Mapping. Proceedings of the Robotics: Science and Systems (RSS), Zurich, Switzerland, 25–28 June 2008; Volume 26.

22. Kaempchen, N.; Buehler, M.; Dietmayer, K. Feature-level Fusion for Free-form Object Tracking Using Laserscanner and Video. Proceedings of the IEEE Intelligent Vehicles Symposium, Las Vegas, NV, USA, 6–8 June 2005; pp. 453–458.

23. Spinello, L.; Siegwart, R. Human Detection Using Multimodal and Multidimensional Features. Proceedings of the IEEE International Conference on Robotics and Automation, Pasadena, CA, USA, 19–23 May 2008; pp. 3264–3269.

24. Oliveira, L.; Nunes, U.; Peixoto, P.; Silva, M.; Moita, F. Semantic fusion of laser and vision in pedestrian detection.*Patt. Recog.* **2010**, *43*, 3648–3659.

25. Gate, G.; Breheret, A.; Nashashibi, F. Fast Pedestrian Detection in Dense Environment with a Laser Scanner and a Camera. Proceedings of the IEEE 69th Vehicular Technology Conference, Barcelona, Spain, 26–29 April 2009; pp. 1–6.

26. Spinello, L.; Triebel, R.; Siegwart, R. Multiclass multimodal detection and tracking in urban environments. *Int. J. Robot. Res.* **2010**, *29*, 1498–1515.

27. Zivkovic, Z.; Krose, B. Part based People Detection using 2D Range Data and Images. Proceedings of the IEEE/RSJ International Conference on Intelligent Robots and Systems, San Diego, CA, USA, 29 October–2 November 2007; pp. 214–219.

28. Musleh, B.; García, F.; Otamendi, J.; Armingol, J.M.; de la Escalera, A. Identifying and tracking pedestrians based on sensor fusion and motion stability predictions. *Sensors* **2010**, *10*, 8028–8053.

29. Platt, J.C. Probabilistic Outputs for Support Vector Machines and Comparisons to Regularized Likelihood Methods. In*Advances in Large Margin Classifiers*; MIT Press: Cambridge, MA, USA, 1999; pp. 61–74.

30. Niculescu-Mizil, A.; Caruana, R. Obtaining Calibrated Probabilities from Boosting. Proceedings of the 21st Conference on Uncertainty in Artificial Intelligence, Edinburgh, Scotland, 26–29 July 2005.

31. Schapire, R.E.; Singer, Y. Improved boosting algorithms using confidence-rated predictions. *Mach. Learn.* **1999**, *37*, 297–336.

32. Friedman, J.; Hastie, T.; Tibshirani, R. Additive logistic regression: A statistical view of boosting (With discussion and a rejoinder by the authors). *Ann. Stat.* **2000**, *28*, 337–407.

33. Lowe, D.G. Distinctive image features from scale-invariant keypoints. *Int. J. Comput. Vis.* **2004**, *60*, 91–110.

34. Cortes, C.; Vapnik, V. Support-vector networks. *Mach. Learn.* **1995**, *20*, 273–297.

35. Garcia, J.; Quintana-Domeque, C. The evolution of adult height in Europe: A brief note. *Econ. Hum. Biol.* **2007**, *5*, 340–349.

36. Tuzel, O.; Porikli, F.; Meer, P. Human Detection via Classification on Riemannian Manifolds. Proceedings of the IEEE Conference on Computer Vision and Pattern Recognition, Minneapolis, MN, USA, 18–23 June 2007; pp. 1–8.

37. Berger, J.O. *Statistical Decision Theory and Bayesian Analysis*; Springer Verlag: Berlin/Heidelberg, Germany, 1985.

38. Zhang, Q.; Pless, R. Extrinsic Calibration of a Camera and Laser Range Finder (Improves Camera Calibration). Proceedings of the IEEE/RSJ International Conference on Intelligent Robots and Systems, Sendai, Japan, 28 September–2 October 2004; Volume 3, pp. 2301–2306.

39. Kassir, A.; Peynot, T. Reliable Automatic Camera-Laser Calibration. Proceedings of the Australasian Conference on Robotics and Automation, Brisbane, Australia, 1–3 December 2010.

40. Oren, M.; Papageorgiou, C.; Sinha, P.; Osuna, E.; Poggio, T. Pedestrian Detection using Wavelet Templates. Proceedings of the IEEE Computer Society Conference on Computer Vision and Pattern Recognition, San Juan, PR, USA, 17–19 June 1997; pp. 193–199.

41. Martin, A.; Doddington, G.; Kamm, T.; Ordowski, M.; Przybocki, M. The DET Curve in Assessment of Detection Task Performance. Proceedings of the Fifth European Conference on Speech Communication and Technology, Rhodes, Greece, 22–25 September 1997.

4

FACE RECOGNITION USING COLOR LOCAL BINARY PATTERN FROM MUTUALLY INDEPENDENT COLOR CHANNELS

Gholamreza Anbarjafari

ABSTRACT

In this article, a high performance face recognition system based on local binary pattern (LBP) using the probability distribution functions (PDFs) of pixels in different mutually independent color channels which are robust to frontal homogenous illumination and planer rotation is proposed. The illumination of faces is enhanced by using the state-of-the-art technique which is using discrete wavelet transform and singular value decomposition. After equalization, face images are segmented by using local successive mean quantization transform followed by skin color-based face detection system. Kullback–Leibler distance between the concatenated PDFs of a given face obtained by LBP and the concatenated PDFs of each face in the database is used as a metric in the recognition process. Various decision fusion techniques have been used in order to improve the recognition rate. The proposed system has been tested on the FERET, HP, and Bosphorus face databases. The proposed system is compared with conventional and the state-of-the-art techniques. The recognition rates obtained using FVF approach for FERET database is 99.78% compared with 79.60 and 68.80% for conventional gray-scale LBP and principle component analysis-based face recognition techniques, respectively.

KEYWORDS

Illumination robust, Local binary pattern, Face recognition Probability distribution function, Discrete wavelet transform, Kullback–Leibler distance

1. INTRODUCTION

Face recognition has been one of the most interesting research topics for over the past half century. During this period, many methods such as principle component analysis (PCA), linear discriminant analysis (LDA), independent component analysis (ICA), etc., have been introduced [1–5]. Many of these methods are based on gray-scale images; however, color images are increasingly being used since they add additional biometric information for face recognition [6–8]. As reported by Demirel and Anbarjafari [6, 8], color probability distribution functions (PDFs) of a face image can be considered as the signature of the face, which can be used to represent the face image in a low-dimensional space. It is known that PDF of an image is a normalized version of an image histogram [9]. PDF recently has been used in many applications of image processing such as object detection, face localization, and face recognition [6, 8–12].

One of the most important steps in a face recognition system is face segmentation. There are various methods for segmentation of the faces such as skin color-based face segmentation [13, 14], Viola–Jones [15] face detection system, local successive mean quantization transform (SMQT)-based face detection [16, 17]. In this study, we are using local SMQT-based face segmentation followed by skin color-based face segmentation. This procedure will reduce the effect of background on the rectangle-shape segmented face image.

In this article, the PDF-based face recognition will be studied analytically and then LBP will be used in order to boost the recognition performance. Also in this article, instead of experimentally choosing PDFs of *HSI* and *YCbCr* color channels [6, 8], analytically specific color channels have been selected. Furthermore, analytical studies of false acceptance rate (FAR) and false rejection rate (FRR) analysis are included in the third section. The head pose (HP) face database [18] with 15 subjects, a subset of 50 subjects from the FERET [19] database with faces containing varying poses changing from –90° to +90° of rotation around the vertical axis passing through the neck (the same subset as Demirel and Anbarjafari used in [6, 8]), and Bosphorus face database [20] with 105 subjects with varying frontal illuminations, poses, expressions, and occlusions were used to test the proposed system.

2. FACIAL IMAGES PRE-PROCESSING

2.1 Image illumination enhancement

In many image processing applications, the general histogram equalization (GHE) is one of the simplest and most effective primitives for contrast enhancement [21], which attempts to produce an output histogram that is uniform [22]. One of the disadvantages of the GHE is that the information laid on the histogram or PDF of the image will be lost. Demirel and Anbarjafari [6] have showed that the PDF of face images can be used for face recognition, hence preserving the shape of PDF of the image is of vital importance. Therefore, GHE is not a suitable technique for illumination enhancement of face images. Also, it is known that GHE often produces unrealistic effects in images. After the introduction of GHE, researchers came out with better technique which deals with equalization of portion of the image at a time, called local histogram equalization (LHE). LHE can be expressed as follows: GHE can be applied independently to small regions of the image. Most small regions will be very self-similar. If the image is made up of discrete regions, most small regions will lie entirely within one or the other region. If the image has more gradual large-scale variation, most small regions will contain only a small portion of the large-scale variation.

However, the contrast issue is yet to be improved and even these days many researchers are proposing new techniques for image equalization. DHE is obtained from dynamic histogram specification [23] which generates the specified histogram dynamically from the input image.

Demirel and Anbarjafari [6, 24] developed singular value decomposition (SVD)-based image equalization (SVE) technique, which is based on equalizing the singular value (SV) matrix obtained by SVD. Since an image can be considered as a numeric matrix, SVD of an image, A, can be written as follows

$$A = U_A \Sigma_A V_A^T \tag{1}$$

where U_A and V_A are orthogonal square matrices known as hanger and aligner, respectively, and Σ_A matrix contains the sorted SVs on its main diagonal. The idea of using SVD for image equalization comes from this fact that Σ_A contains the intensity information of the given image [25]. The objective of SVE [24] is to equalize a low-contrast image in such a way that the mean moves towards the neighborhood of 8-bit mean gray value 128 in the way that the general pattern of the PDF of the image is preserved. Demirel and Anbarjafari [6] used SVD to deal with the illumination problem in their proposed face recognition system. SVE can be described in the following way: the ratio of the largest SV of the generated normalized matrix over a normalized image. This coefficient can be used to regenerate an equalized image. This task is eliminating the illumination problem. It is important to mention that techniques such as DHE or SVE are preserving the general pattern of the PDF of an image.

The proposed method is robust to the frontal homogenous illumination changes and this robustness is achieved by using a state-of-the-art technique which is based on discrete wavelet transform (DWT) and SVD [26]. The two-dimensional wavelet decomposition of an image is performed by applying the one-dimensional DWT along the rows of the image first, and then the results are decomposed along the columns. This operation results in four decomposed sub-band images refer to low-low (LL), low-high (LH), high-low (HL), and high-high (HH). The frequency components of those sub-band images cover the frequency components of the original image. DWT is used to separate the input image into different frequency sub-bands, where LL sub-band concentrates the illumination information. The method is benefiting from the fact that an intensity image (an 8-bit intensity image in a given color channel), A, can be decomposed into multiplication of three matrices, by using SVD. The first SV has the highest impact on the illumination of the image, hence updating this SV will directly effect on the illumination of A. Also it is known that the equalized image by using GHE will result into a visually good looking image [27]. Furthermore, in wavelet domain the illumination information is laid in the LL sub-band. By knowing this information, the method is modifying the SVs by using a correction coefficient, ζ:

$$\zeta = \frac{\max(\Sigma_{LL\hat{A}})}{\max(\Sigma_{LL_A})} \qquad (2)$$

Then, the equalized image is being reconstructed by using the following equation:

$$\bar{\Sigma}_{LL_A} = \zeta\, \Sigma_{LL_A}$$
$$\overline{LL_A} = U_{LL_A} \bar{\Sigma}_{LL_A} V_{LL_A}$$
$$\bar{A} = IDWT\left(\overline{LL}_A, LH_A, HL_A, HH_A\right) \quad (3)$$

SVD is a computationally complex operation. As it is shown in Equation (2) only the highest (the first) SV is used. Also from elementary algebra, it is known that for a matrix, the highest SV is obtained by calculating its norm. Thus, ζ can be calculated by

$$\zeta = \frac{\|LL_{\hat{A}}\|}{\|LL_A\|} \quad (4)$$

Then the equalized image is being reconstructed by using the following equation

$$\overline{LL_A} = \zeta LL_A$$
$$\bar{A} = IDWT\left(\overline{LL}_A, LH_A, HL_A, HH_A\right) \quad (5)$$

Figure 1 shows the block diagram of the proposed technique. One can implement the algorithm in different color channel in order to enhance the illumination of the color images.

Figure 2 shows the visual effect of the DWT-based illumination enhancement on a face image with three different illuminations from OULU face database [28].

3. FACE LOCALIZATION AND SEGMENTATION

A face is naturally recognizable by a human regardless of its many point of variation such as skin tone, facial hair, etc. Face detection is a required first step in face recognition systems [16, 29]. The most straight forward variety of face localization is the detection of a single face at a known scale and orientation, which is yet a non-trivial problem. Efficient fast face detection is an impressive goal, which is subject to face tracking that required no knowledge of previous frames [30]. Another reason that face detection is an important research issue is its role as a challenging case of a more general problem, object detection.

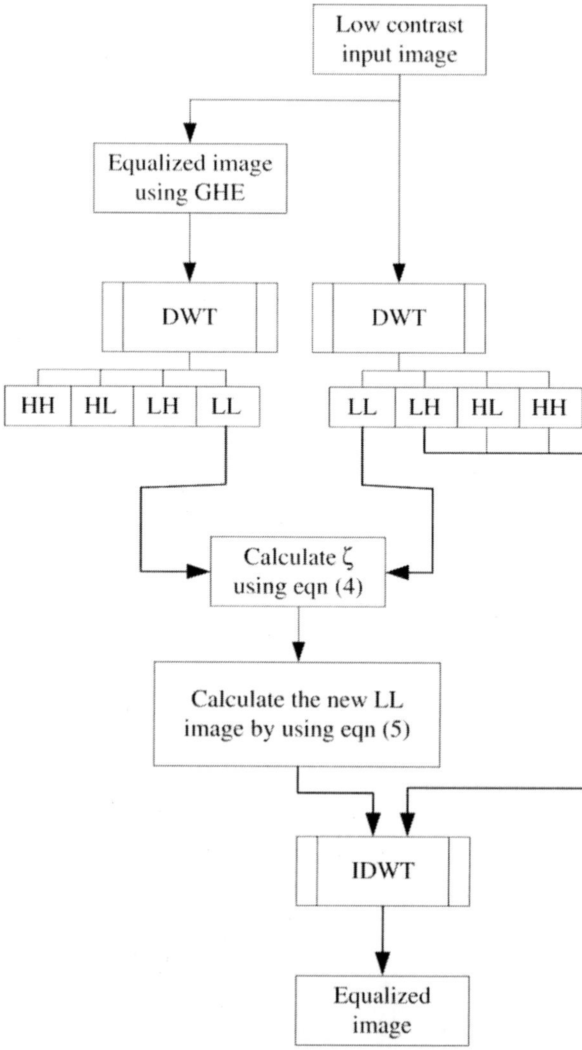

Figure 1 The detailed steps of the image equalization technique.

Skin is a widely used feature in human image processing with applications ranging from face detection [13] and person tracking [31] to content filtering [32]. Human skin can be detected by identifying the presence of skin color pixels. Many methods have been proposed for achieving this. Chai and Ngan [14] modeled the skin color in *YCbCr* color space. In their technique, pixels are classified into "skin" and "non-skin" by using four threshold values, which form a rectangular region in *CbCr* space.

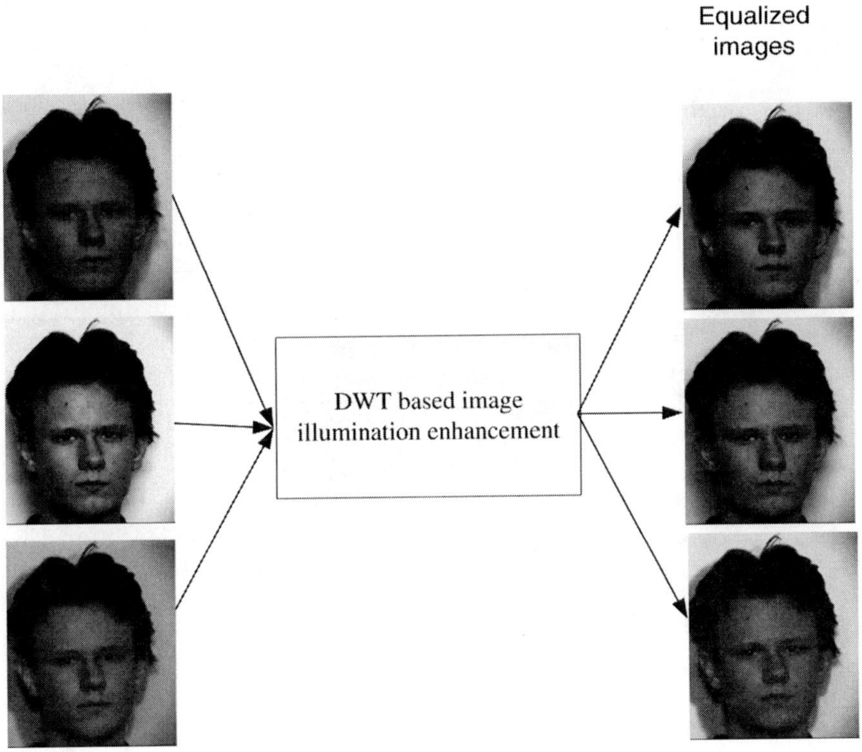

Figure 2 Sample images with different illumination from Oulu face database after and before illumination enhancement.

All color spaces such as *RGB*, *HIS*, and *YCbCr* can be used for face recognition [33]. The advantage of using *HSI* color space is its independence of knowledge of the exact percentage of red, green, or blue. Many applications such as machine vision use *HSI*color space in identifying the color of different objects.

Kjeldson and Kender [34] stated a color preference in *HSI* color space to distinguish skin regions from other segments. Skin color classification in *HSI* color space is based on hue and saturation values.

In [35], the threshold for hue and saturation has been modified from previous work [34] by using 2,500 face samples taken from the FERET dataset, the HP face database, and the Essex University face database. According to these samples, the thresholds for hue and saturation color channels are updated to satisfy the following threshold.

$$(H < 0.17 \quad OR \quad H > 0.63 \quad AND \quad S > 0.1 \tag{6}$$

In order to eliminate the illumination effect from the input images, the intensity component of an image in *HSI* color space has been equalized.

A different approach to separating faces and non-faces in image space is proposed by Osuna et al. [36] and later developed and modified by Romdhani et al. [37]. Both are based on support vector machines (SVM) [38]. The key to the SVM model is the choice of a manifold that separates the face set from the non-face set. Romdhani et al. had chosen a hyperplane which maximizes minimum distance on either side. Romdhani et al. worked further on reducing the vector set in order to improve performance.

In this article, the proposed face recognition system uses local SMQT-based face detection followed by skin tone-based face localization. The SMQT can be considered as an adjustable trade-off between the number of quantization levels in the result and the computational load [39]. Local is defined to be the division of an image into blocks with a predefined size. Let x be a pixel of local D, and let's have the SMQT transform as follows

$$\mathrm{SMQT}_L : D(x) \rightarrow M(x) \tag{7}$$

where $M(x)$ is a new set of values which are insensitive to gain and bias [39]. These two properties are desired for the formation of the intensity image which is a product of reflection and illumination. A common approach to separate the reflection and illumination is based on this assumption that illumination is spatially smooth so that it can be taken as a constant in a local area. Therefore, each local pattern with similar structure will yield the similar SMQT features for a specified level, L. The spare network of winnows (SNoW) learning architecture is also employed in order to create a look-up table for classification [40].

As Nilsson et al. [39] proposed, in order to scan an image for faces, a patch of 32×32 pixels is used and also the image is downscaled and resized with a scale factor to enable the detection of faces with different sizes. The choice of the local area and the level of the SMQT are vital for successful practical operation. The level of the transform is also important in order to control the information gained from each feature. As reported in [39], the 3×3 local area and level $L = 1$ are used to be a proper balance for the classifier. The face and non-face tables are trained in order to create the split up SNoW classifier. Overlapped detections are disregarded using geometrical locations and classification score. Hence, given two detections overlapping each other, the detection with the highest classification score is kept and the other one is removed. This operation is repeated until no overlapping detection is found.

The block diagram of the local SMQT-based face detection is shown in Figure 3.

Figure 4 shows the images of the three faces from Oulu face database enhanced by using DWT + SVE illumination enhancement and the segmented faces by using local SMQT.

The local SMQT-based face detector software has several advantages which promote us in order to use it in this study, which are

- it is fast and very accurate;
- it is a state-of-the-art technique;
- if the input image does not have a face image, there will be no output, therefore in the proposed face recognition system there will be no issue of having a noise image, whose PDF is the same as a face image, as an input.

The output of the local SMQT-based face recognition is that the face image is being cropped in a rectangle frame; hence, some part of background or hair is also included in the frame of the segmented face image. In order to reduce this effect, the output of the local SMQT face detector [17] is passed through a skin color-based face segmentation system [14]. The proposed combination of the aforementioned face segmentation techniques gives an outline of Figure 5, in which a face image from the FERET face database is entered into the system.

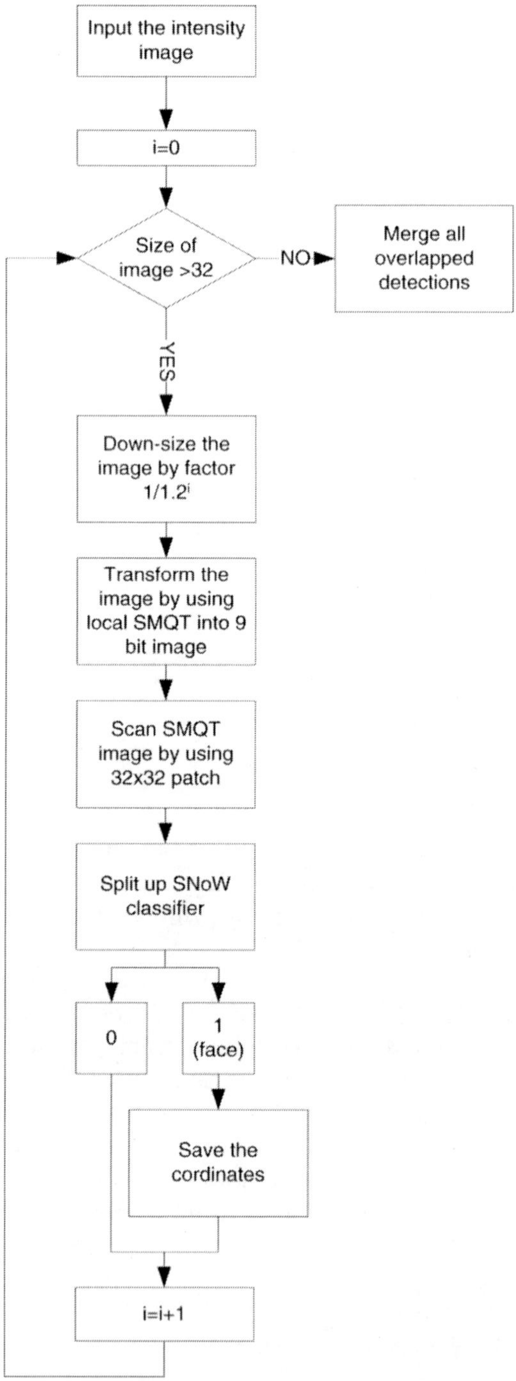

Figure 3 General steps of local SMQT-based face detection **[16]** .

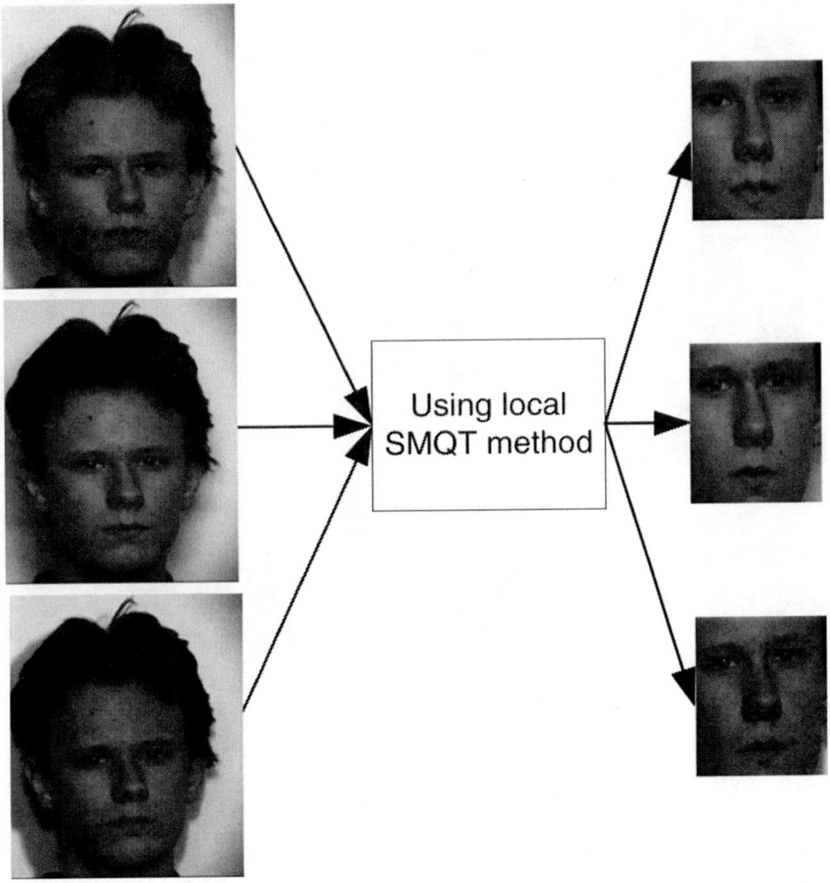

Figure 4 Face detection by using local SMQT for three samples from Oulu face database.

4. PDF BASED FACE RECOGNITION BY USING LBP

4.1 Analytical point of view

In a general mathematical sense, an image PDF is simply a mapping η_i representing the probability of the pixel intensity levels that fall into various disjoint intervals, known as bins. The bin size determines the size of the PDF vector. Given a monochrome image, PDF η_j meets the following conditions, where *N* is the total number of pixels in an image and the bin size is 256:

$$N = \sum_{i=0}^{255} \eta_i \qquad (8)$$

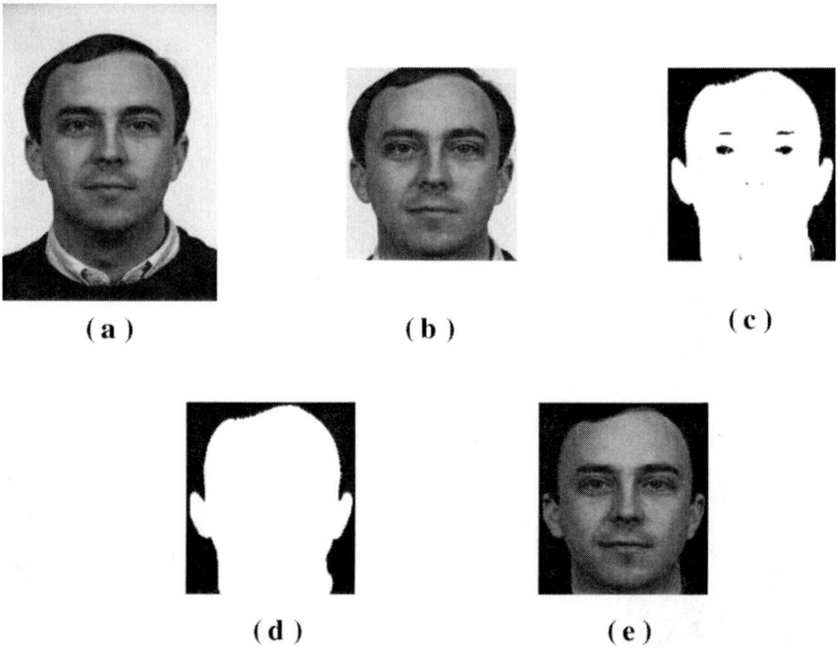

Figure 5 face localization and segmentation (a) A face image from FERET face database, (b) the segmented image by using local SMQT, (c) the mask generated by applying the skin color-based face detection **[14]** , (d) the mask obtained by hole filling of the previous mask, and (e) the final segmented face image.

Then, PDF feature vector, *H*, is defined by

$$H = [p_0, p_1, \ldots, p_{255}]$$

$$p_i = \frac{\eta_i}{N}, \quad i = 0, \ldots, 255 \qquad (9)$$

There are two issues in this point. First one is which metric is more suitable for classification of the PDFs of the faces. For this purpose, L1, L2, cross correlation, and Kullback–Leibler distance (KLD) have been used for the classification of gray-scale faces in the HP face database.

The recognition rate is reported in Table 1. It shows that KLD performs better than the other metrics. Hence in this study, similar to Demirel and Anbarjafari's study [6, 8], we use KLD as a metric for finding the divergence between the PDFs.

Table 1 Recognition rate performance (%) of the PDF-based face recognition system for gray-scale PDFs of HP face database with 15 subjects and 10 samples per each subject obtained by using four different metrics

# of Training Images	L1	L2	Cross Correlation	KLD
1	48.63	36.48	50.81	54.81
2	57.92	48.5	69.54	78.00
3	70.71	61.76	77.6	84.10
4	77.78	71.78	82.26	88.00
5	76.73	67.8	87.78	93.87

The second issue is the number of bin size. What will happen if the bin size drops from 256 into the smaller value? In line of this issue, the bin sizes have been changed and the recognition rate for the gray-scale face images in the HP face database has been obtained. Table 2 reports this result which shows the performance drops as the bin size decreases, due to loss of information laid on the pattern of the PDF.

One of the missing studies in Demirel and Anbarjafari's work was analysis of the discrimination power of the PDF. In order to show the discrimination power of the PDFs by using KLD, the average KLD value within and between-class distances of various databases in different color spaces are given in Table 3.

Table 2 Recognition of face images of the HP face database by using different bin numbers

Number of bins	Recognition rates (%)
256	96.00
128	93.33
64	90.67
32	82.67

Table 3 The discrimination of the PDF by using KLD in different color channels and different databases

DATA BASE		AVERAGE WITHIN CLASS DISTANCE	AVERAGE BETWEEN CLASS DISTANCE	CLASS DISCRIMINATION $\varnothing_c$
FERET	H	0.0542	0.3316	6.12
	S	0.0909	0.4008	4.41
	I	0.0716	0.2396	3.35
	Y	0.0260	0.1300	5.00
	Cb	0.0435	0.1689	3.88
	Cr	0.0364	0.1335	3.67
HP	H	0.0159	0.0818	5.14

DATA BASE		AVERAGE WITHIN CLASS DISTANCE	AVERAGE BETWEEN CLASS DISTANCE	CLASS DISCRIMINATION $\varnothing_c$
	S	0.0097	0.0634	6.54
	I	0.0141	0.0612	4.34
	Y	0.0141	0.0611	4.33
	Cb	0.0132	0.0582	4.41
	Cr	0.0126	0.0573	4.55
BOS	H	0.0083	0.2166	26.11
	S	0.0093	0.9850	106.38
	I	0.0334	0.2793	8.36
	Y	0.0336	0.3385	10.07
	Cb	0.0209	0.6007	28.74
	Cr	0.0243	0.5027	20.70

In Table 3 class discrimination, $\varnothing_c$, is defined to be the ratio of the average between-class distance and the average within class distance which is indicating the discrimination power of different color channels. Class discrimination values show that KLD provides enough separation between classes in different color channels in PDF-based face recognition.

As reported in [6, 8], the PDF-based face recognition system can be implemented in various color channels such as *HSI* and*YCbCr* color spaces in which the luminance and chrominance are separated from each other. These multi decisions can be combined later by using various fusion techniques. But as some of these color channels are highly correlated with each other (they have high mutual entropy), there is no need to include the repeated information in decision making. Table 4 shows the mutual entropy between the channels of *HSI* color space and the *YCbCr* color space.

Table 4 The correlation between ***HSI*** and ***YCbCr*** color channels in percentage

	H	S	I	Y	Cb	Cr
H	100	26.49	9.36	5.28	9.29	16.13
S	26.49	100	25.97	32.91	52.51	65.58
I	9.36	25.97	100	99.05	98.32	93.39
Y	5.28	32.91	99.05	100	96.02	84.63
Cb	9.29	52.51	98.32	96.02	100	92.50
Cr	16.13	65.58	93.39	84.63	92.50	100

Table 4 shows the average mutual information in percentage between the various color channels in *HSI* and *YCbCr* color spaces for Bosphorus face databases where there exist over 4,500 face images. The high correlation between *I-Y*, *I-Cb*, and *I-Cr* color channels shows that instead of using both color spaces, using only *HSI* will have enough information in order to get conclusive recognition rate after the fusion. Also Table 4 indicates that the color channels in *YCbCr* are highly correlated with each other.

5. LOCAL BINARY PATTERN

The local binary pattern (LBP) is a non-parametric operator which describes the local spatial structure of an image [12, 41]. Ojala et al. [41] introduced this operator and showed its high discriminative power for texture classification. At a given pixel position (*xy*), LBP is defined as an ordered set of binary comparisons of pixel intensities between the center pixel and its eight neighbor pixels, as shown in Figure 6.

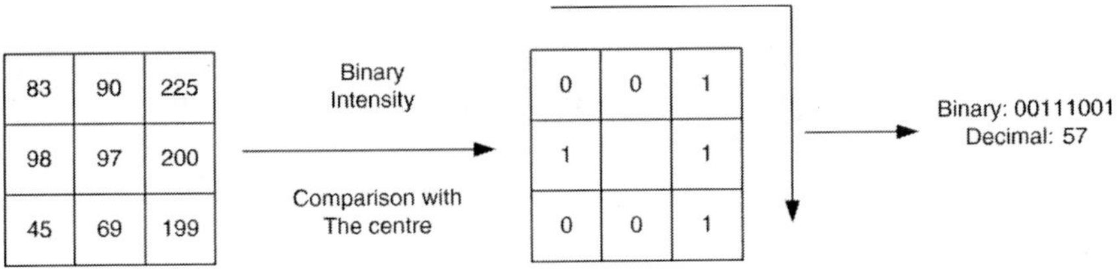

Figure 6 LBP operator.

The decimal form of the resulting 8-bit word of LBP code can be expressed as follows.

$$\mathrm{LBP}(x, y) = \sum_{n=0}^{7} 2^n s\left(i_n - i_{(x,y)}\right) \tag{10}$$

where $i_{(x,y)}$ corresponds to the gray value of the center pixel (*x*,*y*), i_n to the gray values of the eight neighbor pixels, and functions(*x*) is defined as

$$s(x) = \begin{matrix} 1 \text{ if } x \geq 0 \\ 0 \text{ if } x < 0 \end{matrix} \tag{11}$$

By definition, the LBP operator is unaffected by any monotonic gray-scale transformation which preserves the pixel intensity order in a local neighborhood. Note that each bit of the LBP code has the same significance level and that two successive bit values may have a totally different meaning. Sometimes, the LBP code is referred as a kernel structure index.

Ojala et al. [42] extended their previous study to a circular neighborhood of different radius size. They used LBP $_{P,R}$ notation which refers to P equally spaced pixels on a circle of radius R. Two of the main motivations of using LBP are its low computational complexity and its texture discriminative property. LBP has been used in many image processing applications such as motion detection [43], visual inspection [44], image retrieval [45], face detection [46], and face recognition [47, 48].

In most aforementioned applications, a face image was usually divided into small regions. For each region, a cumulative histogram of LBP code computed at each pixel location within the region was used as a feature vector.

Ahnon et al. [48] used LBP operator for face recognition. Their face recognition system can be explained as follows: a histogram of the labeled image $f_1(x\,y)$ can be defined as

$$Hi = \sum_{x,y} I\{f1(x,y) = i\} \quad i = 0, \cdots, n-1 \tag{12}$$

where n is the number of different labels produced by the LBP operator and

$$I\{A\} = \begin{cases} 1 & A \text{ is true} \\ 0 & A \text{ is false} \end{cases} \tag{13}$$

This histogram contains information about the distribution of the local micropatterns, such as edges, spots, and flat areas, over the whole image. For efficient face representation, retaining the spatial information is required; hence, the image is divided into regions R_0, R_1, ..., R_{m-1}, as shown in Figure 7.

The spatially enhanced histogram is defined as

$$H_{i,j} = \sum_{x,y} I\{f_1(x,y) = i\} I\{(x,y) \in R_j\} \quad , \quad \begin{matrix} i = 0, \cdots, n-1 \\ j = 0, \cdots, m-1 \end{matrix} \tag{14}$$

Figure 7 An example of a facial image divided into 8 × 8 windows.

In this histogram, a description of the face on three different levels of locality exists: the labels for the histogram contain information about the patterns on a pixel level, the labels are summed over a small region to produce information on a regional level, and the regional histograms are concatenated to build a global description of the face.

Although Ahnon et al. [48] have mentioned several dissimilarity measures such as histogram intersections, log-likelihood statistics, and Chi square statistics, they used nearest neighbor classifier in their study.

When the image has been divided into several regions, it can be expected that some of the regions contain more useful information than others in terms of distinguishing between people, such as eyes [49, 50]. In order to contribute such information, a weight can be set for each region based on the level of information it contains.

6. THE PROPOSED LBP-BASED FACE RECOGNITION

In this article, the proposed face recognition system uses LBP in order to obtain different PDF of each face in different color channels. Each face images after being equalized and segmented will be divided into sub-images in different color channels. For each sub-image in a specific color channel, the PDF will be calculated. The concatenation of these PDFs will result into a single PDF. Due to high correlation of information of *I* color channel with *YCbCr* color channels, only PDFs of *HSI* color space is used for recognition process by using KLD as it was mentioned earlier. Because several decisions have been obtained from different color channels, the combination of these decisions will boost the final decision. In [51], various decision fusion, data fusion, and source fusion techniques have been studied. In this study, sum rule, median rule, majority voting, and feature vector fusion (obtained by concatenating the PDFs before starting the recognition process) have been used in order to combine the multi decisions obtained from LBP–PDF-based face recognition in *HSI* color channels. Table 5 shows the correct recognition of the aforementioned fusion techniques for the HP face database with 15 subjects and 10 samples per each subject, FERET face database with 50 subjects and 10 samples per each subject, and Bosphorus face database with 105 subjects and 32 samples per each subject.

Table 5 Performance of different decision-making techniques for the proposed face recognition system

	# of training image	**SUM RULE**	**MEDIAN RULE**	**MV**	**FVF**
H	1	82.82	83.37	80.36	79.94
P	2	95.68	95.55	91.75	86.09
	3	96.45	96.31	92.93	95.25
	4	96.84	97.14	95.02	96.85

	# of training image	SUM RULE	MEDIAN RULE	MV	FVF
	5	98.08	98.38	98.70	97.32
F	1	76.63	75.90	75.09	83.32
E	2	86.49	87.74	87.79	89.43
R	3	90.76	89.41	87.72	97.13
E	4	95.81	93.56	92.00	99.01
T	5	96.36	97.17	94.34	99.78
B	1	74.85	74.94	77.54	79.04
O	7	88.60	88.44	88.63	89.81
S	13	89.97	89.32	89.77	90.10
	19	90.07	92.04	93.01	93.12
	25	91.91	94.07	94.31	95.67

In order to show the superiority of the proposed method on available state-of-the-art and conventional face recognition systems, we have compared the recognition performance with conventional PCA-based face recognition system and the state-of-the-art techniques such as, NMF [52, 53], supervised INMF [54], conventional gray-scale LBP [45], and LDA-based face recognition systems [3] for the FERET face database. The experimental results are shown in Table 6. The results clearly indicate that this superiority is achieved by using PDF-based face recognition in different color channels backed by the data fusion techniques. Compared to the state-of-the-art technique proposed by

Demirel and Anbarjafari [8], the recognition rate obtained by using LBP has slightly better performance.

Table 6 Performance of the proposed LBP based face recognition system using FVF, PCA, LDA, conventional gray scale LBP, PDF based face recognition, NMF, and INMF based face recognition system for the FERET face databases with 50 subjects and 10 samples per each subject

# of training images	1	2	3	4	5
FVF	83.32	89.43	97.13	99.01	99.78
FVF [8]	82.89	87.00	96.57	98.80	99.33
PCA	44.00	52.00	58.29	66.17	68.80
LDA	61.98	70.33	77.78	81.43	85.00
LBP	50.89	56.25	74.57	77.67	79.60
NMF	61.33	64.67	69.89	77.35	80.37
INMF	63.65	67.87	75.83	80.07	83.20

Figure 8 shows the FAR and FRR analysis of the proposed face recognition system for the FERET face database. The equal error rate occurs when the recognition rate is about 3.2% which shows that the system can be used in a practical scenario.

The median rule and FVF-based results are 97.17 and 99.78% for the FERET face database, when five samples per subject are available in the training set, respectively. These results are significant, when compared with the recognition rates achieved by conventional PCA and LDA and the state-of-the-art techniques such as LBP, NMF, and INMF-based face recognition system.

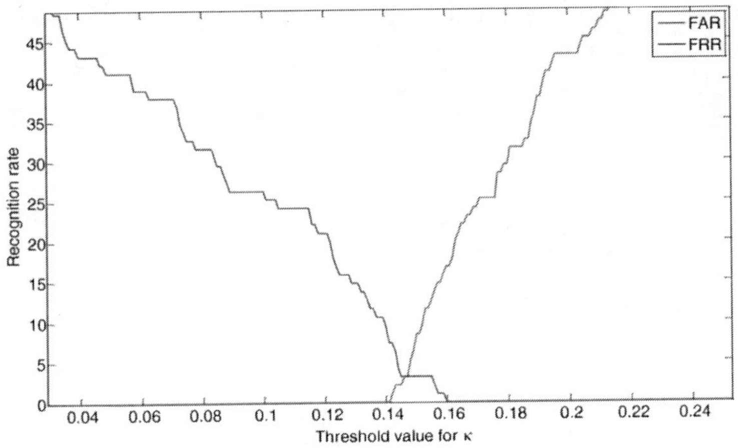

Figure 8 FAR and FRR curves.

7. CONCLUSION

In this article, we have studied a high performance frontal homogenous illumination robust face recognition system using LBP and PDFs in different mutually independent color channels. A face localization which is a combination of local SMQT technique followed by skin tone-based face detection method was employed in this study. DWT + SVD-based image illumination enhancement technique was also applied in order to reduce the effect of illumination. The article analytically analyzed and justified the use of KLD and PDF with a bin size of 256 which was introduced and used in [6, 8]. Several well-known decision fusion techniques have been used in order to combine the decisions obtained from mutually independent color channels. Also an FAR and FRR analysis has been done in this study. Finally, comparison between the proposed method and the conventional and the state-of-the-art techniques has been done which showed the superiority of the proposed method.

ACKNOWLEDGMENTS

The author would like to thank Asst. Prof. Dr. Mikael Nilsson from Blekinge Institute of Technology, for providing the algorithm for local

SMQT-based face recognition. Also the author would like to thank Prof. Dr. Ivan Selesnick from Polytechnic University for providing the DWT codes in MATLAB.

COMPETING INTERESTS

The authors declare that they have no competing interests.

REFERENCES

1. Bledsoe WW: *The Model Method in Facial Recognition, Technical report pri 15.* Panoramic Research, Inc, Palo Alto, California; 1964.

2. Turk M, Pentland A: Face recognition using eigenfaces. In *Proceeding of International Conference On Computer Vision and Pattern Recognition.* Maui, Hawaii: IEEE; 1991:586-591.

3. Belhumeur P, Hespanha J, Kreigman D: Eigenfaces vs. Fisherfaces: Recognition using Class Specific Linear Projection. *IEEE Trans Pattern Anal Mach Intell* 1997, 19: 711-720. 10.1109/34.598228

4. Liu C, Wechsler H: Comparative assessment of independent component analysis (ICA) for face recognition. In *Proceedings of the Second International Conference on Audio- and Video-based Biometric Person Authentication.* Washington D.C., USA; 1999:211-216. 22-24 March

5. Bartlett MS, Movellan JR, Sejnowski TJ: Face Recognition by Independent Component Analysis. *IEEE Trans Neural Netw* 2002, 13(6):1450-1464. 10.1109/TNN.2002.804287

6. Demirel H, Anbarjafari G: Pose Invariant Face Recognition using Probability Distribution Functions in Different Color Channels. *IEEE Signal Process Lett* 2008, 15: 537-540.

7. Marcel S, Bengio S: Improving face verification using skin color information. In *Proceeding 16th International Conference on Pattern Recognition.* Society Press, Quebec, Canada; 2002:378-381.

8. Demirel H, Anbarjafari G: Data fusion boosted face recognition based on probability distribution functions in different colour channels.*EURASIP J Adv Signal Process* 2009, 2009: 1-10.

9. Anbarjafari G, Demirel H: *Face Recognition Using Colour Statistics.* VDM Verlag: Biometric Recognition; 2010.

10. Laptev I British Machine Vision Conference. In *Improvements of object detection using boosted histograms.* Edinburgh, UK; 2006:949-958.

11. Tae-WoongYoo I-SO: A fast algorithm for tracking human faces based on chromatic PDFs. *Pattern Recognit Lett* 1999, 20: 967-978. 10.1016/S0167-8655(99)00053-7

12. Rodriguez Y, Marcel S Proceedings of the 9th European Conference on Computer Vision. In *Face authentication using adapted local binary pattern histograms.* Graz, Austria; 2006:321-332.

13. Yang MH, Kriegman D, Ahuja N: Detecting faces in images: A survey. *IEEE Trans Pattern Anal Mach Intell* 2002, 24: 34-58. 10.1109/34.982883

14. Chai D, Ngan KN: Face segmentation using skin color map in videophone application. *IEEE Trans Circ Syst Video Tech* 9th edition. 1999, 551-564.

15. Viola P, Jones M: Robust real-time face detection. *Int J Comput Vis* 2004, 52(2):137-154.

16. Nilsson M, Nordberg J, Claesson I IEEE International Conference on Acoustics, Speech, and Signal Processing. In *Face detection using local SMQT features and split up snow classifier.* 2nd edition. Hawaii, USA; 2007:589-592.

17. *A face detector software written by Mike Nilsson, provided in MathWorks exchange file.* 2012. http://www.mathworks.com/matlabcentral/fileexchange/loadFile.do?objectId=13701

18. Gourier N, Hall D, Crowley JL: Estimating Face Orientation from Robust Detection of Salient Facial Features. In *Proceedings of Pointing 2004, ICPR, International Workshop on Visual Observation of Deictic Gestures.* Cambridge, UK;

19. Philips PJ, Moon H, Rizvi SA, Rauss PJ: The FERET Evaluation Methodology for Face Recognition Algorithm. *IEEE Trans Pattern Anal Mach Intell* 2000, 22(10):1090-1104. 10.1109/34.879790

20. Savran A, Alyüz N, Dibeklioğlu H, Celiktutan O, Gökberk B, Sankur B, Akarun L: Bosphorus database for 3D face analysis. In *The First COST 2101 Workshop on Biometrics and Identity Management (BIOID 2008)*. Denmark: Roskilde University; 2008:47-56.

21. Kim TK, Paik JK, Kang BS: Contrast enhancement system using spatially adaptive histogram equalization with temporal filtering. *IEEE Trans Consum Electron* 1998, 44(1):82-86. 10.1109/30.663733

22. Weeks AR, Sartor LJ, Myler HR: Histogram specification of 24-bit colour images in the colour difference (C-Y) colour space. *Proc SPIE*1999, 3646: 319-329. 10.1117/12.341098

23. Sun CC, Ruan SJ, Shie MC, Pai TW: Dynamic contrast enhancement based on histogram specification. *IEEE Trans Consum Electron*2005, 51(4):1300-1305. 10.1109/TCE.2005.1561859

24. Demirel H, Anbarjafari G, Jahromi MNS: Image equalization based on singular value decomposition. In *23rd IEEE International Symposium on Computer and Information Sciences*. Istanbul, Turkey: Istanbul, Turkey; 2008:1-5. 27-29 October

25. Tian Y, Tan T, Wang Y, Fang Y: Do singular values contain adequate information for face recognition? *Pattern Recogn* 2003, 36: 649-655. 10.1016/S0031-3203(02)00105-X

26. Ozcinar C, Demirel H, Anbarjafari G: Satellite Image Contrast Enhancement Using Discrete Wavelet Transform and Singular Value Decomposition. *IEEE Geosci Rem Sens Lett* 2010, 7(2):334-338.

27. Kahraman F, Kurt B, Gokmen M: Robust face alignment for illumination and pose invariant face recognition. In *IEEE Conference on Computer Vision and, Pattern Recognition*. Minnesota, USA; 2007:1-7. 17-22 June

28. Abdullah-Al-Wadud M, Kabir MH, Dewan A, Chae O: A Dynamic Histogram Equalization for Image Contrast Enhancement. *IEEE Trans Consum Electron* 2007, 53(2):593-600.

29. Sung KK, Poggio T: Example based learning for view based human face detection. *IEEE Trans Pattern Recogn Mach Intell* 1998, 20: 39-51. 10.1109/34.655648

30. Matsumoto Y, Zelinsky A: Real-time stereo face tracking system for visual interface. In *International Workshop on Recognition, Analysis, and Tracking of Faces and Gestures in Real-Time.* Corfu, Greece; 1999:77-82.

31. Schwerdt K, Crowley J: Robust face tracking using colour. In *4th IEEE International Conference on Automatic Face and Gesture Recognition.* Grenoble, France; 2000:90-95.

32. Huicheng Z, Hongmei L, Daoudi M IEEE Conference on Multimedia and Expo. In *Blocking objectionable images: adult images and harmful symbols.* Lausanne, Switzerland; 2004:1223-1226.

33. Singh SK, Chauhan DD, Vatsa M, Singh R: "A robust skin colour based face detection algorithm". *Tamkang J Sci Eng* 2003, 6(4):227-234.

34. Kjeldsen R, Kender J: Finding skin in colour images. In *Proceedings of the Second International Conference on Automatic Face and Gesture Recognition.* Vermont, USA; 1996:312-317. 14-16 October

35. Anbarjafari G: *A new face recognition system based on colour statistics.* MS Thesis: Eastern Mediterranean University (EMU), Gazimağusa, TRNC; 2008.

36. Osuna E, Freund R, Girosi F: Training support vector machines: an application to face detection. In *Proceedings of the IEEE Conference on Computer Vision and Pattern Recognition (CVPR '97).* San Juan, Puerto Rico; 1997:130-136.

37. Romdhani S, Torr P, Scholkopf B, Blake A 8th IEEE International Conferences on Computer Vision. In *Computationally efficient face detection.* British Columbia, Canada; 2001:695-700.

38. Cortes C, Vapnik V: Support vector networks. *Mach Learn* 1995, 20(3):273-297.

39. Nilsson M, Dahl M, Claesson I IEEE International Conference on Acoustics, Speech, and Signal Processing (ICASSP). In *The successive mean quantization transform.* Philadelphia, USA; 2005:429-432.

40. Roth D, Yang M, Ahuja N Advances in Neural Information Processing Systems. In *A snow based face detector*. Edited by: Solla SA, Leen TK, Muller K-R. MIT Press; 2000:855-861.

41. Ojala T, Pietikainen M, Harwood D: A comparative study of texture measures with classification based on featured distributions. *Pattern Recogn* 1996, 29: 51-59. 10.1016/0031-3203(95)00067-4

42. Ojala T, Pietikainen M, Maenpaa T: Multiresolutiongray-scale and rotation invariant texture classification with local binary patterns. *IEEE Trans Pattern Anal Mach Intell* 2002, 24: 971-987. 10.1109/TPAMI.2002.1017623

43. Heikkila M, Pietikainen M, Heikkila J British Machine Vision Conference. In *A texture based method for detecting moving object*. London, England; 2004:187-196.

44. Turtinen M, Pietikainen M, Silven O: Visual characterization of paper using isomap and local binary patterns. *Conference Mach Vision Applic* 2005, E-89-D: 1-8.

45. Takala V, Ahonen T, Pietikainen M: Block-based methods for image retrieval using local binary patterns. In *14th Scandinavian Conference on Image Analysis*. Joensuu, Finland; 2005:882-891.

46. Jin H, Liu Q, Lu H, Tong X: Face detection using improved LBP under Bayesian framework. In *3rd International Conference on Image and Graphics*. Porto, Portugal; 2004:306-309. 18-20 December

47. Zhang W, Shan S, Gao W, Chen X, Zhang H 10th IEEE International Conference on Computer Vision. In *Local Gabor binary pattern histogram sequence: a novel non-statistical model for face representation and recognition*. Beijing, China; 2005:786-791. 17-21 October

48. Ahnon T, Hadid A: Pietikainen, Face recognition with local binary patterns. In *European Conference on Computer Vision*. Prague, Czech Republic; 2004:469-481.

49. Gong S, McKenna SJ, Psarrou A: *Dynamic Vision, From Images to Face Recognition*. London: Imperial College Press; 2000.

50. Zhao W, Chellapa R, Rosenfeld A, Philips PJ: *Face Recognition: A Literature Survey, Technical report CAR-TR-948*. University of Maryland: Centre for Automation Research; 2002.

51. Polikar R: Ensemble Based Systems in Decision Making. *IEEE Circ Syst Mag* 2006, 6(3):21-45.

52. Lee DD, Seung HS: Learning the parts of objects by nonnegative matrix factorization. *Nature* 1999, 401: 788-791. 10.1038/44565

53. Lee DD, Seung HS: Algorithms for nonnegative matrix factorization. *Adv Neural Inform Process Syst* 2001, 13: 556-562.

54. Chen WS, Pan BB, Fang B, Li M, Tang JL: Incremental nonnegative matrix factorization for face recognition. *Mathematical Problems in Engineering* 2008, 1-17. Vol

5

AN INVERSE PROBLEM APPROACH TO PATTERN RECOGNITION IN INDUSTRY

Ali Sever

University Of North Carolina at Charlotte, Charlotte, NC 28223, USA

ABSTRACT

Many works have shown strong connections between learning and regularization techniques for ill-posed inverse problems. A careful analysis shows that a rigorous connection between learning and regularization for inverse problem is not straightforward. In this study, pattern recognition will be viewed as an ill-posed inverse problem and applications of methods from the theory of inverse problems to pattern recognition are studied. A new learning algorithm derived from a well-known regularization model is generated and applied to the task of reconstruction of an inhomogeneous object as pattern recognition. Particularly, it is demonstrated that pattern recognition can be reformulated in terms of inverse problems defined by a Riesz-type kernel. This reformulation can be employed to design a learning algorithm based on a numerical solution of a system of linear equations. Finally, numerical experiments have been carried out with synthetic experimental data considering a reasonable level of noise. Good recoveries have been achieved with this methodology, and the results of these simulations are compatible with the existing methods. The comparison results show that the Regularization-based learning algorithm (RBA) obtains a promising performance on the majority of the test problems. In prospects, this method can be used for the creation of automated systems for diagnostics, testing, and control in various fields of scientific and applied research, as well as in industry.

KEYWORDS

Artificial neural networks; Inverse problems; Machine learning; Pattern recognition; Regularization

1. INTRODUCTION

No patterns can be derived solely from empirical data (Yee and Haykin, 1993). Some hypotheses about patterns have to be chosen and, from among patterns satisfying these hypotheses, a pattern with a good fit to the data must be sought.

Neurocomputing brought a new terminology to data analysis: searching for parameters of their input/output functions is called learning, and samples of data training sets and a capability to satisfactorily process new data that have not been used for learning is called generalization.

The capability of generalization depends upon the choice of a hypothesis set of input/output functions, in which one searches for a pattern (a functional relationship) that matches the empirical data. So a restriction of the hypothesis set to only physically meaningful functions can improve generalization.

Inverse problems frequently arise in experimental situations when one is interested in the description of the internal structure of a system and is given indirect, noisy data. Estimating the response of a system given a complete specification of the internal structure, on the other hand, is the forward problem.

The modeling problem arises when one is given noisy data, observed over irregular intervals of space and time, and is asked to develop a reasonable model to fit those observed data (Vapnik, 1998).

With the advent of high-speed computers and artificial intelligence techniques, this modeling problem underwent a metamorphosis and emerged as a machine learning problem (Bauer et al., 2007 and Gdawiec and Domanska, 2011). Tikhonov and Lanweber regularized that learning algorithms have recently received an increasing interest due to both theoretical and computational motivations (Abrukov et al., 2006,Kurkova, 2012 and Tiknonov and Arsenin, 1977). Fractal, optimization, and a two-dimensional functional relational model have been used as a feature in several pattern recognition methods (Chang et al., 2010, Lo Gerfo et al., 2008 and Noureddine, in press). Considerable attention is currently being devoted to new possibilities of using artificial neural networks (ANN) in view of their increasing importance for solving the problem of automated reconstruction of the inner structure of an object. Accompanying algorithms that effectively quantify uncertainties, deal with ill-posedness, and fully take the nonlinear model into account are needed Therefore, it is necessary to both look for possible ways to improve the classical learning algorithms already existent in the literature, and to identify new methods which can compete with the traditional ones in speed, robustness, and quality of results.

Inverse problems are often formulated by assuming that the underlying phenomenon is a dynamic system characterized by mathematical equations, although no such assumption is always essential. Often the goal is to build an algorithmic model of the underlying phenomena. In some contexts a model is only a means to an end. The ultimate goal in such cases is to test the validity of a hypothesis. In these cases, the model is used as a classifier (e.g., neural nets and decision trees), and it matters little whether the model is parametric or non-parametric; the classification accuracy becomes more important. From this point of view the entire field of Machine Learning can be treated as an exercise in solving inverse problems (Bauer et al., 2007 and Prato et al., 2007). By their very nature, inverse problems are difficult to solve. Sometimes they are ill-posed. A *well-posed* mathematical problem must satisfy the following requirements: existence, uniqueness and stability. The existence problem is really a non-issue in many realistic situations because the physical reality must be a solution. However, due to noisy and/or insufficient measurement data, an accurate solution may not exist. More often, the major difficulty is to find a unique solution; this especially when solving a parameter identification problem. Different combinations of parameter values (including boundaries and boundary conditions) may lead to similar observations. One useful strategy to handle the non-uniqueness issue is to utilize *a priori* information as additional constraints. These constraints generally involve the imposition of requirements such as smoothness on the unknown solution or its derivatives, or positivity, or maximum entropy or some other very general mathematical property. A more aggressive approach would be the use of regularization. Given an observed data set, genetic algorithms and genetic programming can be used to search a hypothesis space.

In this paper, starting from a reformulation of the pattern recognition as an inverse problem, we introduce an alternative learning algorithm derived by a well-known regularization method. We use a Riesz-type kernel to solve classification tasks by transforming the geometry of input space by embedding them into higher dimensional, inner product spaces, and introducing a regularization method which adds to the derived integral equation a new term, called stabilizer, which penalizes undesired input/output functions. We split the problem into a simpler, ill-posed problem (an integral equation with a Riesz-type kernel) and a well-posed problem. In this way, we isolate and better control the propagation of errors due to the ill-posedness (Noureddine, in press). Then we show that this reformulation can be employed to design a learning algorithm based upon a numerical solution of a system of linear equations.

The rest of the paper is organized as follows: The next Section describes our model and justifies its use. In Section 3, we formulate the proposed regularized learning algorithm. Section IV presents main simulation results. We compare our Regularization-based Algorithm (RBA) with the Support Vector Machine (SVM) and Semanteme-based Support Vector Machine (SSVM) in Section 5. Finally, we conclude the paper with a summary of the work in Section VI.

2. GENERALIZATION MODEL AS REGULARIZATION

Let us formulate the generalized problem as regularization in the following way:

Find a function $\sigma_1 \in L_\infty(\Omega), \Omega \in R^n$, given the function $B(x_k) = w(x_k)$, $x_k \in \Omega_k$, $\Omega_k \in R^n$. Therefore, we have the following integral equation of the first kind

$$A\sigma_1(x) = B(x), \quad x \in \Omega_k \tag{2.1}$$

where $A\sigma_1(x) = \int_\Omega k(x, y)\sigma_1(y)dy$ and $k(x, y) = (1/2\pi)^2|x - y|^{-2}$ and A is considered as an operator from $L_\infty(\Omega)$ into $L_\infty(\Omega_k)$. This integral equation is the Fredholm integral equation of the first kind with a Riesz-type kernel.

First we need to show that Eq. (2.1) represents a severely ill-posed problem. Then we have to prove that a solution $\sigma_1(\alpha)$ to the Eq. (2.2) exists and is unique.

Theorem 1.

Let us assume that Ω and Ω_k are nonintersecting domains in R^3. Then the integral Eq.(2.1) with the Riesz-type kernel represents an ill-posed problem.

Proof.

We should notice that there are no singularities in the Riesz-type kernel with the domains defined above. We then claim that whether $\sigma_1 \in L_2(\Omega)$ is continuous or not, $(A\sigma_1)(x)$ is continuous in the usual sense. In fact,

$$\begin{aligned} |A\sigma_1(x_1) - A\sigma_1(x_2)| &= \left| \int_\Omega |x_1 - y|^{-2} \sigma_1(y)dy - \int_\Omega |x_2 - y|^{-2} \sigma_1(y)dy \right| \\ &\leqslant |\sigma_1(y)| \left| |x_1 - y|^{-2} - |x_2 - y|^{-2} \right| dy \\ &\leqslant \|\sigma_1\|^2 . \int_\Omega \left| |x_1 - y|^\sigma - |x_2 - y|^\alpha \right|^2 . dy \end{aligned}$$

Since the integrand $||x_1 - y|^\sigma - |x_2 - y|^\alpha|$ is uniformly continuous, we have if $|x_1 - x_2| < \delta$,

$$\left| |x_1 - y|^\sigma - |x_2 - y|^\alpha \right|^2 < \varepsilon \text{ for } \forall\, y \in \Omega.$$

Therefore,

$$|A\sigma_1(x_1) - A\sigma_1(x_2)| \leqslant \|\sigma_1\|^2 . \varepsilon . |\Omega|,$$

$|\Omega|$ stands for a certain measure of Ω for any given $\varepsilon > 0$.

Now it is clear that if we take any $B(x)\ \varepsilon\ L_2(\Omega_k)$ which is continuous, then there is no$\sigma_1\ \varepsilon\ L_2(\Omega)$ such that $A\sigma_1 = B$. So the existence requirement of the well-posedness is violated. Therefore the Eq. (2.1) is ill-posed.

For the integral Eq. (2.1), with a Riesz-type kernel and non-intersecting domains Ω and Ω_k, there is uniqueness in $L_2(\Omega)$ Prato and Zanni, 2008. Djatlov's work shows a logarithmic type of stability estimate (Kress, 1989).

We use the Tikhonov regularization method (Kress, 1989 and Sever, 1999) to solve the ill-posed problem in Eq. (2.1). In this method, instead of Eq. (2.1), we solve the following regularized equation:

$$(A^*A+\alpha \boldsymbol{I})\sigma_1(x)=A^*B(x)$$

where $\boldsymbol{I}$ is the identity operator, and α is a regularization parameter. Now we will show the solution $\sigma_1(\alpha)$ and its convergence to the solution B when $\alpha \to 0$, provided σ_1 exists and the uniqueness for the original Eq. (2.1). Now we need to prove the existence of the solution $\sigma_1(\alpha)$ and its convergence to the solution f when $\alpha \to 0$, provided σ_1 exists and is unique.

Theorem 2.

A solution $\sigma_1(\alpha)$ to the Eq. (2.2) exists and is unique. Also $R_\alpha y$ defined as $\sigma_1(\alpha)$ is a regularizer to the Eq. (2.1) on $X = X_M$, provided that the equation $A\sigma_1 = 0$ has only zero solution.

Proof.

First we assume that A is compact, so is A^*A, but A^*A is also self-adjoint. Thus A^*A has a complete eigenfunction system denoted by $\{e_k\}$ with the corresponding eigenvalues $\{\lambda_k\}$.

Then, we have $\sigma_1(\alpha) = \sum_k \sigma_{1k}(\alpha)e_k$, $A^*y = \sum_k B_{Ak}e_k$ using equation, we get

$$(\lambda_k+\alpha)\sigma_{1k}(\alpha)=BAk$$

which implies $\sigma_{1k}(\alpha) = B_{Ak}/(\lambda_k + \alpha)$ is uniquely determined. Uniqueness can be obtained without using the expression of the solution. In fact, since A^*A is positive, we have

$$((A^*A+\alpha)x,x)=(Ax,Ax)+\alpha(x,x)>0 \text{ for } \forall\, x\neq 0. \tag{2.2}$$

Therefore it cannot happen that there is some $\sigma^*_1 \neq 0$ such that

$$(A^*A+\alpha)\sigma_1^*=0$$

which means

$$\text{kernel}(A^*A+\alpha I)=\{0\}.$$

Now we show that $\sigma_1(\alpha)$ is actually a regularizer. To this end, we may assume now$A\sigma_1 = B$ where $\sigma_1 \varepsilon X_M$. Noticing that $A^*A + \alpha I$ is also self-adjoint, we have

$$((A^*A+\alpha))\sigma_1(\alpha),e_k)=(A^*B,e_k)(A^*A\sigma_1,e_k)$$

or

$$(\sigma_1(\alpha),((A^*A+\alpha)e_k)=(\sigma_1,A^*Ae_k)$$

$$((\lambda_k+\alpha)(\sigma_1(\alpha),e_k)=\lambda_k(\sigma_1,e_k)$$

with $\sigma_1(\alpha) = \sum_k \sigma_{1k}(\alpha)\, e_k, \sigma_1 = \sum_k \sigma_k e_k,$ therefore, we get

$$\sigma_{1k}(\alpha)=(\lambda_k/\lambda_k+\alpha)\sigma_1$$

and

$$\sigma_{1k}(\alpha)-\sigma_{1k}=(\lambda_k/\lambda_k+\alpha)\sigma_{1k}-\sigma_{1k}=-(\alpha/\lambda_k+\alpha)\sigma_{1k}.$$

Therefore

$$\begin{aligned}||\sigma_{1k}(\alpha)-\sigma_{1k}||^2 &= \sum_k |\sigma_{1k}(\alpha)-\sigma_{1k}|^2 = \sum_k (\alpha^2/(\lambda_k+\alpha)^2)\sigma_{1k}^2(\lambda_k>0)\\ &< \alpha \sum_{k\leqslant} KK(\lambda_k+\alpha)^{-2}|\sigma_{1k}|^2 + \sum_{k>K}|\sigma_{1k}|^2\end{aligned}$$

Here we assume that $\lambda_k \geqslant \lambda_{k+1} \geqslant \ldots$

For all $\varepsilon > 0$ since $x \in L_2$, $\sum_k|\sigma_{1k}|^2$ converges. We first choose K such that $\sum_k|\sigma_{1k}|^2 < \varepsilon^2/2$.

Then, for the fixed K, we may chose δ such that

$$\alpha \sum_{k\leqslant K} (\lambda_k+\alpha)^{-2}|\sigma_{1k}|^2 < \varepsilon^2/2.$$

Consequently,

$$||\sigma_{1k}(\alpha)-\sigma_{1k}||\leqslant\varepsilon$$

It remains to prove that R_α, i.e., σ_1 is continuous. By observing that

$$\sigma_{1k}(\alpha)-\sigma_{1k}(\alpha_0)=((\alpha_0-\alpha)\lambda_k)/(\lambda_k+\alpha)(\lambda_k+\alpha_0)\sigma_{1k}$$

And using a similar argument to what we had above, we get the continuity of σ_{1k}.

Spectral representation of self-adjoint operators in Hilbert space gives the general case. Assumption $A\sigma_1 = 0$ if and only if $\sigma_1 = 0$ guarantees that the limit of $\sigma_1(\alpha)$ is unique.

3. REGULARIZED LEARNING ALGORITHM

In this section we formulate a regularized learning algorithm based upon the Tikhonov regularization algorithm. For computational reasons, let Ω and Ω_k be the domain in $R^2$and we will regard the integral operator

$$A\sigma_1(x) = \int_{\Omega} \sigma_1(y)/|x-y|^2 dy$$

as defined from $L_2(\Omega)$ into $L_2(\Omega_k)$. By using the definition of an adjoint operator in L_2, we have A^*: $L_2(\Omega_k) \rightarrow L_2(\Omega)$ defined by

$$A^* B(y) = \int_{\Omega k} B(x)/|x-y|^2 dx \quad y \in \Omega \tag{2.3}$$

and $A^*A\sigma_1$ (y) becomes

$$A^* A\sigma_1(y) = \int_{\Omega k} \int_{\Omega} \sigma_1(y')|x-y|^2|x-y'|^2 dy' dx \tag{2.4}$$

where $x \in \Omega_k$, and $y, y' \in \Omega$. By discretizing Eq. (2.4), we have

$$A^* A\sigma_1(y_i) = \sum_{k,j-1}^{n} w_j w_k \sigma_1(y_j')/|x_k - y_i|^2 |x_k - y_j'|^2 y_i, y_j' \in \Omega$$

$$\cong \sum_{j-1}^{n} \Theta_{l,j} \sigma_1(y_j') \tag{2.5}$$

where

$$\Theta_{l,j} \cong \sum_{k,j-1}^{n} w_j w_k / |x_k - y_i|^2 |x_k - y_j'|^2$$

and w_j, and w_k are the weight functions. By discretizing (2.3), we have

$$A^*B(y_i) \cong \sum_{k=1}^{n} w_k B(x_k)/|x_k - y_i|^2 \qquad (2.6)$$

From (2.3), (2.4), (2.5) and (2.6) we have the discretized matrix equation in the form of

$$(\alpha I+\Theta)\sigma_1(y)=A^*B \qquad (2.7)$$

for some regularization parameters, $\alpha > 0$. Now the problem is reduced to solving systems of linear equations.

4. SIMULATION RESULTS

In this section we want to investigate the effectiveness of the regularized learning algorithm introduced in Section 3.

Let us denote 'real object' by σ_t, and 'computed object' by σ_c. To test the method numerically, it is necessary to generate '$B(x)$' in the integral Eq. (2.1). We do this by specifying σ and evaluating the integral numerically. Once we have the numerical values of $B(x)$, we use these as our data and recover the pattern inside the required region. The steps of test calculation are:

(1) specify σ_t,

(2) calculate the integral (2.1),

(3) use (2.7) to find σ_c,

(4) compare σ_t with σ_c.

Our test calculation used

a) smooth surface (Fig. 1)

b) $\sigma_t = \sigma_0 + x_1\sigma_1 + x_2\sigma_2$ (two objects)

where x_i's are characteristic functions of unknown objects, and σ_0 = ½ and σ_l = 1 (Fig. 3). In the case of smooth surface (i), the numerical calculations have shown that whenσ_t is a smooth polynomial, the reconstruction is a very good approximation of σ_c (Fig. 2).

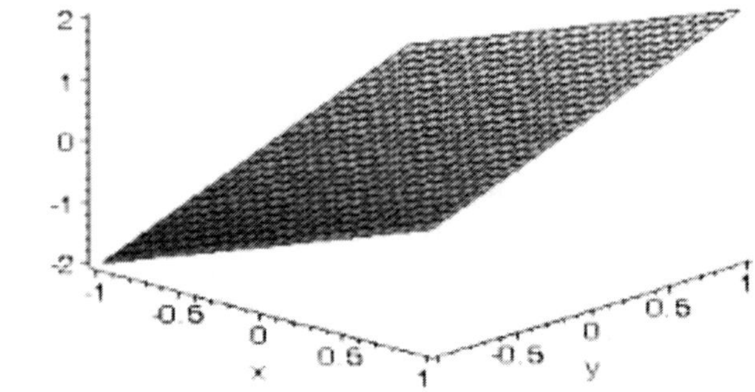

Figure 1. Smooth surface $\sigma_t = x + y$.

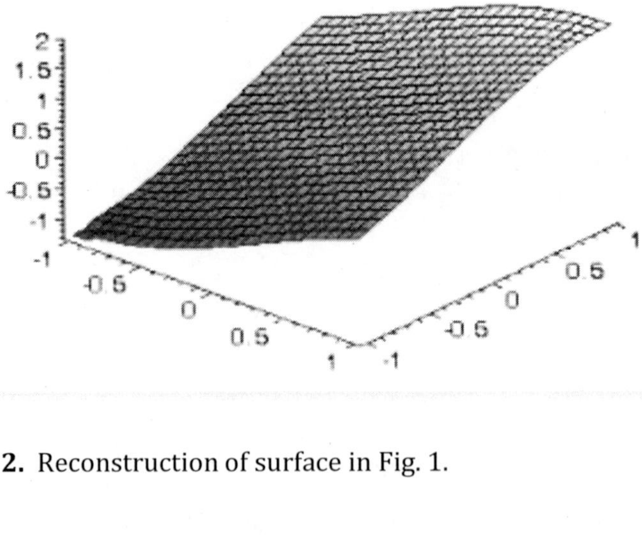

Figure 2. Reconstruction of surface in Fig. 1.

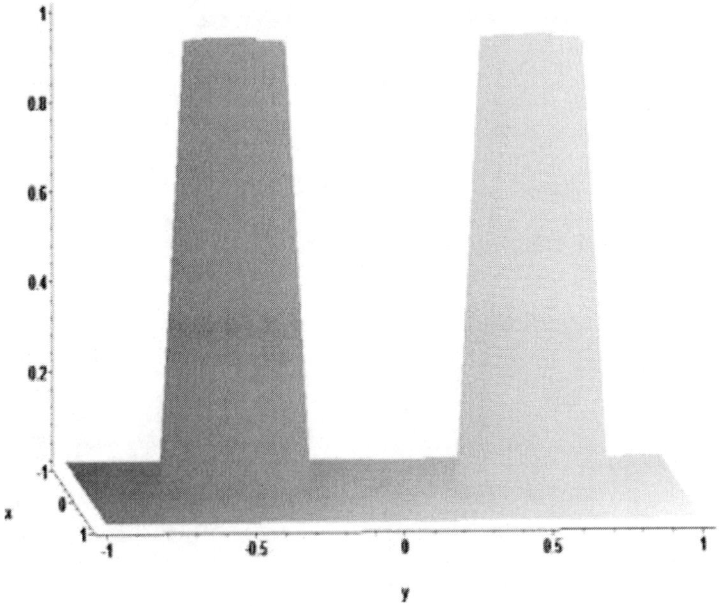

Figure 3. Test domain with two objects.

In case (ii), we used two different regularization parameters for our reconstruction: simply, $\alpha = 10^{-7}$ and $\alpha = 10^{-10}$. We provided the cross sections of σ_t and σ_c. The proposed model was able to distinguish the objects. We observed that the computed σ_c was always smoothed. The location of the objects was well produced by σ_c, and also the shape of theσ_c was a fair indication of the objects (Figure 4 and Figure 5 and Table 1).

Equation (2.7) involves main parameters that must be adjusted for greatest efficiency: the regularization parameter and the number of grid points. Looking at the reconstructions, the numerical experiments described above have shown that the reconstructed surface is smooth and close to the true surface. The reconstruction was usually a fair representation of the shape of the σ.

Summarizing, the simplicity and the reconstruction accuracy make the proposed regularized learning model well suited for the considered application.

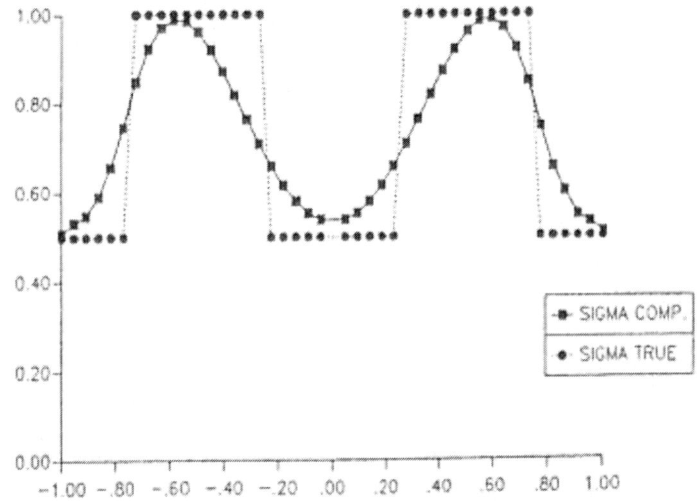

Figure 4. Cross-section from the reconstruction of $\sigma_t = \sigma_0 + x_1\sigma_1 + x_2\sigma_2$ where x_i's are characteristic functions of unknown objects, and $\sigma_0 = ½$ and $\sigma_I = 1$, and $\alpha = 10^{-7}$.

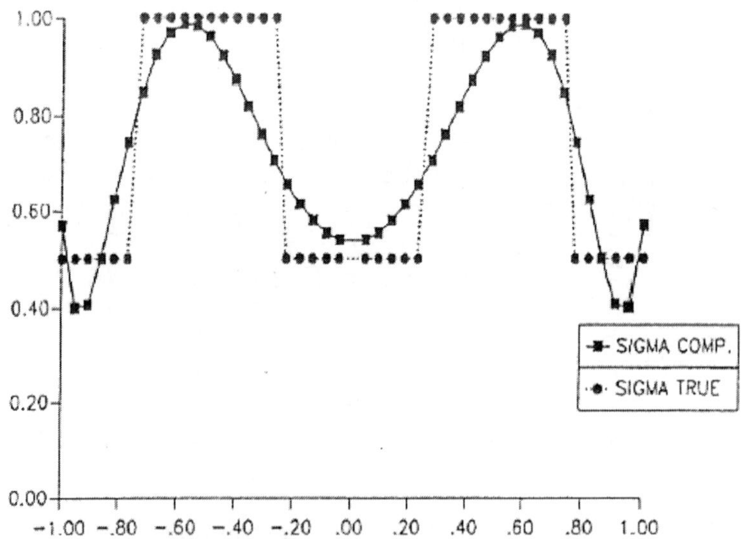

Figure 5. Cross-section from the reconstruction of $\sigma_t = \sigma_0 + x_1\sigma_1 + x_2\sigma_2$ where x_i's are characteristic functions of unknown objects, and $\sigma_0 = ½$ and $\sigma_I = 1$, and $\alpha = 10^{-10}$.

Table 1. Experimental datasets.

Cross-sectional points	$\sigma_0 = 1/2$ and $\sigma_1 = 1$				
	−1	−0.5	0	0.5	1
σ_τ – True value	0.5	1	0.5	1	0.5
$\alpha = 10^{-7}$	0.507	0.982	0.53	0.982	0.507
$\alpha = 10^{-10}$	0.582	0.973	0.532	0.973	0.591
Absolute error for $\alpha = 10^{-7}$ (%)	1	2	6	2	1
Absolute error for $\alpha = 10^{-10}$ (%)	16	3	6	3	18

5. RESULTS AND DISCUSSION

In this section, misclassification rate (Li and Wang, 2009) is used to evaluate the efficiency of our algorithm. Misclassification rate refers to the ratio of the number of misclassified exemplars to the total number of exemplars in the dataset. The ratio is computed using the Formulation (5.3). Correspondingly, the classification accuracy is determined by the Formulation (5.2).

$$\gamma_{\text{error}} = \sum_{i=1,-1} \text{number}_i / n \qquad (5.1)$$

$$\gamma_{\text{error}} = 1 - \gamma(\text{error}) \qquad (5.2)$$

where number_i refers to the number of misclassified exemplars in the positive and negative classes, and n is the total number of X. A smaller γ_{error} value indicates higher classification accuracy and better classification efficiency. Conversely, a bigger γ_{error}value indicates worse classification efficiency.

Experiments are performed on the purely syntactic datasets from the UCI machine learning repository (UCI, 1998). We compare our Regularization-based Algorithm (RBA) with the Support Vector Machine (SVM) and Semanteme-based Support Vector Machine (SSVM) in the Table 2. In each test, all patterns with missing attribute values are initially removed. Continuous Dataset (CDS), Discontinuous Dataset I (DDS-I), and Discontinuous Dataset II (DDS-II) have their fixed real and computed pattern sets. The 9% outliers existing in DDS-II's training patterns are identified, and the dataset is classified as unbalanced. The continuous attributes in datasets are preprocessed using the Formulation (5.3)Li and Wang, 2009.

$$x_{ij} = (x_{ij} - \min_i\{x_{ij}\})(\max_i\{x_{ij}\} - \min_i\{x_{ij}\}) \qquad (5.3)$$

A number of classification algorithms depend on the similarity or dissimilarity of exemplars, such as Euclidean distance and inner production, among others. However, majority of these algorithms only process continuous-attributed data, not discontinuous data. Discontinuous data (surface in our examples) are extreme, having disordered and unbalanced distribution.

Table 2. Misclassification ratio of different algorithms.

Dataset	SVM (%)	SSVM (%)	RBA (%)
CDS	2.9	3.1	5.32
DDS-1	16.3	9.1	4.95
DDS-2	15.5	9.42	9.45
Average	11.5	7.2	6.57

For parameter selection and optimization, regularized learning algorithm faces the problem of selecting parameter α. In many algorithms, the standardization of the selection method for α is rarely performed (Han and Zhao, 2009). The heuristic method or some optimization algorithm is used to select α. In this study, the heuristic method is used in each experiment to standardize datasets. Table 1 shows the relationship between classification accuracy and the value α in the RBA algorithm.

6. CONCLUDING REMARKS AND FUTURE WORK

In this section, we briefly discuss several results obtained and issues related to the proposed RBA learning and recognition technique. Some of these issues may be viewed as merits while others as limitations leading to open research problems for the future.

The implementation of the proposed algorithm shows that the method is reasonably accurate for the reconstruction of two objects, using artificially generated data whose distributions are known. We have seen, both theoretically and experimentally, that pattern classification can be viewed as an ill-posed, inverse problem to which a method of regularization may be applied. As shown in Table 2, our proposed regularized learning algorithm has already shown promising performance in comparison with the state-of-the-art approaches, such as Support Vector Machines (SVMs), on benchmark datasets and real-life test problems.

The information obtained from a preliminary analysis is by no means exhaustive of the method discussed here and suggests several areas of additional investigation. We recognize the clear connection between regularization theory for inverse problems, and pattern recognition as learning, and this allow us to introduce a new learning algorithm. On one front, improvements have to be done both on the algorithm (different regularizer properties must be investigated) and the applications (non-homogeneous 3-D object recognition). More detailed work is needed to improve the effectiveness of the numerics in general. In addition, the answer to exactly how sensitive the method is to moderate amounts of noise is an open question.

REFERENCES

1. Abrukov, V.S., et al., 2006. Artificial Neural Networks and Optical Diagnostics. In: Sixth International Conference on Intelligence Systems Design and Applications.

2. Bauer, F., Preverzev, S., Rosasco, L., 2007. On regularization algorithms in learning theory. J. Complexity 35, 52–72.

3. Chang, Y.F., Lee, J.C., Mohd Rijal, O., Syed Abu Bakar, S.A.R., 2010. Efficient online handwritten Chinese character recognition system using a two-dimensional functional relationship model. Int. J. Appl. Math.

4. Comput. Sci. 20 (4), 727–738. http://dx.doi.org/10.2478/v10006-010-0055-x.

5. Gdawiec, K., Domanska, D., 2011. Partitioned iterated function systems with division and a fractal dependence graph in recognition of 2D shapes. Int. J. Appl. Math. Comput. Sci. 21 (4), 757–767. http://dx.doi.org/10.2478/v10006-011-0060-8, ISSN (Print) 1641-876X.

6. Han, Xian-Pei, Zhao, Jun, 2009. The creation of semantic metadata based on Wikipedia. J. Chin. Inform. Process. 23 (2), 108–114.

7. Kress, R., 1989. Linear integral equation. In: Applied Math. Sciences. Springer-Verlag, Berlin, New York.

8. Kurkova, V., 2012. Complexity estimates based on integral transforms induced by computational units. Nueral Netw. 33, 160–167.

9. Li, Zhi-Hua, Wang, Shi-Tong, 2009. Clustering with outliers-based anomalous intrusion detection[J]. Syst. Eng. Electron. 31 (5), 1227–1230.

10. Lo Gerfo, L., Rosasco, L., Odone, F., De Vito, E., Verri, A., 2008. Spectral algorithms for supervised learning. Neural Comput. 20 (7), 1873–1897.

11. Noureddine, S., in press. An optimization approach for the satisfiability problem, Appl. Comput. Inform.

12. Prato, M., Zanni, L., 2008. Inverse problems in machine learning: an application to brain activity interpretation. J. Phys. 135.

13. Prato, M., Zanni, L., Zanghirati, G., 2007. On recent machine learning algorithms for brain activity interpretation. In: 23rd Annual Review of Progress in Applied Computational Electromagnetics, March 19–23, 2007, Verona, Italy, pp. 1939–1946.

14. Sever, A., 1999. On uniqueness in the inverse conductivity problem. Math. Methods Appl. Sci. 22 (12), 953–966.

15. Tiknonov, A.N., Arsenin, V., 1977. Solutions of Ill-posed Problems Transl from Russian. John Wiley Sons, New York, Toronto.

16. UCI repository of machine learning database [EB/OL], 1998. Available from: <http://www.ics.UCI.edu/~mlearn/ MLRepository. html>.

17. Vapnik, V.N., 1998. Statistical Learning Theory. John Wiley and Sons, New York.

18. Yee, P., Haykin, S., 1993. Pattern classification as an ill-posed, inverse problem: a regularization approach. In: ICASSP'93 Proceedings of the 1993 IEEE International Conference on Acoustics, Speech, and Signal Processing: Plenary, Special, Audio, Underwater Acoustics, VLSI, Neural Networks, vol. I.

6

A VIRTUAL BLIND CANE USING A LINE LASER-BASED VISION SYSTEM AND AN INERTIAL MEASUREMENT UNIT

Quoc Khanh Dang, Youngjoon Chee, Duy Duong Pham and Young Soo Suh *

Department of Electrical Engineering, University of Ulsan, Namgu, Ulsan 680-749, Korea

ABSTRACT

A virtual blind cane system for indoor application, including a camera, a line laser and an inertial measurement unit (IMU), is proposed in this paper. Working as a blind cane, the proposed system helps a blind person find the type of obstacle and the distance to it. The distance from the user to the obstacle is estimated by extracting the laser coordinate points on the obstacle, as well as tracking the system pointing angle. The paper provides a simple method to classify the obstacle's type by analyzing the laser intersection histogram. Real experimental results are presented to show the validity and accuracy of the proposed system.

KEYWORDS

blind; virtual cane; inertial sensor; assisting system; Kalman filter

1. INTRODUCTION

According to an investigation by the World Health Organization, there are 285 million people who are estimated to be visually impaired worldwide: 39 million are blind, and 246 million have low vision as of 2014 [1]. Researchers have been interested in the demand for visually-impaired assistance systems for many years. As a result from Clark-Carter's research [2], all pedestrians have their preferred walking speed that, for them, is the most physically efficient. Blind pedestrians, when accompanied by a sighted guide, will walk at a speed that is close to that of a sighted pedestrian. However, their walking speed decreases when they walk independently. In other words, the mentality while walking effects their walking performance greatly. With the help of visually-impaired assistance systems, blind people can increase their walking speed and avoid the obstacle in their way. The more information the blind persons have about the environment, the more confidence they have on their walks.

In pedestrian travelling, to explore the environment, ultrasonic sensors [3,4], infrared sensors [5] and cameras [6,7,8] are typically used to help the visually impaired find obstacles within the sensor's working range. Ultrasonic or infrared sensors can measure the distance from a blind person to an obstacle, but only provide binary information of whether the obstacle exists or not. This limitation makes the system become large if we want to know more detailed information about the obstacle position. For instance, the system in [3] is the combination of five ultrasonic sensors for spectacles and a waist belt, and the system in [5] has three IR sensors attached on a stick and the user's hat. Most importantly, it is hard to define the obstacle shape with these sensor systems. In another approach, the camera systems [6,7] were successful in finding possible paths for the blind by extracting free spaces from environmental images. However, when an image contains many objects, the extraction may not work accurately. In a similar research, Kim *et al.* [8] use a stereo camera to detect the user's pointing finger in 3D using color and disparity data, then the object within the estimated pointing trajectory in 3D space is detected, as well as the distance to the object. The drawbacks of this system are its computation cost and limited range of detection. The accuracy depends heavily on the finger gesture process, and the working range is limited in a virtual cylinder around the finger. Another method is using a laser source to investigate the environment, which is the main interest of this paper.

Some related works that use a laser source to scan the environment have been proposed previously [9,10]. Yuan and Manduchi [9] have proposed a system consisting of a laser pointer and a camera, which acts like a virtual white cane, using triangulation, that can measure distances at a rate of 15 measurements per second. The authors used a laser beam and a camera to scan the environment by swinging the system vertically. This could be a simple system with a simple scanning method that analyzes the laser-measured range by the time profile. However, the users need much time to scan the environment. For example, to scan an ascending or descending step, the system needs 2–3 s for a scan, including upward and downward swinging motions. The problem comes from the fact that the laser pointer only provides a single beam. Therefore, to inspect the environment, the user must swing the system vertically, since only a slice of the obstacle is obtained in one swing. Another system that uses a laser source was proposed by Pallejà *et al.* [10]. Light detection and ranging (LiDAR) is used with an accelerometer to investigate the environment in front of the user. The system is installed on the user's wrist, and the LiDAR points horizontally. The authors considered that the position of the system did not change much while walking. By pointing the system towards the ground, a frontal line created from the intersection of the laser plane and the ground plane is analyzed to estimate the information of the obstacle. The limitation is that only a partial slice of the object is estimated, making it difficult for the user to predict the type of obstacle. Since the system only provides a horizontal laser line with respect to the user, the user has to move forward, so that the laser can scan the whole obstacle. For example, to be informed that there are stairs ahead, the user must walk for at least two seconds, so that the change in the laser distance could be analyzed. This could sometimes be dangerous for the user. Besides, the assumption that the position and the orientation of the system are not changing much while walking could lead to a large error.

To overcome these limitations, we propose an indoor system that includes a laser line, a camera and an inertial measurement unit (IMU). The user scans the environment by swinging a vertical laser line horizontally as the user's hand movement is estimated using an inertial sensor unit. By scanning, the visually impaired can obtain more information from the environment, which will help them be more confident while walking and increase the chance of avoiding obstacles. Different from [9], our system can provide instant information of the environment instead of swinging a laser beam vertically. Additionally, unlike the system in [10], where the system only provides a slice of the obstacle, our system can provide the information of the obstacle shape while walking.

The main objectives of the system are to classify the obstacles and to estimate the distance from them to the user. The obstacle type is recognized by analyzing the laser projection shape on the obstacle, while the distance to the obstacle is calculated based on the distance of the closest laser point that belongs to the object. From the inertial sensor, the system pointing angle is tracked with respect to the navigation coordinate frame. This estimated pointing angle is combined with the laser stripe on the obstacle's surface to compute the laser point coordinates in the navigation coordinate frame. If we analyze the histogram of the laser point coordinates by height, the obstacle can be classified into wall, stairs or other obstacles. In addition to this, the obstacle distance is also estimated. To provide this environment information to the visually impaired, simple sound feedback using a single tone that has a volume inversely proportional to the distance to the obstacle can be used. Some voice indications can also be provided to give environmental danger warnings. The advantage of the proposed system is that it provides more information, since a vertical laser line is used to scan the environment horizontally with respect to the user.

This paper is organized into five main parts. Section 2 gives an overview of the proposed system. In Section 3, the obstacle classification and obstacle distance estimation methods are explained in detail. Section 4 describes the experimental procedures and results. Finally, some conclusions are discussed in Section 5.

2. SYSTEM OVERVIEW

The system consists of a camera, a laser line source and an IMU. There are three coordinate systems in the paper that are the camera coordinate frame, the IMU coordinate frame and the temporary world coordinate frame, which will be introduced later. The camera coordinate frame has the origin at the pin hole of the camera; the x and y axes make a plane that is parallel with the camera CCD screen, and the z axis points out and is orthogonal to the CCD screen. The IMU coordinate frame has the xy plane parallel with the sensor's bottom, and the z axis points up. The IMU is mounted so that its x coordinate axis coincides with the z axis of the camera coordinate frame, as in Figure 1. The laser line generates a laser stripe when intersecting with an obstacle, and this stripe is observed by the camera. Since all devices in the system are fixed, the laser plane equation can be computed and is unique in the camera coordinate frame. Therefore, for each two-dimensional (2D) laser point observed in the camera image frame, its coordinates can be computed in three dimensions with respect to the camera coordinate frame. If we know the position of the system corresponding to the blind person, the three-dimensional (3D) position of the scanned object can be estimated.

The system is held at the blind person's front and close to the waist (Figure 1). This is a comfortable position, such that the blind person only needs to swing his or her wrist to scan the environment. The laser line is placed so that its projection on the floor is a vertical stripe. When the user swings the system horizontally, the vertical light can scan a large space in front of the user.

The information of the environment is analyzed in each image frame. In each frame, the laser points are extracted based on their intensities, since the laser provides a brighter source than other environmental light sources. A set of laser points is then divided into a basic line and obstacle members. The basic line consists of laser points that lie on the floor, while the obstacle members are the laser point coordinates on the obstacle surface. From this separation, obstacles can be classified into walls, stairs and other obstacles by analyzing their laser shapes. Furthermore, from the laser point coordinates, the distance from the user to the obstacle is also calculated. While the system is swung, its orientation with respect to the navigation coordinate frame can be tracked using a Kalman filter [11]. The estimated orientation is used to approximate the pointing angle of the system in the navigation coordinate frame. It can also be used to detect the case when the user points the system horizontally to turn off the laser (to avoid harmful effects on others' eyes).

3. VIRTUAL BLIND CANE OPERATION

In addition to the camera and IMU coordinate frames, we consider a temporary world coordinate frame whose origin coincides with the IMU coordinate frame origin at the beginning and ending of a swing. The z axis of the temporary world coordinate frame is chosen to be upward, while the x and y axes are arbitrary.

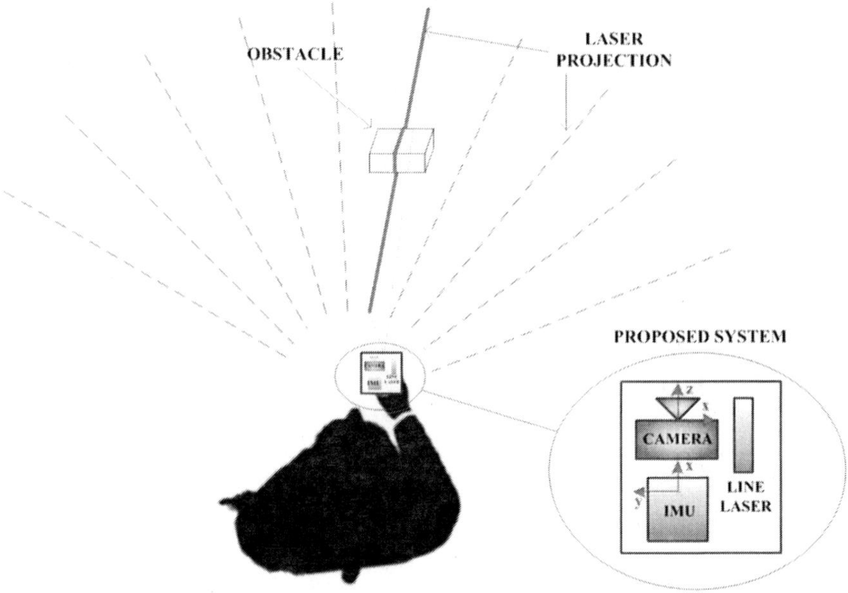

Figure 1. System overview.

Our goals are to classify the obstacle types and estimate the obstacle distance while swinging the system to scan the environment. To achieve these goals, sensor calibration and initial system height estimation are necessary. While the system is in use, the swing movement is estimated based on the IMU data. This movement is then combined with the laser information computed in the camera coordinate frame to give the 3D coordinates of the laser intersection points with respect to the temporary world coordinate frame. Based on this expression, an obstacle can be recognized by analyzing the laser point histogram, and the distance to the obstacle is computed.

3.1. Initial Estimations

Since the system is a combination of multiple sensors, a calibration step to estimate the relative position and orientation of each sensor is required. IMU-camera calibration has been studied many times. In [12], a turntable was used with a robot arm to estimate the relative pose (position and orientation) between the IMU and the camera. Another method used the observed positions and orientation analyzed from the camera while capturing a known checkerboard to compare to the trajectory obtained from the IMU in order to optimize the IMU-camera relationship. This paper used the IMU-camera calibration proposed in [13], since it is easy to use, but still gives an accurate result.

The laser plane equation in the camera coordinate frame is obtained in the camera-laser calibration. This calibration consists of capturing a known checkerboard at different positions, as in Figure 2. In each position, two images are taken, where one image contains the laser line and the other does not (the laser is turned off). By subtracting one image from the other, a new image that only contains the laser line is obtained. These laser coordinate points belong to the laser line plane, as well as the planar checkerboard. Since the position and orientation of the checkerboard is known in the camera coordinate frame, the extracted laser point coordinates can be computed with respect to the camera coordinate frame. This method can be found in many research papers about cameras and structured light calibration, such as [14,15].

After the calibration steps, the relationships between the camera, IMU and laser plane have been defined. The camera and line laser now become a unified system, which can be called the line laser-based vision system. This system has a coordinate frame that coincides with the camera coordinate frame. Since all sensors are fixed on a board, their relative positions and orientations are also constant. Therefore, the calibration process only needs to be done once.

The blind person scans the environment by swinging the system horizontally. Based on this fact, it is assumed that the height of the system with respect to the ground does not change much while the system is swinging. This height can be estimated based on the orientation of the IMU and the laser stripe distance.

Before using, to compute the system's height from the ground, the system is held stably for a few seconds. We note that the height from the ground to the system only needs to be estimated one time before using. In this state, the IMU observes the gravitational force to calculate the rotation matrix from the IMU coordinate frame to the temporary world coordinate frame. Let the temporary world coordinate frame coincide with the navigation coordinate frame; then, we have the rotation matrix RWI from the IMU to the temporary world coordinate frame based on the accelerometer outputs. Let P be the intersection point of the camera coordinate frame Z axis and the ground. The distance from the IMU coordinate frame origin to $P(|r_P|_W)$ is computed based on the IMU-camera translation tIC and [rPC], where [$rP]C$ is the position of P in the camera coordinate frame. The system height $h0$ is computed as:

$$h_0 = \begin{bmatrix} 0 & 0 & 1 \end{bmatrix} |r_P|_W = \begin{bmatrix} 0 & 0 & 1 \end{bmatrix} R_I^W \left(R_C^I |r_P|_C + t_C^I \right) \quad (1)$$

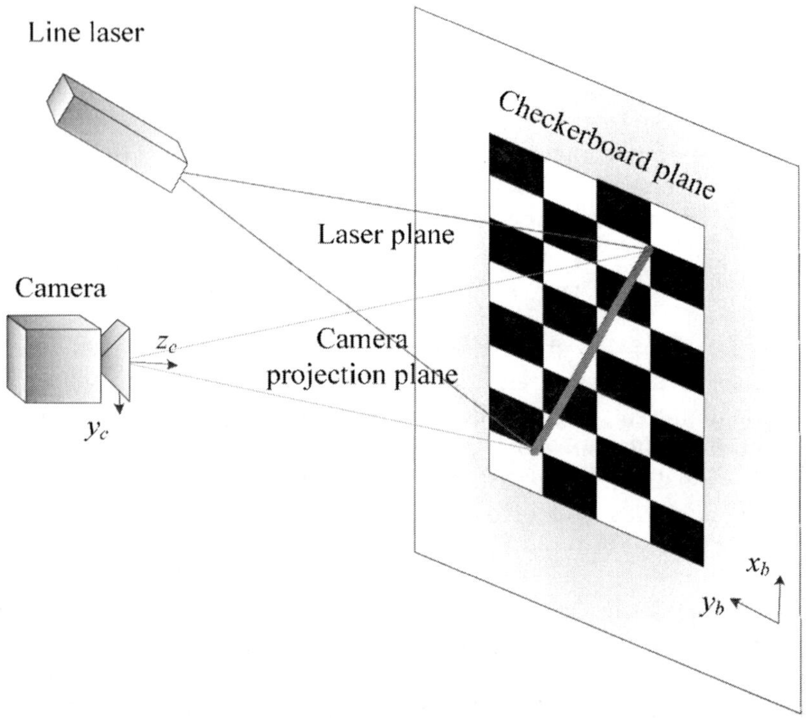

Figure 2. Line-structured light and camera calibration.

3.2. User's Swing Analysis

Normally, the walking speed of visually-impaired people is much smaller than normal vision people. The result in [16] showed that the walking speed of a blind person was about 0.4 m/s. Another research work on the association between visual impairment and mobility performance in older adults [17] concluded that the walking speed of visually-impaired people was on average 0.6 m/s. With the help of an aiding system, the visually-impaired people can increase their walking speeds, which range from 0.6 m/s to 0.8 m/s [18].

The motion of the blind person's hand while scanning the environment is described as in Figure 3. This motion consists of a moving interval (swing interval) and two stationary intervals (the beginning and ending of the swing intervals) with respect to the blind person's body. The motion of the hand is tracked using a Kalman filter with the initial position at the "stationary point" of the *k-th* swing and the stopping point at the (*k*+1)-*th* swing in the temporary world coordinate frame. The temporary world coordinate frame is reset at each swing (see Figure 3 for details), as well as Kalman filter parameters to avoid accumulated errors. The motion estimation is only considered in each swing separately. In other words, the accumulated error at the*k-th* swing does not affect the (*k*+1)-*th* swing, since it is reset to zero when the temporary world coordinate frame is reset.

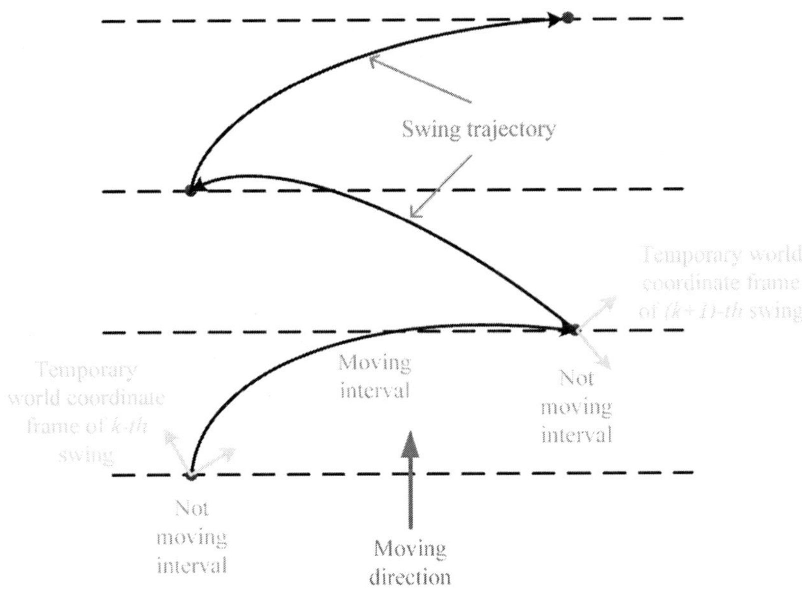

Figure 3. User's swing motion.

In this system, the IMU has two main roles. Firstly, the stationary interval of the IMU can be detected when gyroscope values for all three coordinates are approximately zero. In this stationary interval, the accelerometer measures the body acceleration and the gravity. Since the movement of the blind person is slow and the acceleration is small during stable walking, it is assumed that the IMU only observes gravity at stationary points. The error given by this assumption was small enough that it does not affect the estimation result much (see [10] for a similar error). Based on this assumption, the orientation of the system to the temporary world coordinate frame at the initial position of each swing can be computed using a triad algorithm [19]. In the second role, the IMU provides the acceleration and angular rate of the system while moving. This information is used in a Kalman filter-based motion tracking algorithm, which uses the system's initial orientation as the initial value to track the orientation of the system in each swing. Once the orientation of the system is tracked, the pointing angle of the system can also be computed. We note that only the roll and pitch angles are estimated if we observe gravity. However, in this paper, the heading angle is not important since the users intuitively know where their hands are pointing, and only the pitch angle affects the estimation result.

The inertial navigation motion tracking in this paper uses the errors in quaternion, position and velocity as the states of an indirect Kalman filter. The states consist of the errors in $\hat{q}$, $\hat{v}$ and $\hat{r}$ as follows:

$$x(t) = \begin{bmatrix} \overline{q}_e \\ r_e \\ v_e \end{bmatrix} \in \Re^9 \tag{2}$$

where " ^" denotes estimation and q, v and r stand for the quaternion, velocity and position of the system in the temporary world coordinate frame, respectively.

From the assumption that $\overline{q}_e$ is small, we obtain the following [20]:

$$\dot{x}(t) = Ax(t) + \begin{bmatrix} -\frac{1}{2}n_g \\ 0 \\ -R^T(\hat{q})\, n_a \end{bmatrix} \tag{3}$$

where:

$$A \triangleq \begin{bmatrix} [-y_g \times] & 0 & 0 \\ 0 & 0 & I \\ -2R^T(\hat{q})\lfloor y_a \times \rfloor & 0 & 0 \end{bmatrix}$$

and n_a and n_g are accelerometer and gyroscope noise, respectively. $R(\hat{q})$ is the estimated rotation matrix from the IMU coordinate frame to the temporary world coordinate frame, and y_g and y_a are the gyroscope and accelerometer outputs, respectively. Equation (3) is discretized with the sampling period *T* [11]:

$$x_{k+1} = A_{d,k} x_k + w_k \quad (4)$$

where $A_{d,k} \approx \exp(A(kT)T)$ and w_k is a Gaussian white noise with covariance $Q_{d,k} = E\{w_k w_k^T\}$. Since there is no physical measurement during the motion, the zero velocity during the stationary intervals can be used as a virtual measurement to improve the accuracy of the estimation:

$$z_{zero,k} = H_{zero} x_k + n_{v,k} \quad (5)$$

where $z_{zero,k} = [0 - \hat{v}_k]$ and $H_{zero} = \begin{bmatrix} 0_3 & 0_3 & I_3 \end{bmatrix}$ at the discrete time *k* with a small Gaussian white noise $n_{v,k}$ with covariance $R_{v,k} = E\{n_{v,k} n_{v,k}^T\}$.

In the case of swinging, it can be assumed that there is no movement at the starting and stopping points of a swing due to the slow and stable walking of the blind person. This assumption can affect the accuracy of estimation. However, the error is still acceptable for detecting the tilt angle of the system and finding separate histogram bins of laser points in the temporary world coordinate frame.

We can also utilize the laser information as in Figure 4. The position of a point *P* in the temporary world coordinate frame in a moving period is:

$$[r_P]_W = C(q)^T [r_P]_I + r \quad (6)$$

where $C(q)$ and r are the rotation from the IMU coordinate frame to the temporary world coordinate frame and the position of the IMU in the temporary world coordinate frame, respectively. Then, $[r_P]_I$ is the position of point P in the IMU coordinate frame. The height of the IMU is calculated as [21]:

$$\begin{aligned} h_0 &= \begin{bmatrix} 0 & 0 & 1 \end{bmatrix} [r_P]_W \\ &= \begin{bmatrix} 0 & 0 & 1 \end{bmatrix} \left(C(q)^T [r_P]_I + r \right) \\ &= \begin{bmatrix} 0 & 0 & 1 \end{bmatrix} \left(C(\hat{q})^T [r_P]_I + 2C(\hat{q})^T [q_e \times] [r_P]_I + \hat{r} + r_e \right) \end{aligned} \quad (7)$$

and can be rewritten as:

$$z_{height,k} = H_{height,k}\, x_k + n_{z,k} \quad (8)$$

where $z_{height,k}$ is the measurement and $n_{z,k}$ is a measurement noise at the time k:

$$z_{height,k} = h_0 - \begin{bmatrix} 0 & 0 & 1 \end{bmatrix} \left(\hat{r} + C(\hat{q})^T [r_P]_I \right) \quad (9)$$

and $H_{height,k}$ is:

$$H_{height,k} = \begin{bmatrix} 0 & 0 & 1 \end{bmatrix} \begin{bmatrix} -2C(\hat{q})^T [[r_P]_I \times] & I_3 & 0_3 \end{bmatrix} \quad (10)$$

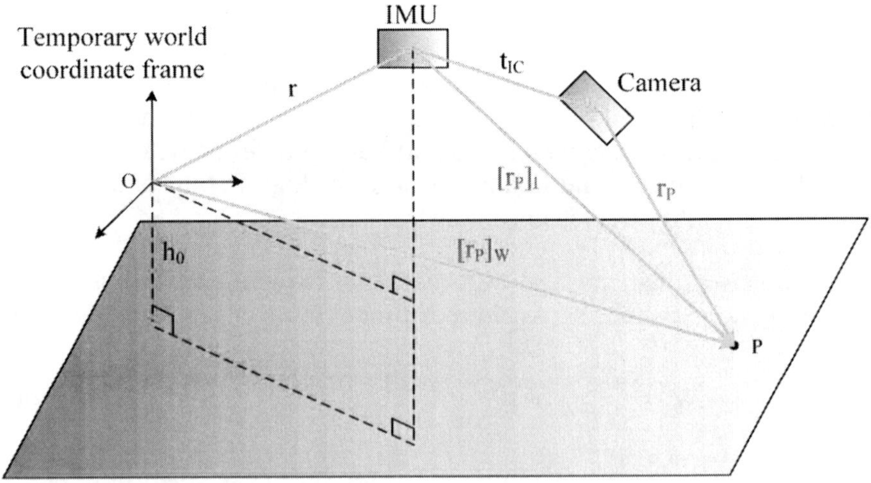

Figure 4. Position updating from laser point coordinates.

3.3. Obstacle Classification

This part describes the obstacle classification process. It could be assumed that the usual indoor obstacles are walls, stairs and blocks. The obstacle classification process is illustrated in Figure 5. Starting at the "stationary point", the motion of the hand is estimated using a Kalman filter. The information of interest from the hand motion tracking is the system orientation. From the system orientation, the inclination angle of the hand can be computed. This inclination is used together with the laser information to define an obstacle and is later used in detecting the horizontal pointing pose of the system.

In each camera image, we can separate the laser points into the ground and obstacle members, since the laser point coordinates are known in the camera coordinate frame. By forming a basic line from some of the laser points closest to the user, the laser points can be divided into two cases by comparing their distances to the basic line. The first case is when all of the laser points belong to the basic line (see Figure 6a), while in the second case, the laser points are separated into those belonging to the basic line and those associated with an object (see Figure 6b). When the image only contains the basic line, there is a chance that the entire laser line is on the floor or on a plane, such as a wall or large obstacle. In this case, the inclination angle of the basic line (not in the image, but in the 3D space) is checked to define whether the laser line is on the floor or on a wall. The inclination angle α of the basic line in the temporary world coordinate frame can be calculated from the angle of the basic line direction vector $v\rightarrow$ and the z axis unit vector:

$$\alpha = \frac{\pi}{2} - \arccos\left(\left(\vec{v}, \begin{bmatrix} 0 & 0 & 1 \end{bmatrix}^T \right) \right) \tag{11}$$

The basic line direction vector $v\rightarrow$in the temporary world coordinate frame is the normalization of:

$$v_W = C(q)' R_C^I v_C \tag{12}$$

where v_C is the basic line direction vector in the camera coordinate frame, which is formed by two arbitrary points in the basic line, and $C(q)$ represents a rotation matrix corresponding to q. If the inclination angle α of the basic line is larger than a threshold value, it can be inferred that all of the laser points are on a wall or on a large plane. Otherwise, they lie on the floor. It is easy to define a wall or a floor based on the laser stripe inclination angle since the inclination of a wall is about 90° while a floor's inclination angle is approximately 0°.

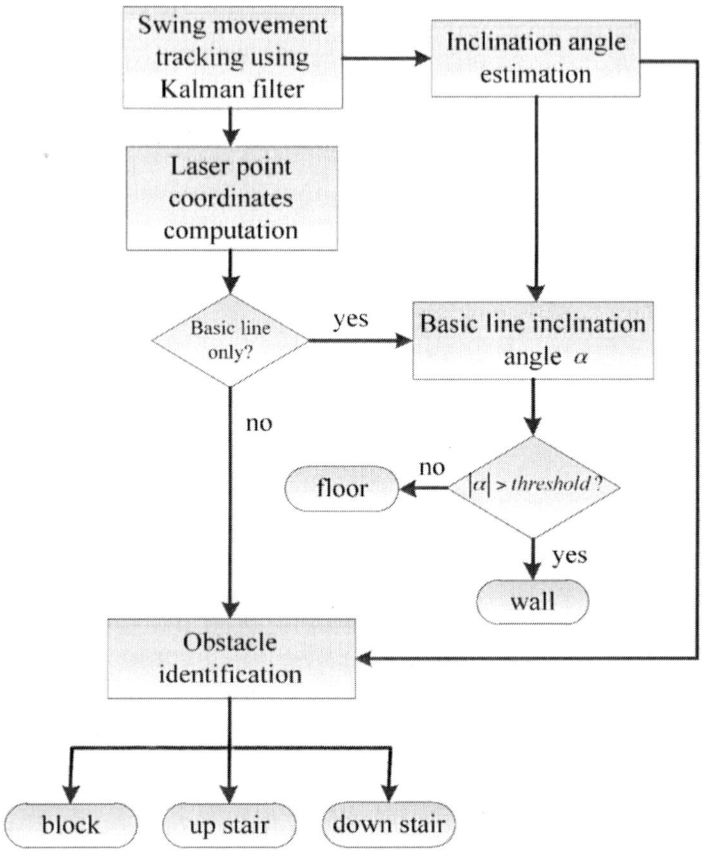

Figure 5. Obstacle classification process.

When some laser points' distances to the basic line are greater than a threshold, or in other words, the laser points are separated into ground and obstacle members, as in Figure 6b, an obstacle classification process is used to distinguish the obstacles. As shown in Figure 7, different obstacles have different laser intersection shapes. However, they are mainly formed of vertical and horizontal planes, which become laser lines in the camera images. Thus, in the obstacle identification process, we analyze the distribution of the laser points expressed in the temporary world coordinate frame by height to determine an obstacle's type. Since almost all obstacles in the building, such as blocks and stairs, are formed by vertical and horizontal surfaces, different obstacles provide different histogram forms, as in Figure 7.

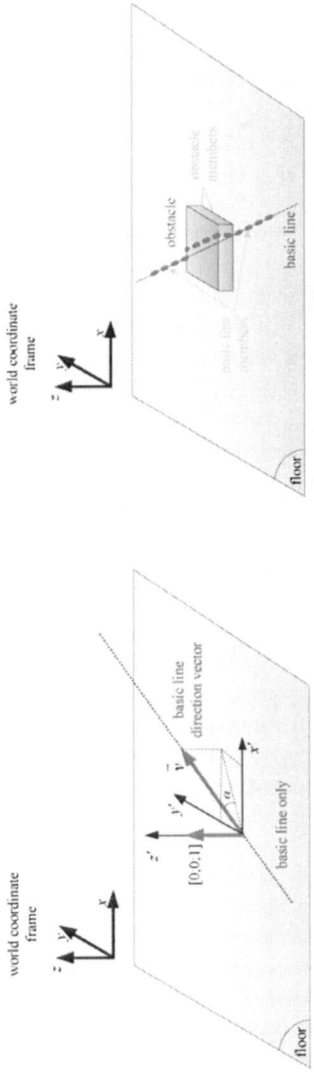

Figure 6. Laser points' contribution. (**a**) Floor or wall case: only a basic line exists; (**b**) Obstacle case: the laser stripe contains an obstacle and basic line members.

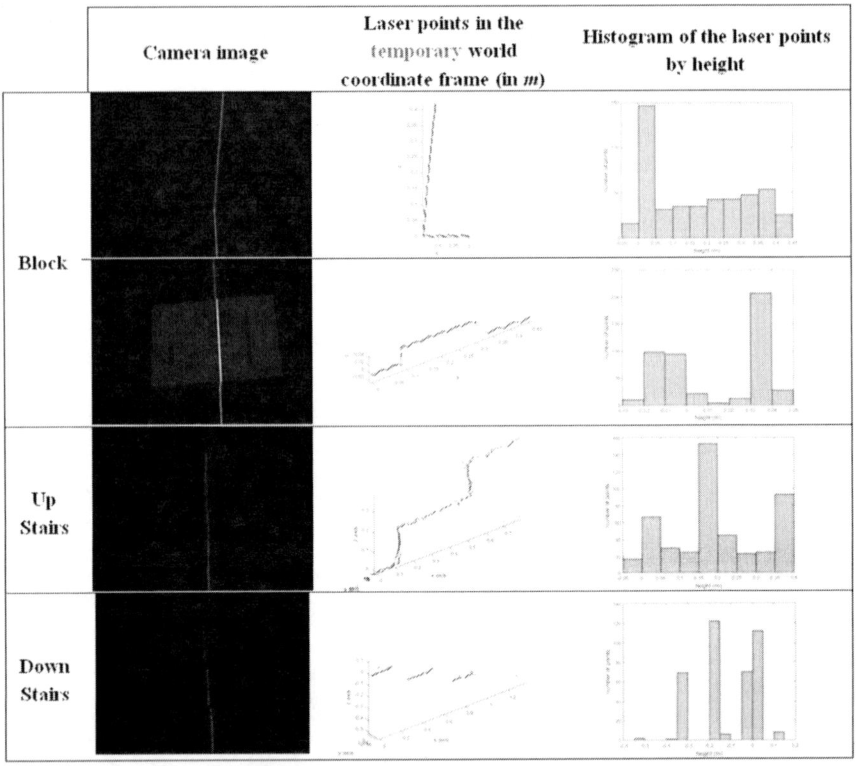

Figure 7. Laser stripe formation on various obstacles.

The positions of the laser points can be obtained in the IMU coordinate frame, since the relative pose (position and orientation) between the IMU and the camera is known. Once the pose of the IMU has been tracked using an inertial navigation algorithm, the laser point coordinates can be expressed in the temporary world coordinate frame. In Figure 7, to make the histogram analysis by height have an easier view, all of the laser point coordinates are shifted so that the first point of the basic line is at the origin of the temporary world coordinate frame (see the "laser points in the temporary world coordinate frame" column). In the obstacle identification process, the algorithm finds separate histogram bins whose values are greater than a threshold. In other words, the algorithm divides the laser points into groups based on theirs height values. We assume that if a bin's value (number of points) is greater than a threshold, it represents a horizontal plane that forms the obstacle. After finding histogram bins, two bins are considered to be one bin if they stand next to each other. For example, in Figure 7, in the "down stairs" case, if a threshold of 60 points is set, the histogram bins of laser points that are greater than the threshold are Bins 3, 4, 6 and 7. Since Bin 6 stands next to Bin 7 in the height axis, they are considered to be a single bin; while Bins 3 and 4 are split to be two separate bins. Therefore, the total number of separated bins that can be found in the laser histogram is three. This means that the obstacle is formed by three horizontal planes. We can conclude that it is stairs.

Generally, a block is detected with one or two separate bins, as shown in Figure 7, while stairs normally have three separate bins. In some cases, the histogram bin number for stairs can be two. In these cases, the height of the last laser point with respect to the blind person is compared to the height values of two bins to determine whether the scanned object is stairs or a block. Up or down stairs have a final laser point height much larger or smaller, respectively, than the bin's height.

3.4. Distance to the Obstacle

In addition to the obstacle identification, the other important information from the environment that needs to be determined is the distance from the obstacle to the blind person. The distance d from the system to the obstacle is computed based on the system height h_0 and the laser distance l_P, as depicted in Figure 8. In this system, we chose 40 mm as the threshold for determining whether a laser point belongs to the basic line or not. Assuming that the point P in Figure 8represents the first point of the obstacle from the view of the blind person, we can determine P as the closest laser point to the blind person that does not lie on the basic line. Since the laser distance l_P can be derived from the coordinates of P in the IMU coordinate frame, the distance d can be calculated as:

$$d = \sqrt{l_P^2 - h_0^2} \qquad (13)$$

4. EXPERIMENTS AND RESULTS

The experimental setup is shown in Figure 9. The system consists of a Firefly camera, an Xsens IMU and a laser line projector. The camera and the IMU are synchronized using a microprocessor. For processing, a

2.09-kg HP ProBook 6460 b laptop with a configuration of Core i5 2.5 GHz CPU, 4 GB RAM, was used with this experimental system. The experimental system weight is about 250 g. In the experiments, the laptop was carried by a volunteer, while the proposed system was held by hand in front of the volunteer and close to his waist.

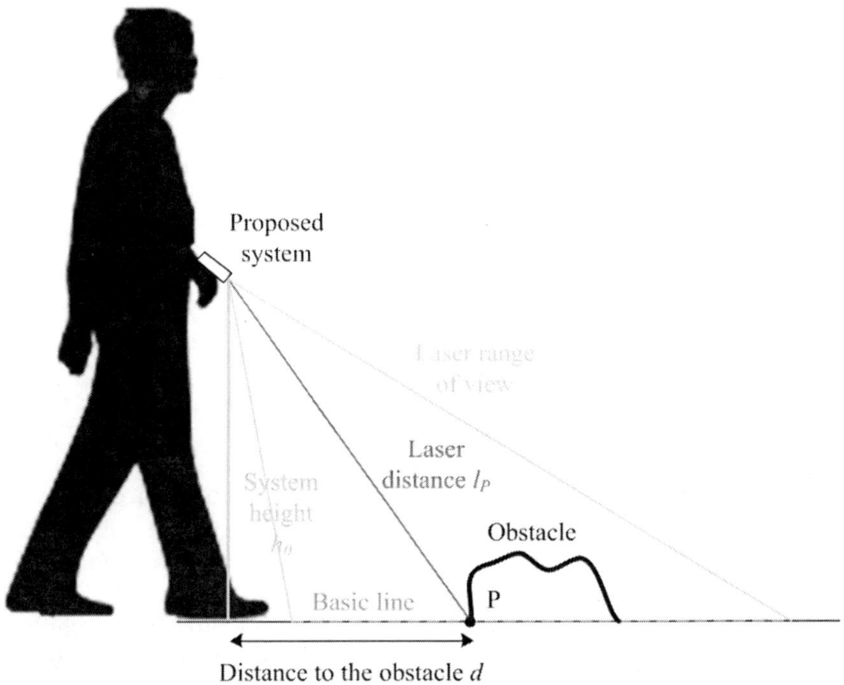

Figure 8. Distance estimation for the obstacle.

4.1. System Height Estimation Experiment

Since the system height is used to compute the distance from the user to the obstacle, it is necessary to estimate the system height. To verify the accuracy of the system height estimation with respect to the ground, the system was pointed toward a flat floor at different heights and orientations in each recording process. The position of the system was first calculated based on the method proposed in Section 3.1 and was then compared to the ground truth value tracked by the OptiTrack system [22]. The experiment results verifying the IMU's height estimation are given in Table 1.

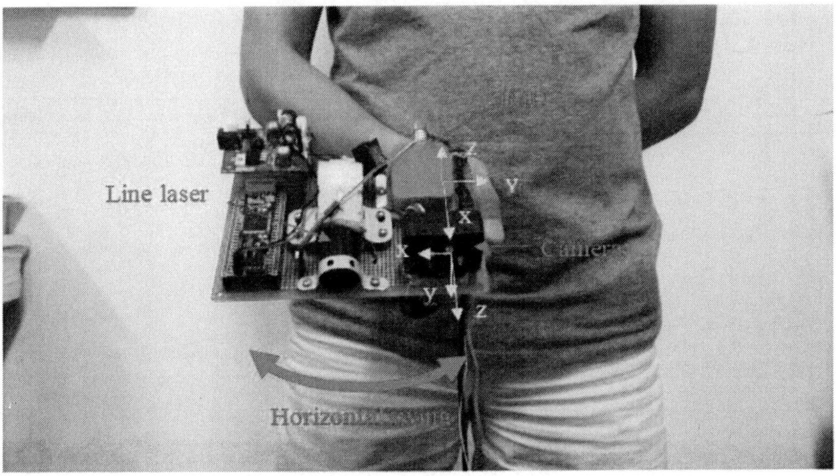

Figure 9. Experimental system.

During operation, the system height can be changed a certain amount. However, this variation affects the distance estimation only moderately. For example, if the system is held close to the user's belt, the system height could be around 1 m. With a normal pointing angle of 45° with respect to the horizontal plane, the laser distance could be around 1.4 m. If the system height is changed by 10 cm, then the distance error from the user to the obstacle is smaller than 10 cm. This is an acceptable error compared to the walking distance.

4.2. Obstacle Classification Experiment

In this experiment, the proposed algorithm was tested in offices and corridors with typical obstacles, such as chairs, tables, walls and stairs. With the current configuration, the effective working range of the system was about 1.8 m from the user, because the laser point extraction was affected by the environmental illumination. We conducted an experiment to find the effective working range of the system. The distance from the object to the system was changed after the object classification process was completed. The results are given in Figure 10, which shows the relationship between the distance from the system to the object and the successful classification percentage.

Table 1. Height estimation by the IMU.

Number of Experiment	Ground Truth Height (cm)	Estimated Height (cm)	Error (cm)
1	66.50	66.37	0.13
2	71.00	71.40	0.40
3	75.00	75.00	0.00
4	80.00	80.43	0.43
5	82.00	81.99	0.01
6	85.50	85.96	0.46
7	90.00	89.94	0.06
8	92.00	92.16	0.16
9	95.00	94.41	0.59
10	100.00	99.51	0.49
	Average Error (cm)		0.273
	Standard Deviation (cm)		0.193

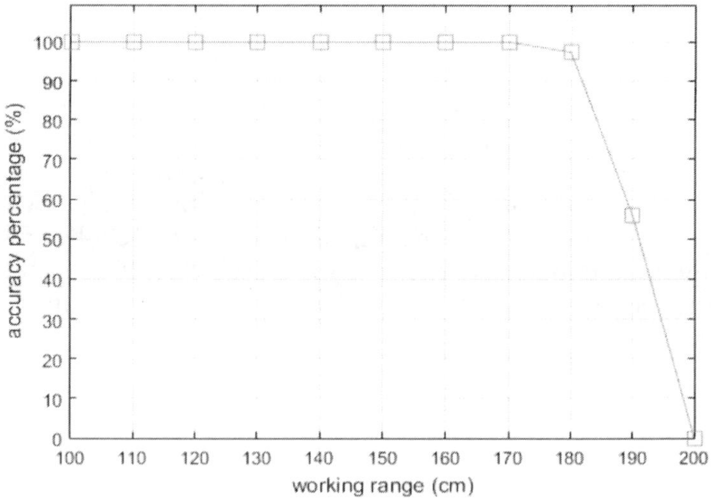

Figure 10. Working range accuracy.

The working range is also affected by the baseline between the camera and the line laser due to the error given by a small parallax. To verify the accuracy of the object classification of the system using the current configuration, an experiment was carried out with three boxes with heights of 4, 8 and 13.5 cm, respectively. Boxes were captured by the system at different distances ranging from 1 m to 1.9 m. The laser stripes on box surfaces were analyzed to estimate the box's heights, which, in other words, represents the change in laser point coordinates. The accuracy of the system (in cm) is shown in Table 2.

The result indicates that with the proposed configuration, the system can recognize obstacles with the current camera-laser baseline. Increasing the baseline of the camera and the laser will provide a better object estimation. However, the limitation is that the size of the system will be increased. As a handheld device, we chose this baseline to balance the object estimation error and the size of the system.

A volunteer was asked to scan the environment while walking. The experiment was repeated five times for each environment. The sampling rate of the camera is 20 Hz. We note that all experiments were done within the effective working range of the system. The laser shapes on the obstacles were analyzed, and the classification results are given in Table 3, in which the accuracies are expressed as percentages. Table 3 shows that the system can accurately recognize walls and floors. Other obstacles, such as stairs and a block, could also be detected with a high accuracy of up to 96%.

Since the wall and floor only contained the basic line, they were the easiest to recognize. The obstacles used in the room experiment were blocks, which were formed by one vertical and two horizontal planes. Therefore, sometimes, they were recognized as stairs. For the stairs case, when the laser stripe was not fully captured, the laser point histogram only contained two separate bins, causing the stairs to be classified as a block.

4.3. Distance to Obstacle Estimation

The distance to the obstacle estimation experiment was set up with a block lying on a flat floor. Before this experiment, the system height was estimated. Then, the user swung the system to scan the environment while standing in certain marked positions. The position of the block was marked on the floor, and the distance from the user to the block was measured directly. These ground truth distances were used in comparison to the estimated distances calculated based on Section 3.4.Table 4 summarizes the ground truth and estimated distances.

Table 2. A result of estimating different obstacle heights (in cm) at different distances (in m).

Object (cm)	Distance										Mean	Error
	1 m	1.1 m	1.2 m	1.3 m	1.4 m	1.5 m	1.6 m	1.7 m	1.8 m	1.9 m		
4	4.76	4.81	4.04	4.13	4.69	5.03	4.78	4.59	5.01	4.50	4.63	0.63
8	8.70	8.14	8.04	7.60	7.69	8.06	9.53	7.86	9.57	9.18	8.44	0.44
13.5	12.70	11.77	11.07	12.32	11.35	13.35	14.03	13.00	14.34	13.44	12.74	0.76

Table 3. Obstacle classification accuracy (%) within the effective working range (1.8 m).

		Real Features				
		Wall	Floor	Up Stairs	Down Stairs	Block
Number of Samples (Images)		1315	753	846	1101	785
Detected as (%)	Wall	100	0	0	0	0
	Floor	0	100	0	0	0
	Up Stairs	0	0	96.27	0	3.85
	Down Stairs	0	0	0	96.11	0
	Block	0	0	3.73	3.89	96.15

The maximum error was 11.15 cm, while the minimum error was 4.08 cm. These errors are acceptable compared to the distance of a normal stride. The mean error of 6.17 cm shows that the system is feasible for real life application.

Table 4. Estimation of distance to the obstacle.

Number of Experiment	Ground Truth Distance (cm)	Estimated Distance (cm)	Error (cm)
1	60	55.92	4.08
2	75	70.15	4.85
3	90	84.38	5.62
4	105	101.02	3.98
5	120	126.95	6.95
6	135	139.50	4.5
7	150	141.97	8.03
8	165	171.33	6.33
9	180	191.15	11.12
	Average error (cm)		6.17
	Standard deviation (cm)		2.18

4.4. Dynamic Experiment with the OptiTrack Camera System

In this experiment, the volunteer scanned the environment with the system while the system position was observed by the OptiTrack cameras. A box was placed in a known location with respect to the OptiTrack camera system's coordinate frame. Since the purposes of the system are to recognize the obstacle's type and to estimate the distance from the user to it, an OptiTrack marker was attached to the IMU to record the system position. Once the marker's position was known, the distance from the marker (also the system) to the box was computed. This ground truth value was compared to the distance that was estimated by the system based on Section 3.4.

The overview of the experimental results is given in Figure 11, which shows the positions of the system and the corresponding laser stripes. The system scanned the floor until it met a box. There were 136 images captured, where eight images contained the box, and the rest (129 images) were floor images. The system successfully recognized the box in seven images (87.5%) and the floor in 129 images (100%). One image was incorrectly classified as a down stair case.

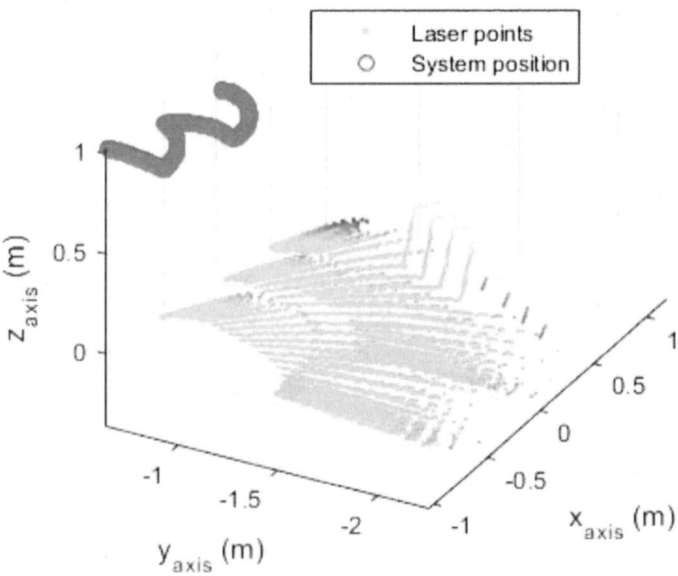

Figure 11. Results of the dynamic experiment.

The distance from the obstacle to the system was also computed, based on the images that contained the box. Compared to the real distances, which were obtained from the marker's position relative to the box, the estimated distances had an average error of 11.58 cm; the best estimation was 2.79 cm, and the worst estimation was 22.36 cm.

Besides, the assumption that h_0 is not changing much while swinging is also shown in Figure 11. As can be seen from the figure, the system height, which is observed by the OptiTrack system, does not change much. The height at the starting point is 1.012 m, while the height at the ending point is 1.018 m. The minimum height value is 0.9837 m, and the maximum height value is 1.028 m.

5. DISCUSSION

This paper proposes a blind navigation assistance system consisting of an IMU, a laser line and a camera. The objectives of the system are to recognize an obstacle and to find the distance from the user to the obstacle. The obstacle's type is classified by investigating the laser point distribution by height, while the distance to the obstacle is computed by combining the swing movement analysis with the 3D laser point coordinates. Some experiments have been done to verify the accuracy, as well as the feasibility of the system. The results showed that the obstacles can be classified accurately, and the distance to the obstacle has a small error. When the system is applied in a real environment, the estimated distance error is acceptable compared to a normal walking step. The advantages of the system are its simplicity, low cost and accuracy. It can be easily implemented by attaching a line laser to a smartphone or other PDA devices, which already have a built-in IMU and a camera.

However, the limitation of the system is that it is easily affected by strong illumination. Therefore, the system working range is limited, as shown in Figure 10. This led to some large errors in estimating the distances to the obstacles in the dynamic experiment, because some laser points are out of effective working range while the system is swinging. This limitation can be reduced by applying some laser filters or using a stronger laser line.

Another limitation of the system is that the laser light is harmful for the eyes. To avoid this danger, the system gives some indications when the user points the system horizontally. To do this, the system pointing angle is tracked by a Kalman filter, as mentioned in Section 3.2. Although there is an error in the system pointing angle estimation due to the swing of the hand and the movement of the body, the horizontal and ground pointing angles are much different (about 90° for horizontal pointing and about 40° for ground pointing). Therefore, the estimated system pointing angle is used to identify the horizontal pointing case.

At the starting point of a swing, the system pointing angle ρ of the system is calculated based on Equation (55) in [23]:

$$\rho = \frac{\pi}{2} - arccos\frac{a_z}{\sqrt{a_x^2 + a_y^2 + a_z^2}} \tag{14}$$

where $a = \begin{bmatrix} a_x & a_y & a_z \end{bmatrix}^T$ is the accelerometer output at that moment. The system pointing angle ρ is then tracked in each swing movement to give the system pointing angle at every sampling point in the swing.

Since the z axis of the IMU coordinate frame is pointing upward and its xy plane is parallel to the horizontal plane, the value of the inclination angle, which is computed based on Equation (55) in [23], varies from 90° (when the system is pointed orthogonally to the ground or upward) to 0° (when the system is pointed horizontally). Therefore, we used Equation (14) to express the system pointing angle by subtracting the inclination angle from $\pi/2$ to have the pointing angle ranging from 0° to 90°. A demonstration is given in Figure 12 below (note that $\cos(\alpha) = \cos(-\alpha)$; thus, inclination angles in the case of the OA and OB directions have the same value).

As an example, in Figure 13, the user was walking while scanning the ground from zero to 15 s before the system swung horizontally from 15 to 25 s. As shown in Figure 13, the tracked system pointing angle of the ground scanning period was about 45°, while in the second period, the horizontal swing angle was about 87°. With a large change, the difference between the ground and horizontal swinging can be easily recognized. The system turns off the laser when it detects horizontal pointing.

The last thing to discuss is the system height. There is an assumption that the system height does not change much while walking ,since the system is held in front of the users, close to their waist, which is the most comfortable place for long holding and similar to the usual blind cane position. An experiment was done within the range of the OptiTrack system view, where a volunteer used the proposed system while a marker was attached on the system to observe the system height h_0 The h_0 at each stationary point in this experiment can be calculated based on the inclination angle of the system and the laser distance. The result is given in Figure 14.

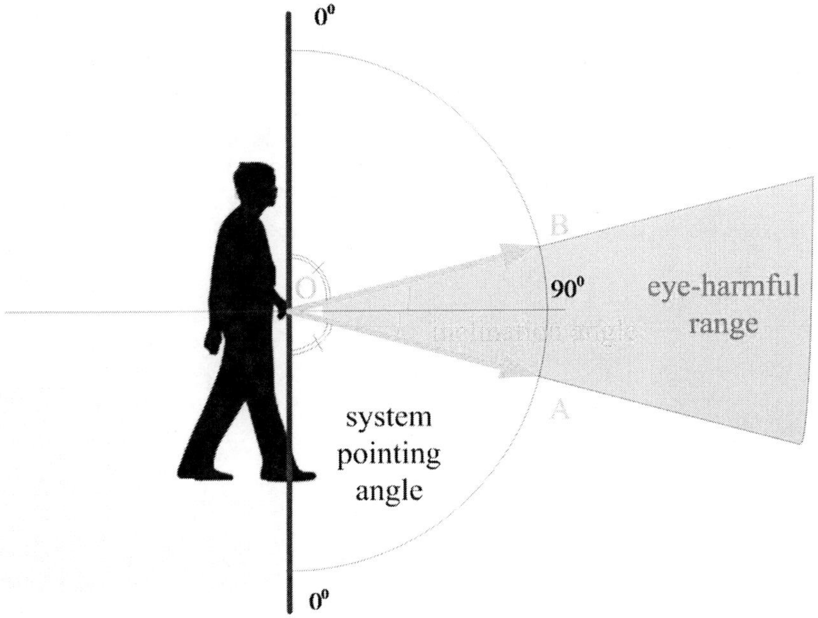

Figure 12. System pointing angle.

The maximum absolute error was about 5 cm, while the average absolute error was 2.2 cm. This result implied that the system height does not change much during walking.

Since the system is used by blind people, sound feedback can be selected to give the indications to the users. Sound feedback has been studied for many years. A well-known sound feedback system is the image to sound technique, which was proposed by Meijer in 1992 [24]. In this method, an image is scanned by the pixel column. In each column, one pixel row position corresponds to a frequency, while the sound amplitude is proportional to the pixel color. This representation provides a sound combined from many frequencies and their own amplitudes. The audience can visualize an image by listening to the column sound, which moves from the left to the right of the image.

However, to use this system, the user needs to be trained, and the continuous sounds may disturb the user.

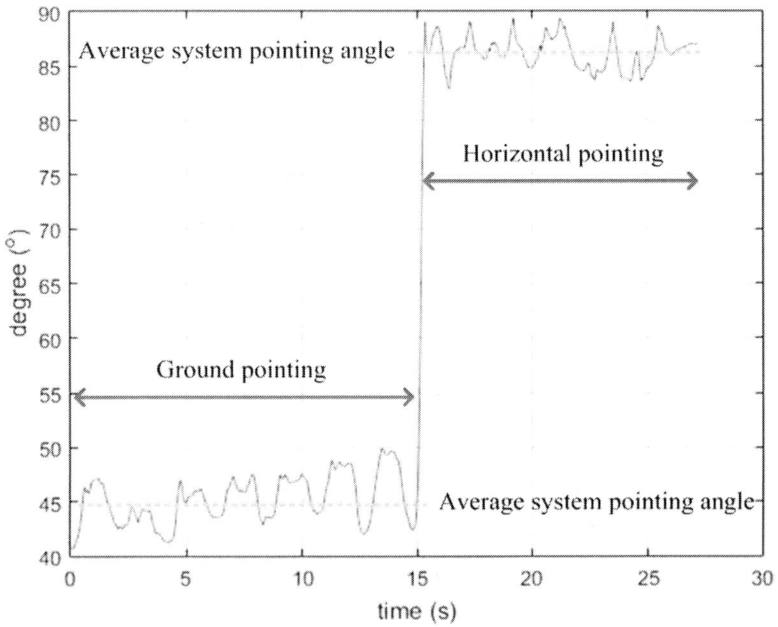

Figure 13. System pointing angle estimation example.

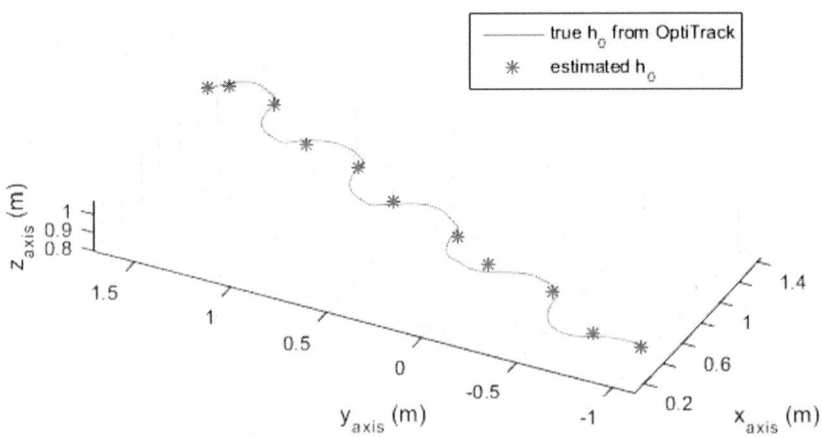

Figure 14. Estimated and true h_0.

As can be seen from Figure 14, the estimated h_0 is close to the true value obtained from the OptiTrack camera system. The error between estimated h_0 and the true value is given in Table 5 below.

Table 5. Estimated and true h_0 at stationary points.

Stationary Point Order	1	2	3	4	5	6	7	8	9	10	11
True h_0 (m)	1.0009	1.0178	1.0267	1.0356	1.0196	1.0350	1.0399	1.0442	1.0439	1.0395	1.0362
Estimated h_0 (m)	1.0104	1.0395	1.0791	1.0795	0.9772	1.0553	1.0499	1.0167	1.0435	1.0277	1.0377
Absolute Error (m)	0.0095	0.0217	0.0524	0.0439	0.0424	0.0203	0.0100	0.0275	0.0004	0.0118	0.0015
Absolute Mean Error (m)						0.0219					

In this system, a simple feedback method can be used. The feedback includes sound feedback and voice description. The sound feedback presented here is a single tone sound with a magnitude proportional to the distance from the blind person to the object, while the voice description gives an indication for some special cases, such as “up stairs two meters ahead”, “horizontal pointing”, *etc.* A higher tone indicates that the user is closer to the obstacle. To avoid sound annoyance, the sound only exists when the system detects certain obstacles.

ACKNOWLEDGMENTS

This work was supported by National Research Foundation of Korea Grant funded by the Korean Government (No. 2011-001978).

AUTHOR CONTRIBUTIONS

Quoc Khanh Dang proposed the idea and developed the algorithm under the supervision of Youngjoon Chee and Young Soo Suh. Youngjoon Chee provided the verification method while Duy Duong Pham and Quoc Khanh Dang developed the system and collected experiment data. Young Soo Suh contributed the inertial navigation and position measurement update algorithms. The paper was written by Quoc Khanh Dang and revised by Youngjoon Chee and Young Soo Suh.

CONFLICTS OF INTEREST

The authors declare no conflict of interest.

REFERENCES

1. WHO. Visual Impairment and Blindness—Fact Sheet n° 282. Available online: http://www.who.int/mediacentre/factsheets/fs282/en/ (accessed on 1 August 2015).

2. Clark-Carter, D.D.; Heyes, A.D.; Howarth, C.I. The efficiency and walking speed of visually impaired people.*Ergonomics* **1986**, *29*, 779–789.

3. Bhatlawande, S.S.; Mukhopadhyay, J.; Mahadevappa, M. Ultrasonic spectacles and waist-belt for visually impaired and blind person. In Proceedings of the 2012 National Conference on Communications (NCC), Kharagpur, India, 3–5 Feburary 2012; pp. 1–4.

4. Niitsu, Y.; Taniguchi, T.; Kawashima, K. Detection and notification of dangerous obstacles and places for visually impaired persons using a smart cane. In Proceedings of the 2014 Seventh International Conference on Mobile Computing and Ubiquitous Networking (ICMU), Singapore, 13–17 September 2014.

5. Al-Fahoum, A.S.; Al-Hmoud, H.B.; Al-Fraihat, A.A. A smart infrared microcontroller-based blind guidance system.*Act. Passiv. Electron. Comp.* **2013**, *2013*.

6. Tang, J.; Jing, X.; He, D.; Liang, S. Blind-road location and recognition in natural scene. In Proceedings of the 2009 WRI World Congress on Computer Science and Information Engineering, Los Angeles, CA, USA, 31 March–2 April 2009; pp. 283–287.

7. Velazquez, R.; Fontaine, E.; Pissaloux, E. Coding the environment in tactile maps for real-time guidance of the visually impaired. In Proceedings of the 2006 International Symposium on Micro-NanoMechatronics and Human Science, Nagoya, Japan, 6–8 November 2006; pp. 1–6.

8. Kim, D.; Kim, K.; Lee, S. Stereo camera based virtual cane system with identifiable distance tactile feedback for the blind. *Sensors* **2014**, *14*, 10412–10431.

9. Yuan, D.; Manduchi, R. Dynamic environment exploration using a virtual white cane. In Proceedings of the IEEE Computer Society Conference on Computer Vision and Pattern Recognition, San Diego, CA, USA, 20–25 June 2005; Volume 1, pp. 243–249.

10. Palleją, T.; Tresanchez, M.; Teixidó, M.; Palacin, J. Bioinspired electronic white cane implementation based on a lidar, a tri-axial accelerometer and a tactile belt. *Sensors* **2010**, *10*, 11322–11339.

11. Brown, R.G.; Hwang, P.Y.C. *Introduction to Random Signals and Applied Kalman Filtering*; John Wiley & Sons: New York, NY, USA, 1997.

12. Lobo, J.; Dias, J. Relative pose calibration between visual and inertial sensors. *Int. J. Robot. Res.* **2007**, *26*, 561–575.

13. Fleps, M.; Mair, E.; Ruepp, O.; Suppa, M.; Burschka, D. Optimization based imu camera calibration. In Proceedings of the IEEE/RSJ International Conference on Intelligent Robots and Systems, San Francisco, CA, USA, 20–25 September 2011; pp. 3297–3304.

14. Zhang, B.; Li, Y.F.; Wu, Y.H. Self-recalibration of a structured light system via plane-based homography. *Pattern Recogn.* **2007**, *40*, 1368–1377.

15. Zhou, F.; Zhang, G. Complete calibration of a structured light stripe vision sensor through planar target of unknown orientations. *Image Vis. Comput.* **2005**, *23*, 59–67.

16. Guerrero, L.A.; Vasquez, F.; Ochoa, S.F. An indoor navigation system for the visually impaired. *Sensors* **2012**, *12*, 8236–8258.

17. Swenor, B.K.; Muñoz, B.; West, S.K. A longitudinal study of the association between visual impairment and mobility performance in older adults: The salisbury eye evaluation study. *Am. J. Epidemiol.* **2013**, *179*, 313–322.

18. Shoval, S.; Ulrich, I.; Borenstein, J. Navbelt and the guide-cane obstacle-avoidance systems for the blind and visually impaired. *IEEE Robot. Autom. Mag.* **2003**, *10*, 9–20.

19. Black, H.D. A passive system for determining the attitude of a satellite. *AIAA J.* **1964**, *2*, 1350–1351.

20. Suh, Y.S. Orientation estimation using a quaternion-based indirect kalman filter with adaptive estimation of external acceleration. *IEEE Trans. Instrum. Meas.* **2010**, *59*, 3296–3305.

21. Pham, D.D.; Suh, Y.S. Foot pose estimation using an inertial sensor unit and two distance sensors. *Sensors* **2015**, *15*, 15888–15902.

22. Optitrack. Available online: http://www.optitrack.com/ (accessed on 1 August 2015).

23. Pedley, M. Tilt Sensing Using a Three-Axis Accelerometer. Available online: http://cache.freescale.com/files/sensors/doc/app_note/AN3461.pdf?fpsp=1 (accessed on 1 August 2015).

24. Meijer, P.B.L. An experimental system for auditory image representations. *IEEE Trans. Biomed. Eng.* 1992, *39*, 112–121.

7

EXPLORE SEMANTIC PIXEL SETS BASED LOCAL PATTERNS WITH INFORMATION ENTROPY FOR FACE RECOGNITION

Zhenhua Chai Heydi Mendez-Vazquez, Ran He, Zhenan Sun and Tieniu Tan

1National Laboratory of Pattern Recognition, Institute of Automation, Chinese

Academy of Science, P.O. Box 2728, Beijing 100190, People's Republic of China.

2Advanced Technologies Application Center, 7th Avenue #21812 b/ 218 and 222, Havana, Cuba.

ABSTRACT

Several methods have been proposed to describe face images in order to recognize them automatically. Local methods based on spatial histograms of local patterns (or operators) are among the best-performing ones. In this paper, a new method that allows to obtain more robust histograms of local patterns by using a more discriminative spatial division strategy is proposed. Spatial histograms are obtained from regions clustered according to the semantic pixel relations, making better use of the spatial information. Here, a simple rule is used, in which pixels in an image patch are clustered by sorting their intensity values. By exploring the information entropy on image patches, the number of sets on each of them is learned. Besides, Principal Component Analysis with a Whitening process is applied for the final feature vector dimension reduction, making the representation more compact and discriminative. The proposed division strategy is invariant to monotonic grayscale changes, and shows to be particularly useful when there are large expression variations on the faces. The method is evaluated on three widely used face recognition databases: AR, FERET and LFW, with the very popular LBP operator and some of its extensions. Experimental results show that the proposal not only outperforms those methods that use the same local patterns with the traditional division, but also some of the best-performing state-of-the-art methods.

1 INTRODUCTION

Face recognition is a popular biometric technique, mainly because it is considered as non-intrusive and it can be applied in a wide range of applications such as access control, video surveillance and human computer interaction[1]. Feature extraction is one of the most important steps in the face recognition process, but to obtain discriminative and robust features for describing face images is still an open problem[2]. Several methods have been proposed toward this aim, that can mainly be divided into two groups: local feature-based methods and global appearance-based methods[1]. In general, local feature-based methods exhibit a better behavior and have some advantages over the global ones[3–5]. Among existing local descriptors, Gabor wavelet-based methods are one of the best performing, mainly due to their spatial locality and orientation selectivity[6]. However, although different strategies have been proposed, they are still computationally intensive and consume too much time in feature extraction[7], being not suitable for real-time and mobile applications. On the other hand, histograms of local patterns, such as Local Binary Patterns and its different extensions, which are also very popular local descriptors[8], are very simple and fast to compute.

The Local Binary Patterns (LBP) operator was first proposed for texture classification and was then applied to face recognition using a regular regions division[9]. Many extensions of the original operator have appeared afterwards[10–16]; however most of them have focused on obtaining more discriminative descriptors, while few methods have been proposed to get a more robust division strategy.

Recently, the semantic pixel set-based LBP (spsLBP)[17] was proposed for this aim. By clustering the pixels in an image region into a number of sets according to their semantic meanings instead of using a regular division, it makes better use of the spatial information when constructing the local histograms. It was shown in[17] that this strategy can alleviate to some extent the pixel-shifting problem caused by some face deformations like variations in expression. However, only the original LBP operator was tested with the proposed strategy in[17], while more robust LBP variants can be used for improving the overall performance.

In this paper, we aim at extending the proposal in[17] to a more general framework, in which more robust local operators can be applied, such as Local Ternary Patterns (LTP) and Three-Patch LBP (TP-LBP). Moreover, we believe that the amount of information in different face regions is different, then using a fixed number of sets for all regions, like in[17], could not be appropriate. Hence, a different number of sets should be used in different regions according to their specific information quantity. Taking this into account, we propose in this paper a method for automatically learning the number of sets in which each region should be divided, by using information entropy. When including more sets, the feature vector dimensionality increases, so a dimensionality reduction method is needed. We have considered to apply the Principal Component Analysis with a Whitening process (WPCA)[18] in our framework. This method not only reduces the dimension of the feature vector, making it more compact, but also can be used even on small-sample-size cases[18].

The rest of this paper is organized as follows: in section 2, related work is analyzed; in section 3, the proposed framework is introduced, and the strategy to learn the number of clusters in a region is presented; section 4 shows experimental results of the proposed method in comparison with some related state-of-the-art descriptors; finally, conclusions are given in section 5.

2 RELATED WORK

LBP is one of the most popular face image descriptors[19, 20]. It was introduced in this area in 2004, motivated by the fact that faces can be seen as a composition of micro-patterns which can be well described by this operator[9]. The original LBP[21] describes these local texture patterns by thresholding the comparison results between the intensity value of the center pixel and its 3×3 neighborhood. The resulted binary values are then concatenated together and encoded as an integer. This encoding process is illustrated on Figure1. The operator is invariant to grayscale monotonic variations since it only takes into account if the surrounding pixels values are brighter or darker than the center pixel value. The original method was later extended for using a circular neighborhood of different radius sizes and considering different numbers of equally spaced pixels on the defined circle[22]. In the same work[22], it was shown that more than 90% of the texture information (lines, edges, corners) is contained on 58 patterns which have at most two bitwise 0 to 1 or 1 to 0 transitions; so these patterns were called uniform LBP and, in this case, a single label is assigned to all remaining patterns.

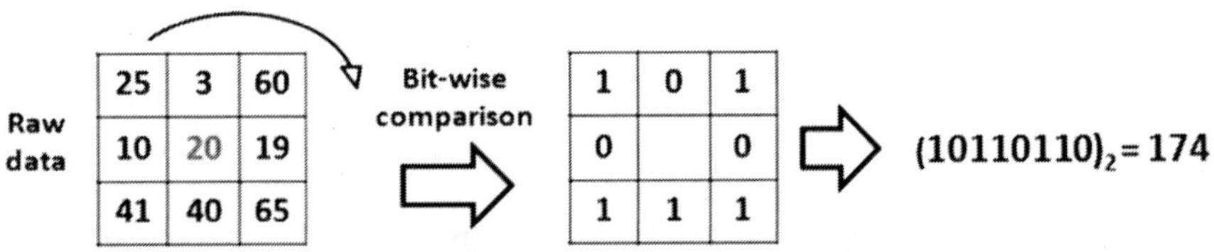

Figure 1 LBP encoding process. This figure describes the LBP encoding process in which each pixel is compared with its eight neighbor pixels and the comparisons are encoded in a binary number representing the LBP code.

In the past few years, a number of variants of the original operator have been proposed for improving different aspects of the method[20]. Some of the extensions aim at enhancing the discriminative capability of the operator, such as the improved LBP (ILBP)[10], in which both the pixels in the circular neighborhood and the center pixel are compared against the mean intensity value of them. Another is the extended LBP (ELBP)[23], which encodes the gradient magnitude image in addition to the original image in order to represent the velocity of local variations. There are some extensions that have been proposed for improving the robustness, such as the local ternary patterns (LTP)[16] which includes a 3-level generalization coding scheme and is more resistance to noise. However, this operator is no longer invariant to monotonic grayscale transformations. There are also some extensions which have concentrated on choosing an appropriate neighborhood for the encoding process (e.g. the number and distribution of the sampling points as well as the shape and size of the neighborhood). One of the examples is the Multi-scale Block LBP (MB-LBP)[24], in which the average intensity values of neighboring rectangular blocks are compared rather than single pixels. This allows to capture macro-structures of face images. Three-Patch LBP and Four-Patch LBP[25] are also patch-based operators, and their experimental results are very promising.

Most of the descriptors mentioned above use the original strategy of Ahonen et al.[9] for facial representation. The scheme consists of dividing the face image into rectangular regions, from which local histograms of the extracted local patterns are obtained. Afterwards, the histograms of all regions are concatenated into a single spatially enhanced feature histogram that encodes both the local texture and the global shape of face images. Under this strategy, deciding the number and size of blocks is usually a problem, especially when there are different appearance variations on the face. A finer division usually makes the descriptor more discriminative but sometimes, for example when there are expression variations, will bring some problems. This is illustrated on Figure2, where it can be appreciated that in the case of expression variations, a finer division can affect the recognition process because small blocks around some face areas, such as mouth and eyes, are shifted to neighbor blocks. Just a few methods on the literature aim at modifying the spatial division strategy. In[26] and[27], many subregions are obtained by shifting and scaling a rectangular region over the face image and boosting is used for selecting the most discriminative regions of different sizes at different positions. Overlapped subregions have also been used[28]; as well as circular[29] and triangular[30] regions.

The spsLBP method[17] is another approach proposed to solve the blocks division problem. It uses a simple clustering method to segment the pixels in a region by considering their intensity values. In spsLBP, the face image is first divided into a few coarse rectangular regions and then the pixels in each region are regrouped by their semantic meanings. Histograms of LBP codes are computed from the obtained sets and concatenated as in the traditional scheme. It is a very simple idea in which the local patterns are associated with their semantic meaning instead of their spatial position only. This strategy allows to group most of the relevant pixels into corresponding sets even in the presence of some shifting. It should be noticed that, for simplicity, intensity values were used for associating the pixels, but some other attributes such as contrast, luminance, texton, etc., could also be used. It was shown in[17] that this strategy outperforms the traditional regular division. However, more robust LBP variants were not considered in that work. On the other hand, the number of pixel sets for each region was set equal which can be inappropriate in some cases. In Figure3, it is shown that different face regions can contain a different amount of variable information. By intuition, some regions rich in texture, like areas around eyes, should contain more information; thus, a large number for pixel groups with different semantic meanings should be set while others, like cheek, can be almost homogenous. Hence, we believe both, more robust descriptors and proper number of sets for each region, can boost the performance of this framework.

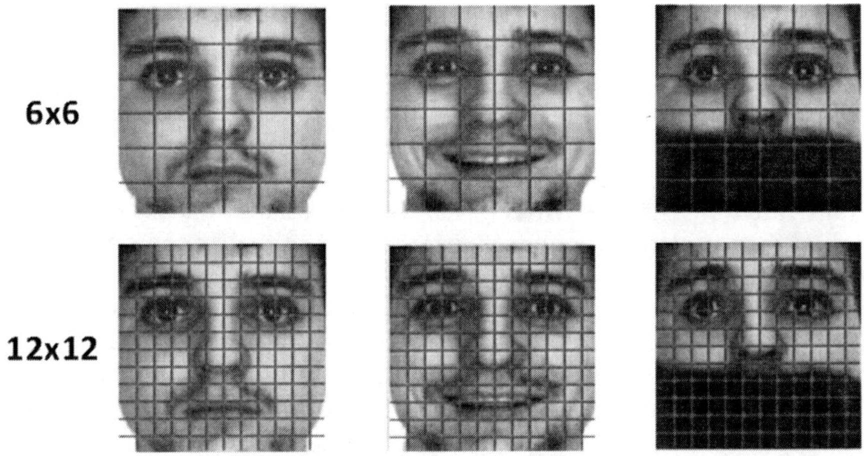

Figure 2 Traditional regular face blocks division. This figure illustrates the effect of using different sizes for regular blocks division. It is shown that when there are occlusions on faces, a finer division allows to have more blocks for comparisons (valid areas); meanwhile, in the case of expression variations, a finer division produces a decrease on the recognition rates because small blocks around some face areas, such as mouth and eyes, are shifted to neighbor blocks.

3 FACE FEATURE EXTRACTION USING SEMANTIC PIXEL SET-BASED LOCAL PATTERNS

The most often used strategy for obtaining face descriptors is based on spatial histograms of local patterns. However, the grouping statistical process only considers the spatial information of the pixels, and this may be the reason for non-corresponding sub-blocks matching when there are large expression variations. Hence, we present a strategy for associating local patterns in a face region by their semantic meaning in an adaptive way, in order to exploit better the information within each rectangular face region.

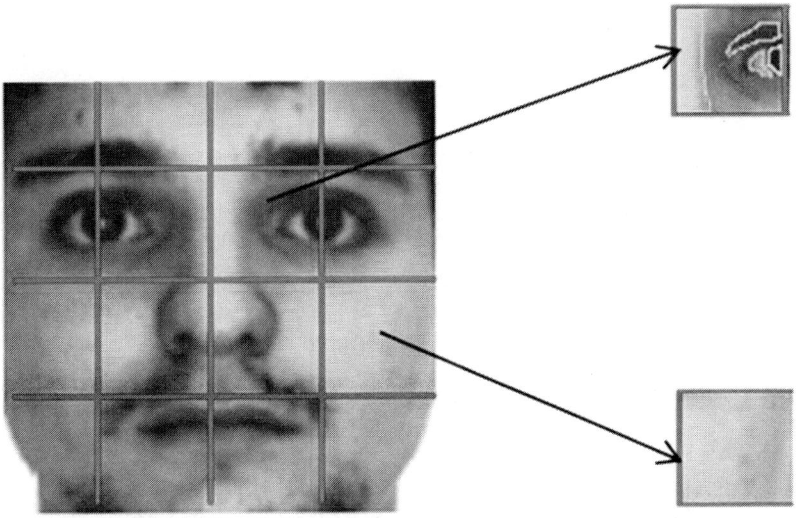

Figure 3 Illustration of the different amount of information contained in different face regions. The figure shows an example of the amount of information contained in different face regions. It can be seen that in regions around eyes, there are more variations according to pixel intensities than in cheek regions.

The process of face feature extraction using the general framework of semantic pixel set-based local patterns is illustrated on Figure4. First, a face image is divided into a few regular blocks of a given size, and the number of pixel sets (N_i) for block *i*, is learned according to the information entropy of the block. Then, pixels in this block are re-grouped into N_i sets according to their semantic meaning. Once we have different sets of pixels for each block, histograms of local patterns are extracted from each of them. Finally, all features are concatenated together and enhanced by the WPCA method.

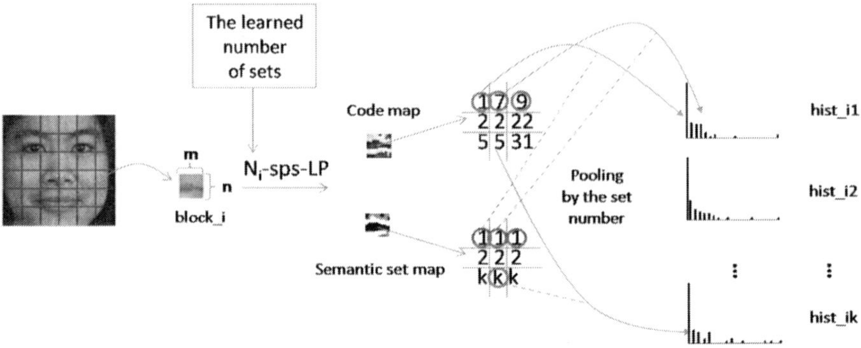

Figure 4 The flowchart of the semantic pixel set-based local patterns using information entropy. This figure describes the complete flowchart of the proposed method. First, a face image is coarsely divided into a few blocks of a given size. With the learned number of pixel sets for each face block according to the information entropy, pixels are re-grouped to different sets according to their semantic meaning. Histograms of local patterns are then extracted from each set. Finally, all features are concatenated together and enhanced by the WPCA method.

3.1 Learning the number of sets based on the information entropy

The entropy is a term defined in information theory as a measurement of the uncertainty associated with a random variable[31]. It is relevant to the quantity and variability of the information. Here, we assume that the pixel intensity value is a random variable; thus, we can use the histogram of the intensities in each face block to approximate the probability density function (PDF) for computing the information entropy. Applied to our case, the larger the entropy value is, the more information a face block should contain, and thus more clusters should be set.

The entropy value of the face block *i* can be then defined as

$$S(i) = \sum_{k=1}^{n} p(x_k) \log_2 \left(\frac{1}{p(x_k)} \right) = -\sum_{k=1}^{n} p(x_k) \log_2 p(x_k) \tag{1}$$

where $p(x_k)$ is the probability of the pixel x with intensity value k in the histogram of the block.

In our proposal, the entropy following Equation 1, is computed from the intensity histograms of the coarse-divided regions for all face images in the training set. Then, the average entropy value of a block in all images is used as the corresponding regional entropy. Although some images in the training set might be affected by noise, the average entropy values can still reflect the information quantity differences among different facial regions. Finally, a monotonic transform function is used for mapping the entropy value to the number of sets. The whole process is described in Figure5.

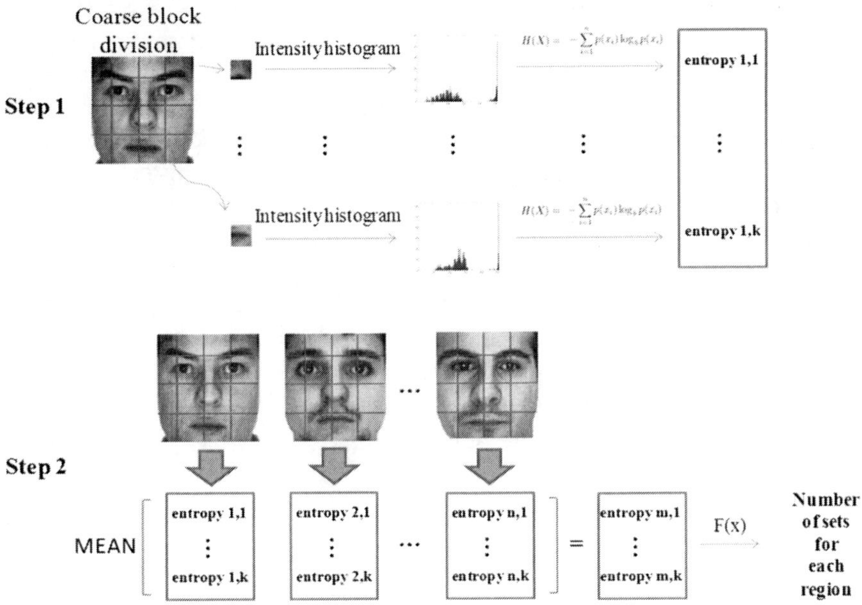

Figure 5 The details for learning the number of sets in each face block using information entropy. This figure describes the process of learning the number of sets for each face block using the information entropy. First, the pixel intensity value in each face block is treated as a random variable; thus, we can use the histogram of the intensities in each face block to approximate the probability density function (PDF) for computing the information entropy. Then, the average entropy value of all face images is used as the regional corresponding entropy. Finally, a linear function is used as a mapping from the entropy value to the number of sets.

The monotonic transform function $F(x_i)$ in this paper, is implemented by using a linear function as follows:

$$F(x_i) = (x_i - x_{\min})/(x_{\max} - x_{\min}) \times (\mathrm{new}_{\max} - \mathrm{new}_{\min}) + \mathrm{new}_{\min}, \quad (2)$$

where x_i is the average entropy for block i, $x_{\min}$ and $x_{\max}$ are the minimum and the maximum entropy values from all regions, $\mathrm{new}_{\min}$ is the least sets the region should be divided while $\mathrm{new}_{\max}$ is the maximum number of sets that can be obtained in a region. If the output of $F(x_i)$ is not an integer number, it can be rounded to be an integer value.

In this work, we have decided to use $\mathrm{new}_{\min} = 2$ and $\mathrm{new}_{\max} = 8$ and a coarse blocks division of 6 × 6, aiming at having a good trade-off between the computational cost and the proper use of the local spatial information. Illustrated in Figure6 is the number of sets learned with the proposed algorithm, using the mentioned configuration, for a given training set. In the image, the brightest parts represent those regions with number of sets equal to 8 and the darkest parts correspond to the number of sets 2, while the gray parts represent integers between 2 and 8. It can be seen that those blocks corresponding to the eyes and nose contain more information than the rest of the parts. This corresponds to our intuition and also obeys the traditional weighted maps used for face recognition. Hence, we believe that using different number of sets for each block will enhance the discriminant ability of the method proposed in[17], where a fixed number of sets was used. Besides, it can also help to make better use of the spatial information.

3.2 Semantic pixel sets based local patterns

Once the number of pixel sets (N_i) in each face block is learned on the training phase, the proposed semantic pixel set-based strategy for obtaining the histogram features can be used in the recognition process. First, the pixel intensity values on block i are sorted and clustered uniformly in N_i sets, as it is illustrated in Figure7. Under this strategy, for a fixed number of sets, the division of a block will always be the same although some have monotonic variations; so if the used local pattern operator, such as LBP, is invariant to monotonic grayscale variations, the final descriptor will also inherit this property (Additional file1).

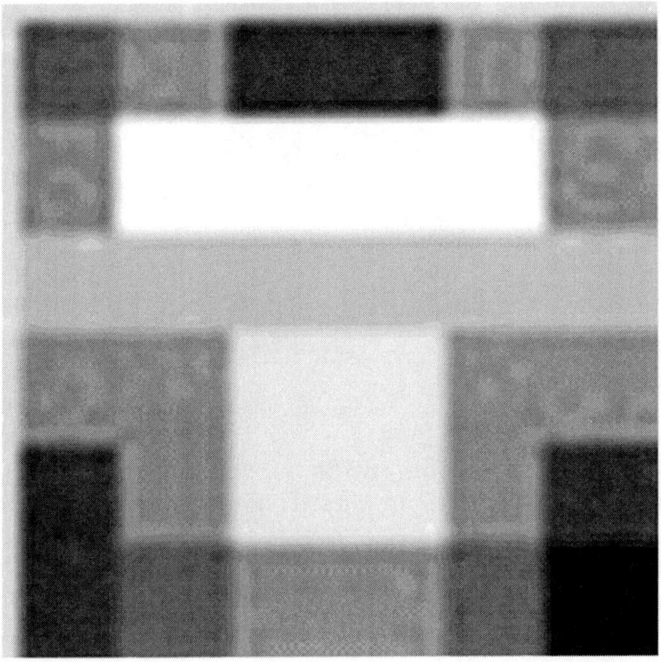

Figure 6 The learning results of set number in each face block. In the figure, the number of sets learned with the proposed algorithm based on entropy, for a given face division, is shown. It can be seen that those blocks corresponding to the eyes and nose contain more information than the rest of the parts.

As was mentioned before, not only the LBP operator but also any other local pattern-based encoding method can be used with our strategy since the final representation will be given by the histograms of codes computed from each pixel set. So, we will have for each coarse block the corresponding semantic set map and the codes map computed by the encoding method (e.g. LBP, LTP, TPLBP, etc.).

Using both, the semantic set map and the computed codes map, the histogram for the set $S(i,n)$, with $n \in [1,..,N_i]$, can be obtained by

$$H_{i,n}(l) = \sum_{x,y \subset S(i,n)} I\left\{\text{codes\_map}(x,y) = l\right\}, l = 0, 1, \ldots, m-1 \quad (3)$$

where codes _map(x,y) is the local pattern obtained at position (x,y) and m is the number of code labels.

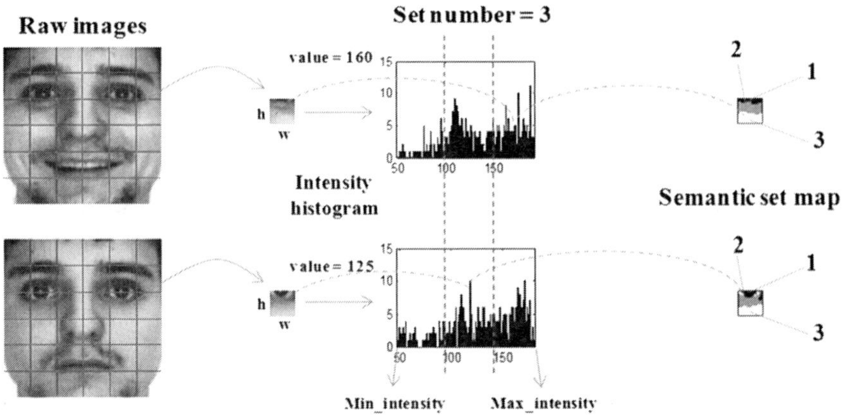

Figure 7 The details of computing the semantic set map. This figure shows the detailed process for clustering the semantic pixel sets in one face block. First, the pixel intensity value distribution is computed. It can be viewed as a simplified sorting process. Then, it is quantified into *k* sets according to the learned number. Finally, according the raw pixel intensity values and the sets they belong to, a semantic set map for one face block can be obtained.

Finally, all feature vectors from all sets of all blocks (1:*t*) will be concatenated together to represent a face image:

$$X = \left[H_{1,1}\ H_{1,2}\ \ldots\ H_{1,N_1}\ \ldots\ H_{t,N_t} \right]. \tag{4}$$

In the following, we will call this face image descriptor, semantic pixel set-based local patterns using information entropy (en-spsLP). As have been explained, the local patterns (LP) can be any histogram descriptor based on a local operator such as LBP and its different extensions.

3.3 Dimensionality reduction using WPCA

In order to take more advantage of the spatial information, overlapping regions can be used to extract the en-spsLP features. However, this increases the total dimension of the feature vector and can bring the curse of dimensionality. Hence, a feature reduction method should be applied in this case, in order to get a more compact representation.

There are different methods in the literature for dimensionality reduction. Most of the supervised methods usually applied in face recognition like LDA, although have shown good results, require more than two images per person for training, which cannot be always satisfied in real applications. It was proposed in[18] to apply Principal Component Analysis with a Whitening process (WPCA) to solve the so-called 'Single Sample per Person' problem. This method has been recently used with different face descriptors such as Local Gabor Binary Patterns[32] and POEM[33], showing a very good performance even when only one or a few images are available per person. For those reasons, we decided to apply WPCA for the dimensionality reduction in our framework.

Under this method, after a feature vector, *X*, is projected into the lower dimensional feature space found by PCA, $u = W_{PCA}X$, it is normalized with a whitening transformation:

$$w = \Lambda_M^{-1/2} u, \tag{5}$$

Where $\Lambda_M^{-1/2} = \mathrm{diag}\left\{\lambda_1^{-1/2}, \lambda_2^{-1/2}, \ldots, \lambda_M^{-1/2}\right\}$ and λ_i are the eigenvectors of the covariance matrix. This process aims at reducing the negative influences of the leading eigenvectors, as well as magnifies the discriminating details encoded in the trailing ones.

4 EXPERIMENTAL EVALUATION

Verification and identification experiments were conducted in order to evaluate the performance of the proposed method. Two popular databases: FERET[34] and AR[35], were used for identification experiments, while the LFW[36] database was used for verification. In those experiments where WPCA was not applied, the χ^2 distance was used to compare the obtained descriptors from face images, otherwise cosine distance will be used. In the case of identification, the nearest neighbor classifier was applied, and the top-rank recognition rate was used to measure the performance of the methods. In the case of verification on LFW, we have followed the evaluation protocol, and the estimated mean classification accuracy with the standard error (u^±SE$\hat{u} \pm \mathrm{SE}$) was used for the evaluation. All images were photometric normalized with the preprocessed sequence proposed by Tan and Triggs[16].

The two databases used for identification are composed by images captured under controlled environments. The FERET database[34] contains images with a lot of variations in expression, lighting and aging, divided into five subsets: Fa (gallery set), composed by frontal images of 1,196 subjects; Fb containing 1,195 face images with variations in expression; Fc subset, which contains 194 images with variations in lighting; Dup-I with 722 face images taken with an elapsed time with respect to the images in the gallery set; and Dup-II, a subset of Dup I, which contains 234 images in which the elapsed time is at least 1 year. On the other hand, the AR database[35] was created to test face recognition methods in front of various expressions, different illuminations and occlusions. It contains more than 3,200 face images of 126 people captured on two different sessions. Each person has up to 13 images per session. We randomly selected 100 different subjects (50 males and 50 females) and the neutral expression image of every person in each session was used as gallery and the rest of them with different expressions, lighting and occlusions were used for testing. Images from both databases were cropped to 114 × 114. Thus, using a coarse block division of 6 × 6, the blocks size will be 19 × 19.

Different from the former two databases, the LFW[36] database contains 13,233 images that were obtained under different unconstrained environments. The images are from 5,749 different individuals, and 1,680 of them have two or more images. In our experiment, we follow the standard training and testing protocol. We have used here the 'View 1' for learning the number of sets for each face block, and the 'View 2' for the final testing. Under this protocol, 6,000 pairs of images are compared in the evaluation; the half of them correspond to images from the same person and the other half not. The testing data are divided into 10 evenly distributed sets and the test is repeated 10 times, using one set for testing and the others for training. It should be noted that our proposal was tested with the original data, without correcting the few labeling errors in the database. Besides, the aligned version (provided by[37]) of face images was used, and all of them were cropped to 126 × 110. In this case, overlapped coarse blocks of 18 × 22 were used.

4.1 The contribution of semantic pixel sets to different LBP based descriptors

The aim of the first experiment is to show that the semantic pixel set (sps)-based strategy, makes not only the original LBP but also other

LBP-based descriptors, more robust and stable under different variations of facial appearance. It is expected that by using more robust descriptors, better results can be achieved. In order to make a fair comparison with[17], we use in this experiment the same fixed number of sets for each region, i.e. 6 or 8 sets. Besides, the original uniform LBP, the Local Ternary Patterns (LTP)[16] and the Three-Patch LBP (TP-LBP)[25] with the coarse initial division are tested. The obtained results on the FERET database are listed on Table1. It can be seen that almost on all cases, the sps outperforms the traditional regular division. Moreover, the more robust the descriptor, the better the results achieved with our proposal. In general, the best performing descriptor is LTP.

Table 1 Top rank recognition rates on the FERET database

Method	Fb	Fc	DupI	DupII	Average
uLBP	91.96	93.29	58.86	49.14	77.61
6-spsLBP	95.73	95.36	69.52	62.39	84.30
8-spsLBP	95.56	95.36	68.28	60.68	83.66
LTP	95.73	96.90	69.39	61.96	84.34
6-spsLTP	97.07	96.90	72.71	67.94	86.65
8-spsLTP	97.15	96.90	71.88	65.38	86.18
TPLBP	91.54	88.14	65.51	55.55	79.65
6-spsTPLBP	95.73	92.26	71.32	64.10	84.77
8-spsTPLBP	95.56	91.23	70.08	62.39	84.05

The contribution of semantic pixel sets to different LBP-based descriptors.

In order to have an in-depth comparison between the sps strategy and the traditional block division, we test the LTP descriptor, with each strategy during histogram estimation. In order to make the comparison fair, we do not use the illumination preprocessing in this experiment. Given a coarse blocks division of 6 × 6, we compare the results of using LTP directly over this division (LTP), dividing those coarse blocks into more *n* sub-blocks (*n*-blockLTP) and dividing them into *n* sets according to our proposal (*n*-spsLTP). The results obtained in each subset of AR database with different kinds of variations are listed on Table2.

Table 2 Top rank recognition rates on the AR database

Method	Expression	Lighting	Scarf	Sunglasses	Average
LTP	88.66	94.66	74.00	64.83	79.70
6-blockLTP	83.50	99.66	93.83	91.16	92.04
8-blockLTP	82.83	99.33	92.66	89.33	91.04
6-spsLTP	90.00	98.66	91.33	88.83	91.83
8-spsLTP	90.66	99.33	92.33	86.66	92.63

The advantage and disadvantage between sps and regular blocks division.

As was explained in the Introduction, a finer regular block division is good for some cases (e.g. occlusions) but degrades for some others, especially for expression variations. It can be seen from Table2, that although the blockLTP presents slightly better results than our proposal for occlusion variations, in the case of expressions, the performance drops off by a significant margin, even worse than the original LTP. In general, our sps strategy has a more stable behavior. In any case, we have to admit the disadvantages of our method in the case of unpredicted occlusions. For instance, the pixel intensities of the original cheek region occluded by sunglasses will not be as dark as the black sunglasses. This will definitely change the sorting results of the pixel intensity values. The pooling process will thus go wrong. So, in the future, we will try some appearance-based methods for clustering in order to get a more stable block division result.

4.2 The contribution of entropy-based learning algorithm for estimation the number of sets in each block

The aim of the this experiment is to demonstrate the contribution of using the information entropy for learning the number of sets for each face block. In this case, we compare the results of the same three descriptors with a fixed number of sets for each block (best results from Table1) and using information entropy for learning the number of sets (en-sps). The obtained results are shown on Table3. It can be appreciated that by using different number of sets for each region, better results are achieved in almost all cases. Besides, it can be said that the proposed learning method is useful for deciding the number of sets in each face block.

4.3 Face recognition using information entropy based spsLTP

In order to further exploit the capabilities of the proposed descriptor and to make better use of the spatial information, in this experiment we use the overlapping regions to derive the face features. Since in both experiments above, the LTP-based descriptor performs the best, we are going to use it in this experiment. In this case, keep the same blocks size but with five pixels of overlapping between neighbor blocks. When more blocks are involved, the final feature vector size becomes many times the original one. Hence, the use of a feature reduction method is needed. As it was explained above, the WPCA method is applied in this case. The obtained results, compared with some other face descriptors on FERET database are shown on Table4. It can be seen that for spsLTP, better results can be achieved with the overlapping version (spsLTP-ov). Besides, when the learned number of sets for each block is used, the results can get further improvement, compared with the results obtained by using a fixed number of sets for all blocks. Moreover, the benefits of using WPCA are demonstrated. In this database, when using overlapping blocks, we have found a total of 1,298 sets. This means that the descriptor (en-set-spsLTP-ov) has a dimension of 153,164 ($1{,}298 \times 59 \times 2$). We have selected only 850 features by using WPCA (en-set-spsLTP-ov-WPCA) and a better result is obtained. So, by applying WPCA, we get a more compact and discriminative descriptor.

Table 3 Top rank recognition rates on the FERET database

Method	Fb	Fc	DupI	DupII	Average
6-spsLBP	95.73	95.36	69.52	62.39	84.30
en-spsLBP	96.31	96.39	71.60	67.52	85.84
6-spsLTP	97.07	96.90	72.71	67.94	86.65
en-spsLTP	97.23	96.39	74.93	70.94	87.67
6-spsTPLBP	95.73	92.26	71.32	64.10	84.77
en-spsTPLBP	97.74	96.90	72.02	65.38	86.52

The contribution of entropy based learning algorithm for the estimation of the number of sets in each face block.

Table 4 Top rank recognition rates on the FERET database

Method	Fb	Fc	DupI	DupII
LGBPHS[32]	94.00	97.00	68.00	53.00
LGBPWP[18]	98.10	98.90	83.80	81.60
POEM[33]	97.60	96.00	77.80	76.50
POEM + WPCA[38]	99.60	99.48	88.78	85.00
LLGP[39]	99.00	99.00	80.00	78.00
HOGOM[40]	98.10	99.50	83.60	82.00
DLBP[41]	99.00	99.00	86.00	85.00
6-spsLTP-ov	97.65	99.48	76.73	72.22
en-spsLTP-ov	98.41	99.48	79.36	76.92
6-spsLTP-ov + WPCA	99.41	99.48	84.90	81.62
en-spsLTP-ov + WPCA	99.74	99.48	88.78	85.89

Face recognition using entropy based spsLTP-ov + WPCA in controlled environment.

It can also be seen on the table that our results are comparable with some of the state-of-the-art methods such as the Local Gabor Binary Patterns Histograms Sequence (LGBPHS)[32], the Learned Local Gabor Patterns (LLGP)[39], the Histograms of Gabor Ordinal Measures (HOGOM)[40], the Patterns of Oriented Edge Magnitudes (POEM)[42] and Discriminative Local Binary Patterns (DLBP)[41].

4.4 Descriptors comparison in unconstrained environment

The aim of this last experiment is to show the effectiveness of our proposal in a more challenging face database, the LFW, for the uncontrolled face verification task. Since our method is unsupervised, only related works are compared. All images of the aligned version[36] are cropped to be 126 × 110 around the center. Blocks of 18 × 22 pixels are used to extract the en-spsLTP features, overlapped by six pixels in the rows and eight pixels in the columns. During model selection, the training set in 'View 1' was used to learn the number of sets for each block by using the information entropy. For testing in 'View 2', the training set is used to train the WPCA axes and find the best threshold for determining if a comparison corresponds to the same person or not. In Table5, we compare our method with other descriptors evaluated in[37] and[43] under the same protocol. We can find that in the list of unsupervised methods, our proposed method is comparable with the other descriptors. Since this dataset is very challenging, we believe our method can achieve a better result by using a more complex nonlinear classifier learned from a supervised way.

Table 5 Mean scores on the LFW database on 'image-restricted configuration' and aligned images

Method	Performance
uLBP[37]	0.6824
Gabor (C1)[37]	0.6849
TPLBP[37]	0.6926
FPLBP[37]	0.6818
SIFT[37]	0.6986
V1-like[43]	0.6421 ± 0.0069

Method	Performance
V1-like+[43]	0.6808 ± 0.0044
LARK[44]	0.7223 ± 0.0049
POEM[33]	0.7520 ± 0.0073
POEM + WPCA[45]	0.8113 ± 0.0053
en-spsLTP-ov + WPCA	0.8050 ± 0.0033

Face recognition using entropy based spsLTP-ov + WPCA in uncontrolled environment.

5 CONCLUSIONS

This paper proposes a face representation framework called histogram of semantic pixel set-based local patterns using information entropy (en-spsLP). First, the number of pixel sets is learned according to the information entropy in each face block. Then, during the histogram estimation, the code of the local pattern is pooled according to the original pixel intensity distribution. Finally, all the histograms are concatenated together and enhanced by the WPCA. The proposed method is easy to implement and the speed of the feature extraction is very fast. At the same time, the results are comparable with some of the state-of-the-art methods. Future work is to try other clustering criterion (e.g. by texton) in order to achieve more robustness to unpredicted occlusions. Besides, the optimal values for initial block size and position based on face landmarks can be further analyzed.

ACKNOWLEDGEMENT

This work is funded by the Strategic Priority Research Program of the Chinese Academy of Sciences (Grant No. XDA06030300), National Basic Research Program of China (Grant No. 2012CB316300), National Natural Science Foundation of China (Grant No. 61075024, 61273272, 61103155) and International S&T Cooperation Program of China (Grant No.2010DFB14110).

COMPETING INTERESTS

The authors declare that they have no competing interests.

REFERENCES

1. Jain AK, Li SZ: *Handbook of Face Recognition*. Secaucus, NJ, USA,: Springer-Verlag New York, Inc.; 2005.

2. Zhao W, Chellappa R, Phillips PJ, Rosenfeld A: Face recognition: a literature survey. *ACM Comput. Surv* 2003, 35(4):399-458. 10.1145/954339.954342

3. Heisele B, Ho P, Wu J, Poggio T: Face recognition: component-based versus global approaches. *Comput. Vis. Image Underst* 2003, 91(1–2):6-21.

4. Tan X, Chen S, Zhou Z, Zhang F: Face recognition from a single image per person: a survey. *Pattern Recognit* 2006, 39(9):1725-1745. 10.1016/j.patcog.2006.03.013

5. He R, Hu BG, Zheng WS, Kong XW: Robust principal component analysis based on maximum correntropy criterion. *IEEE Trans. Image Process* 2011, 20(6):1485-1494.

6. Serrano Á, de Diego IM, Conde C, Cabello E: Recent advances in face biometrics with Gabor wavelets: a review. *Pattern Recognit. Lett*2010, 31(5):372-381. 10.1016/j.patrec.2009.11.002

7. Lei Z, Liao S, Pietikäinen M, Li SZ: Face recognition by exploring information jointly in space, scale and orientation. *IEEE Trans. Image Process* 2011, 20: 247-256.

8. Pietikäinen M, Hadid A, Zhao A, Ahonen T: *Computer Vision Using Local Binary Patterns*. London Ltd: Springer-Verlag; 2011.

9. Ahonen T, Hadid A, Pietikãinen M: Face recognition with local binary patterns. *European Conference on Computer Vision (ECCV)* Prague, Czech Republic, 11–14 May 2004, pp. 469–481

10. Jin H, Liu Q, Lu H, Tong X: Face detection using improved LBP under Bayesian framework. *International Conference on Image and Graphics (ICIG)* Hong Kong, 18–20 Dec 2004, pp. 306–309

11. Liao S, Chung ACS: Face recognition by using elongated local binary patterns with average maximum distance gradient magnitude. *Asian Conference on Computer Vision (ACCV)* Tokyo, 18–22 Nov 2007, pp. 672–679

12. Liao S, Zhu X, Lei Z, Zhang L, Li SZ: Learning multi-scale block local binary patterns for face recognition. *International Conference on Biometrics (ICB)* Seoul, 27–29 Aug 2007, pp. 828–837

13. Guo Z, Zhang L, Zhang D, Mou X: Hierarchical multiscale LBP for face and palmprint recognition. *International Conference on Image Processing (ICIP)* Hong Kong, 26–29 Sept 2010, pp. 4521–4524

14. Liao S, Law M, Chung A: Dominant local binary patterns for texture classification. *IEEE Trans. Image Process* 2009, 18(5):1107-1118.

15. Guo Z, Zhang L, Zhang D: A completed modeling of local binary pattern operator for texture classification. *IEEE Trans. Image Process*2010, 19(6):1657-1663.

16. Tan X, Triggs B: Enhanced local texture feature sets for face recognition under difficult lighting conditions. *IEEE Trans. Image Process*2010, 19(6):1635-1650.

17. Chai Z, Mendez H, He R, Sun Z, Tan T: Semantic pixel sets based local binary patterns for face recognition. *acepted in Asian Conference on Computer Vision (ACCV)* Daejeon, 5–9 Nov 2012

18. Deng W, Hu J, Guo J: Gabor-eigen-whiten-cosine: a robust scheme for face recognition. *AMFG* Beijing, 16 Oct 2005, pp. 336–349

19. Marcel S, Rodriguez Y, Heusch G: On the recent use of local binary patterns for face authentication. *Tech. Rep* 06-34,. Idiap, 2006

20. Huang D, Shan C, Ardabilian M, Wang Y, Chen L: Local binary patterns and its application to facial image analysis: a survey. *IEEE Trans. Syst. Man Cybernetics-Part C: Appl. Rev* 2011, 41(6):765-781.

21. Ojala T, Pietikãinen M, Harwood D: A comparative study of texture measures with classification based on featured distributions. *Pattern Recognit* 1996, 29: 51-59. 10.1016/0031-3203(95)00067-4

22. Ojala T, Pietikäinen M, Mäenpää T: Multiresolution gray-scale and rotation invariant texture classification with local binary patterns. *IEEE Trans. Pattern Anal. Mach. Intell* 2002, 24(7):971-987. 10.1109/TPAMI.2002.1017623

23. Huang X, Li SZ, Wang Y: Shape localization based on statistical method using extended local binary pattern. *International Conference on Image and Graphics (ICIG)* 2004, 184-187.

24. Liao S, Zhu X, Lei Z, Zhang L, Li SZ: Learning multi-scale block local binary patterns for face recognition. *International Conference on Biometrics (ICB)* Seoul, 27–29 Aug 2007, pp. 828–837

25. Wolf L, Hassner T, Taigman Y: Descriptor based methods in the wild. *Faces in Real-Life Images workshop at the European Conference on Computer Vision (ECCV)* Marseille, 12–18 Oct 2008

26. Zhang G, Huang X, Li S, Wang Y, Wu X: Boosting local binary pattern (LBP)-based face recognition. In *Advances in Biometric Person Authentication, Volume 3338 of Lecture Notes in Computer Science.* Edited by: Li S, Lai J, Tan T, Feng G, Wang Y. Heidelberg: Springer Berlin; 2005:179-186.

27. Shan C, Gong S, Owan McP: Conditional mutual information based boosting for facial expression recognition. *Proceedings of British Machine Vision Conference* Oxford, UK, Sept 2005

28. Gritti T, Shan C, Jeanne V, Braspenning R: Local features based facial expression recognition with face registration errors. *Proceedings of*

IEEE International Conference on Automatic Face and Gesture Recognition Amsterdam, The Netherlands, 17–19 Sept 2008

29. Ahonen T, Hadid A, Pietikãinen M: Face description with local binary patterns: Application to face recognition. *IEEE Trans. Pattern Anal. Mach. Intell* 2006, 28(12):2037-2041.

30. Mendez-Vazquez H, Garcia-Reyes E, Condes-Molleda Y: A new image division for LBP method to improve face recognition under varying lighting conditions. *Proceedings of International Conference on Pattern Recognition* Tampa, Florida, 8–11 Dec 2008, pp. 1–4

31. Cover TM, Thomas JA: *Elements of Information Theory (Wiley Series in Telecommunications and Signal Processing)*. New York: Wiley; 2006.

32. Zhang W, Shan S, Gao W, Chen X, Zhang H: Local Gabor binary pattern histogram sequence (LGBPHS): a novel non-statistical model for face representation and recognition. *International Conference on Computer Vision (ICCV)* Beijing, 17–20 Oct 2005, pp. 786–791

33. Vu NS, Caplier A: Face recognition with patterns of oriented edge magnitudes. *European Conference on Computer Vision (ECCV)*Heraklion, Crete, 5–11 Sept 2010, pp. 313–326

34. Phillips JP, Moon H, Rizvi SA, Rauss PJ: The FERET evaluation methodology for face-recognition algorithms. *IEEE Trans. Pattern Anal. Mach. Intell* 2000, 22(10):1090-1104. 10.1109/34.879790

35. Martínez A, Benavente R: The AR face database. *Tech. Rep. #24, CVC* 1998

36. Huang GB, Ramesh M, Berg T, Learned-Miller E: Labeled faces in the wild: a database for studying face recognition in unconstrained environments. *Tech. Rep* 07-49,. (University of Massachusetts, Amherst, 2007)

37. Wolf L, Hassner T, Taigman Y: Similarity scores based on background samples. *Asian Conference on Computer Vision (ACCV)* Xi'an, China, 23–27 Sept 2009, pp. 88–97

38. Vu NS, Caplier A: Enhanced patterns of oriented edge magnitudes for face recognition and image matching. *IEEE Trans. IP* 2012, 21(3):1352-1365.

39. Xie S, Shan S, Chen X, Meng X, Gao W: Learned local Gabor patterns for face representation and recognition. *Signal Process* 2009, 89(12):2333-2344. 10.1016/j.sigpro.2009.02.016

40. Chai Z, He R, Sun Z, Tan T, Mendez-Vazquez H: Histograms of Gabor ordinal measures for face representation and recognition. *IAPR International Conference on Biometrics (ICB),* New Delhi, India, 29 March–1 April 2012, pp. 52–58

41. Maturana D, Mery D, Soto A: Learning discriminative local binary patterns for face recognition. *International Conference on Automatic Face and Gesture Recognition (FG)* Santa Barbara, CA, 21–25 March 2011, pp. 470–475

42. Vu NS, Dee HM, Caplier A: Face recognition using the POEM descriptor. *Pattern Recogn* 2012, 45(7):2478-2488. 10.1016/j.patcog.2011.12.021

43. Pinto N, DiCarlo JJ, Cox DD: Establishing good benchmarks and baselines for face recognition. *Faces in Real-Life Images workshop at the European Conference on Computer Vision (ECCV)* Marseille, 12–18 Oct 2008

44. Seo HJ, Milanfar P: Face verification using the LARK representation. *IEEE Trans. Inform. Forensics Secur. (TIFS)* 2011, 6(4):1275-1286.

45. Vu NS, Caplier A: Enhanced patterns of oriented edge magnitudes for face recognition and image matching. *IEEE Trans. Image Process*2012, 21(3):1352-1365.

8

ON UNIFIERS, DIVERSIFIERS, AND THE NATURE OF PATTERN RECOGNITION ☆

Gavin Brown

School of Computer Science, University of Manchester, Manchester, UK

ABSTRACT

We study a dichotomy of scientific styles, *unifying* and *diversifying*, as proposed by Freeman J. Dyson. We discuss the extent to which the dichotomy transfers from the natural sciences (where Dyson proposed it) to the field of *Pattern Recognition*. To address this we must firstly ask what it means to be a "unifier" or "diversifier" in a field, and what are the relative merits of each style of thinking. Secondly, given that Dyson applied this to the *sciences*, does it also apply in a field known to be a blend of science and engineering? Parallels are drawn to Platonic/Aristotelian views, and to Cartesian/Baconian science, and questions are asked on what drives the Kuhnian paradigm shifts of our field. This article is intended not to marginalise individuals into categories (unifier/diversifier) but instead to demonstrate the utility of philosophical reflection on our field, showing the depth and complexities a seemingly simple idea can unearth.

KEYWORDS

Nature of pattern recognition; Unifying; Diversifying; Dyson

1. INTRODUCTION

In his 1988 book, *Infinite in All Directions*, the theoretical physicist Freeman J. Dyson discusses two distinct styles of scientific thinking: *unifying*, and *diversifying*, claiming that most sciences are dominated by one or the other in various periods of their history.

"**Unifiers** *are people whose driving passion is to find general principles which will explain everything. They are happy if they can leave the universe looking a little simpler than they found it.*"

"**Diversifiers** *are people whose passion is to explore details. They are in love with the heterogeneity of nature* [...]*They are happy if they leave the universe a little more complicated than they found it.*" [1, chap. 3, p. 44]

When I first read these quotes, and showed them to colleagues, there were a number of immediate assumptions. For example, some assumed that unifiers are *theoreticians*, and the diversifiers are *experimenters*. Others took the dichotomy to be equivalent to*scientists* vs *engineers*, or to *academia* vs *industry*. In association with intellectual endeavour, the terms *unifying* and *diversifying* seem to come with a certain semantic "baggage". This is exemplified by the media-fuelled furore surrounding 20th century physics, with science celebrities seemingly promoting a unifier viewpoint and the search for the 'ultimate laws of the universe'.

Dyson's treatment of this is relatively short, at just one 18-page chapter [1]. It is therefore important to moderate our contemporary biases, if we are to understand what he intended. It seems appropriate to engage in a conceptual analysis of these terms, with a major question being whether they have the same meaning in *natural* sciences (where Dyson conceived them) as they do in a *computational* science like our own.

Whilst Dyson expands upon his view with examples from physics and biology spanning 400 years, our own field of Pattern Recognition[1] is relatively young. If physics is the old man of science, then we are the spotty teenagers. This considered, it is good to look back and consider how far we have come, where we are going, and whether we can learn something from the older disciplines. This type of philosophical reflection allows us to plan objectives, to understand our motivations, successes and failures, both as a collective and in our individual pursuits. The purpose of this article is to reflect in this way, on how the dichotomy transfers from the natural sciences to a science of *computation*, and more specifically, *Pattern Recognition*.

1.1. What are we?

Pattern Recognition is a multifarious field. We study the science and engineering elements of *data*. We are interested in automating the understanding of data, including*prediction* and *description* of phenomena. The construction of both heuristic and formal mathematical models forms the backbone of our culture. The field was spawned from the dreams of Artificial Intelligence, though the reality has encompassed a far broader scope of study than originally envisioned at the Dartmouth Conference [2]. However, we are not tackling the wider integrative challenge of A.I., but instead focused on a restricted (yet immensely challenging) problem: the automated processing and inference problems that arise from diverse sources of data. At present, we encompass aspects of pure/applied statistics and mathematics, computer science, and biologically-inspired mechanisms, among others.

1.2. Structure of this article

As mentioned, Dyson's terminology of 'unifiers' and 'diversifiers' lends itself to a number of potential implicit meanings—a deeper analysis of these is a necessary first step, tackled in 2 and 3 of this article. Section 4 will explore how the dichotomy transfers over to Pattern Recognition. For example, something quite explicit from Dyson's writings is that he equates *unifying* with *simplicity*. This reflects his training in physics, where the belief is widespread that beautiful (or simpler) theories are more likely to be correct. But what does this mean in Pattern Recognition, and how is it different than in natural sciences like physics or chemistry? Sections 5–7 consider the nature of work in our field, and of how revolutions in a field come about—are they driven by unifiers, or diversifiers, or both?

Finally, Section 8 will play Devil's Advocate, and ask *why study this?* What is the *value* of the dichotomy as a conceptual tool? What benefits may come, to the individual or to the community, from addressing these philosophical questions?

2. TWO STYLES OF THINKING

Dyson states that *unifiers* (citing Albert Einstein as the exemplar) believe the universe can be reduced to a finite set of principles—a simple, elegant framework, couched in the language of mathematics—and have the pursuit of this as their primary goal in science. On the other hand, *diversifiers* (citing Emil Wiechert, a geophysicist who discovered the layered structure of the Earth) prefer to explore the infinite diversity of details in the universe, often creating new phenomena and tools simply for the sake of exploring those details. Wiechert delivered a lecture in 1896 in which he stated:

"So far as modern science is concerned, we have to abandon completely the idea that by going into the realm of the small we shall reach the ultimate foundations of the universe. I believe we can abandon this idea without any regret. The universe is infinite in all directions, not only above us in the large but also below us in the small. If we start from our human scale of existence and explore the content of the universe further and further, we finally arrive, both in the large and in the small, at misty distances where first our senses and then even our concepts fail us."

Einstein, as a unifier, believed the large and small of the universe could be *abstracted*into a single unified theory. Wiechert, as a diversifier, believed the universe is inexhaustible and potentially incomprehensible to the human mind—that no matter how long or far we look into the "misty distances", the universe *will not conform to abstractions.* For a diversifier, the details matter more than the simple explanations. Where a unifier prefers abstract structure and the aesthetics of a unified theory, the diversifier focuses on the concrete variations of nature, the exceptions to the theory.

This dichotomy could be (mis-)interpreted in several ways. One could read it as equivalent to theoretician/experimenter, to academia/industry, or to scientist/engineer. Or, taking in a broader philosophical context: to Platonic/Aristotelian views, Cartesian/ Baconian science, or analysis vs synthesis as processes for generating knowledge. The following sections will argue that none of these is exactly isomorphic to Dyson's dichotomy; but, on deeper reflection, all provide fascinating perspectives for our own field.

2.1. Theoreticians and experimenters?

On a first reading, it could be perceived that Dyson's unifiers are *theoreticians*, whilst diversifiers are *experimenters*. This is reinforced by his naming of the great experimenter Ernest Rutherford as a diversifier. Rutherford was an outstanding experimental physicist, but according to Dyson, disrespectful of academic learning, more interested in facts than theories. Rutherford was well known for statements such as *"If your experiment needs statistics, you ought to have done a better experiment"*, and referring to theoretical physicists he once joked *"they play games with their symbols, but we turn out the real solid facts of nature"*. Rutherford's diversifier perspective on scientific research provided new capabilities, such as determining the size of an individual atom, or counting the number of atoms in a given volume of gas. To be clear: his purpose was *science*, not engineering, but he was interested in the "real solid facts of nature". Dyson states that Einstein and Rutherford held such opposing views, greater than the normal rift between theorist/experimenter, that they could barely talk to each other—explained by the fact that they held fundamentally different philosophies on the nature and purpose of science.

However, assuming Einstein/Rutherford as the definitive unifier/diversifier split does not appear to be Dyson's intention. The simple mapping of *unify =theory* and *diversify =experiment* is far too naïve. He explicitly names a theoretical physicist, John Wheeler, as a diversifier. Wheeler (1911–2008) was one of the most prolific and accomplished theoretical physicists of the 20th century, a pioneer in quantum gravity and the theory of nuclear fission, he also introduced the term 'black hole', and 'wormhole' to describe hypothetical tunnels through space-time. He was also an early advocate of the "anthropic principle"—that the laws of physics are fine-tuned for the existence of life in the universe. However, Wheeler suggested a stronger extension, the *participatory* anthropic principle, in which the laws of physics are not primary, but derivative, and *brought into being* by the presence of conscious life in the universe. Here, Einstein's pure reductionist approach to physics, hunting for a single unifying set of laws, is turned on its head—the laws themselves are *mutable*, and are a function of our observation. Thus the search for unifying laws may be futile, since we cannot observe other laws that may have come into existence without us. Of course, it could be that Wheeler saw a deeper set of*developmental* governing laws. But, the very fact that the rest of the physics community was converging on a single unifying theory, and Wheeler challenged their viewpoint by bringing into the equations the 'tiny' detail of their own consciousness, makes him a*diversifier*. In Dyson's words:

"Among contemporary physicists, John Wheeler is unique in taking seriously the possibility that the laws of physics may be contingent upon the presence of life in the Universe." [...]

"Wheeler's colleagues love him more than they listen to him. The physics of the unifiers has no room for his subversive thoughts."

So, now we have a theoretician-diversifier. It is also easy to think of the converse, a unifier who relies on experimental observation. Charles Darwin's approach was almost exclusively observational and empirical in nature; in his autobiography he reflects on his career as so:

"Therefore, my success as a man of science, whatever this may have amounted to, has been determined, as far as I can judge, by complex and diversified mental qualities and conditions. Of these the most important have been [...]*industry in observing and collecting facts, and a fair share of invention as well as of common-sense."* [3, p. 144]

It is widely acknowledged that by the word 'invention', Darwin meant invention of hypotheses that can be experimentally tested. Darwin held a unifier mindset, reducing our very existence to the result of a single principle (natural selection) yet every step of the work relied on observation and experiment.

It is equally easy to name an experimental *physicist* with a unifier mindset. Though Dyson did not explicitly name him, one posits that James Prescott Joule (1818–1889) would be a typical unifier in his mind. Joule determined equivalencies between thermal, electrical, and mechanical phenomena, through rigorous experimentation. His principle of energy conservation is not a product of esoteric mathematics, but careful control of external factors that could have affected his experimental observations. This work unified numerous competing viewpoints, laying the foundation for the modern theory of thermodynamics. So, we have a theoretician-diversifier, and an experimenter-unifier, and the converse for each case.

	Theoretician	Experimenter
Unifier	Einstein	Darwin/Joule
Diversifier	Wheeler	Rutherford

Whilst Dyson makes clear that instances of theorist-diversifiers are possible, it seems to be his contention that in his own field they are rare, and 20th century theoretical physicists are more likely to be unifiers. Equivalently, though we have two examples (Darwin/Joule), one posits that experimenter-unifiers (in any field) are rare. Thus, it may be that *most* unifiers are theory-oriented, but not all, and *most* diversifiers are more experimental, but again, not all.

2.2. Academia and industry?

To underline the nature of his unifier/diversifier dichotomy, Dyson presents an analogy, rephrasing it in social terms.

"The first academic city in the world was Athens, and the first industrial city was Manchester, so I like to use the names of Athens and Manchester as symbols of the two styles of scientific thinking." [1, p. 37]

He clarifies later,

"The science of Athens emphasises ideas and theories; it tries to find unifying concepts which tie the universe together. The science of Manchester emphasises facts and things; it tries to explore and extend our knowledge of nature's diversity." [1, p. 40].

To clarify, he is not stating that all academics are unifiers, nor that all of industries are diversifiers. Neither is he explicitly stating that Manchester's *industry* was the home of the diversifiers he refers to. In fact he refers equally to the practice of science no matter where it occurs, within academic walls or in industry.

"Science belongs to both worlds, but the style of academic science is different from the style of industrial science. The science of the academic world tends to be dominated by unifiers, while the science of the industrial world tends to be dominated by diversifiers." [1, p. 36].

The qualification "tends to be" is important here. Whist he says industry "tends to be dominated" by diversifiers, it is interesting to consider the cause of this—whether diversifier-style science is *a function of industrial requirements*. The Manchester exemplar is particularly illuminating in this respect, given a deeper look at its historical context. Manchester, situated in the North of England, was the birthplace of the Industrial Revolution, and the growth of its intellectual capital is well documented by Thackray [4]. In the late 18th century, a number of learned societies[2] were founded by a group of dissatisfied intellectuals driven by a common vision—to escape the constraints forced upon the North from the wealthy elite in the South of England, typified by men with classical Oxford and Cambridge educations. Whilst the industrial revolution was an obvious driver of science in this period, Thackray argues that the immense scientific innovation of the age was as much a means for

"the social legitimation of marginal men, [...]the adoption of science as a means of cultural expression by a new social class" [4, p. 678].

Dyson summarises neatly that *" the atmosphere of Manchester was saturated with contempt for the ancient universities".* The style of science in these learned societies (and ultimately the University) was mirrored by these geo-social pressures.

"Science did flourish in Manchester during the crucial formative years of the industrial revolution, but [...]did not arise in response to the needs of industrial production. The driving force of the Manchester scientific renaissance were not technological and utilitarian; they were cultural and aesthetic." [1, p. 38]

He argues that, although Manchester's industrial needs were evident, the diversifier scientific style was not a strict function of this need. Instead it was borne out of a need for cultural distinction from the traditional Universities; and, in the wider city "to raise the aspirations of leadings citizens to a loftier level", showing that it was possible to live in Manchester and still be a gentleman. One element of Dyson's diversifier seems therefore to be a "rebellious" nature, to sit in opposition to convention, finding exceptions where others assume none.

Dyson names his archetypal diversifier of 19th century Manchester as Ernest Rutherford, whose academic work in understanding the structure of the atom was wholly curiosity-driven, without thought of immediate applications. Rutherford was well known to challenge convention, to ignore elegant theories in favour of observable facts. This combination of traits seemed to work for him, providing strong foundations for the emerging field of thermodynamics. This of course had great implications for the industrial revolution, though the industrial side was in full swing before Rutherford came along.

One notable omission from Dyson's argument is the distinction between *science* and*engineering*. Given the discussion on Manchester being the first industrial city, with many aspects of its activity oriented towards engineering, this is surprising. This is also especially relevant if we are to see whether this applies to Pattern Recognition, commonly viewed as a field straddling both science *and* engineering.

2.3. Science and engineering?

It is here we must be careful with our dichotomies. Academia and industry are *venues*, not practices. Science and engineering are *practices*. Unifying and diversifying are *styles of practice*. These, according to Dyson, occur in both academia and industry in the practice of science, and as will be argued here, also the practice of engineering.

Dyson made no explicit statements on whether his dichotomy was intended to apply only to science, but we can speculate. The debate over the definition of *science* versus*engineering* could form an entire article by itself, and an excellent example is to be found within this special issue [5]. Acknowledging this, but for the purposes of simplicity, I will adopt a distinction as so:

science is a practice primarily concerned with *truth*,

engineering is a practice primarily concerned with *utility*.

A naïve step would be to assume unifiers = scientists; however, Dyson's concept of a unifier does not seem to preclude the possibility of them having an engineering mindset. A unifier is someone who thinks about the relations *between* artefacts, rather than artefacts themselves. A unifier is, like Einstein and Darwin, concerned with how much of the universe can be brought under their metaphorical umbrella. One can imagine an engineer taking on the challenge of building a bridge, but with a unifier's view. This engineer would be concerned with characteristics of bridges that make them all strong, with the physics of how they can be modelled in a variety of situations, as opposed to the nuances of how one particular bridge should be built. In our own field of Computer Science, a unifier-engineer may be concerned with building *frameworks* of software/hardware or mathematics, for others to use, incorporating as many general principles as possible. This may sacrifice functionality in favour of having a clean single interface to a number of underlying tools. A diversifier-engineer in our field is more concerned with pushing limits, testing when and where individual techniques do or do not work—for example, they may demonstrate how parameter settings can be found automatically using efficient mechanisms imported from other fields, or evaluating scenarios where the mode of application for a predictive model is not so clear-cut.

In conclusion, Dyson's dichotomy easily applies across the science/ engineering boundary. Whether one is interested in the pursuit of pure scientific knowledge, or of more practical goals, this does not limit a person to one *style* of research thinking.

2.4. Summary

Unpicking Dyson's dichotomy, a unifier is someone who is comfortable making abstractions or assumptions in order to reach a broader conclusion; where unifiers tolerate abstractions, diversifiers question them, and pursue the details; unifiers emphasise *similarities*, whilst diversifiers emphasise *differences*. Both these styles can be followed in academia or in industry, by theorist or experimentalist, by scientist or engineer. Whilst mathematics is a strong element of a unifier's toolbox, it is not *the*defining element.

The unifier's assumptions may be questionable, but the reasoning process followed from them is not. This approach allows great leaps of thought, by abstracting away from potentially flawed observations to an idealised form. Diversifiers on the other hand, cannot ignore the concrete variations of nature. To them, compromise or conformity to dogma seems alien, ignoring the observable facts as they can plainly be seen. They love the details, they see and enable things unifiers cannot, simply by persistence, fertile imagination, and systematic thought.

Given this breakdown of the concepts, some parallels to established dichotomies in classical and modern philosophy can be seen. In particular the idea of unquestionable reasoning from base assumptions is effectively the deductive process, championed by Descartes, and the idea of abstracting away details to have an "idealised form" is reminiscent of Plato's worldview. In the following section we will discuss these parallels.

3. PARALLELS TO PHILOSOPHICAL LITERATURE

3.1. Plato's forms versus Aristotle's empiricism?

Dyson states that the science of Athens (unifiers) emphasises "ideas and theories", whereas the science of Manchester (diversifiers) emphasises "facts and things". The most immediate philosophical parallel here is Plato versus Aristotle.

At his most fundamental, Plato's position was that, progress towards new knowledge only begins when we come to think of our world experiences as flawed and possibly irrelevant, and it is only by processes of abstract thinking that we generate true understanding. Plato believed that humans were superior, born with *innate* knowledge, from which the full truth and knowledge of the universe (including theories of society, justice and government) could be reached by deduction alone, thus reference to empirical data was unnecessary, even distracting.

Aristotle on the other hand believed inductive processes could be used to establish first principles, combined with abstractions only when justified, from which deduction could be trusted and results later tested. This fits better with modern scientists arguably of the unifier mindset—Hawking, Feynman, and Dyson himself, proposed theories that can be tested, built on the foundations of observable phenomena. Feynman once delivered a memorable speech on the meaning of the modern scientific method:

"If it disagrees with experiment, it's WRONG. In that simple statement is the key to science. It doesn't make any difference how beautiful your guess is, it doesn't matter how smart you are, who made the guess, or what his name is. If it disagrees with experiment, it's wrong. That's all there is to it." [6]

Whilst Feynman's Nobel prize-winning work (Quantum Electrodynamics) undoubtedly involved a "unifier" perspective on physics, he did not require the level of abstraction in thought that Plato would have insisted upon. On the other hand, Aristotle's writing on science (natural philosophy) was wholly qualitative, he simply did not have access to quantitative tools like clocks or thermometers to *measure* the universe. As a consequence Aristotle was observational but not strictly in the sense of modern scientific method. Thus, in his own temporal context, Aristotle was probably a diversifier, but the details that would be scrutinised by a modern diversifier were perhaps unintentionally glossed over by the Aristotelean worldview.

3.2. Cartesians and Baconians?

Almost at the outset of his essay, Dyson seems to equate his dichotomy with Cartesian versus Baconian science:

"Historians of science are accustomed to call these two traditions in science Cartesian and Baconian, since Descartes was the great unifier and Bacon the great diversifier at the birth of modern science in the seventeenth century." [1, p. 40]

However it is doubtful that Dyson believes these are exact synonyms for his terminology. In later a communication he states that only *"roughly speaking, unifiers are following the tradition of Descartes, diversifiers are following the tradition of Bacon"* [7]. The "rough" correspondence between unifier/diversifier and Cartesian/Baconian is supported by further unpicking of the concepts.

Descartes followed the *rationalist* view, that the universe has an inherently logical structure, and its entirety could be deduced from first principles. The belief in the strength of the deductive process, and a belief that there exists an underlying logical structure to pursue, are strong unifier traits. However, the defining tenet of Descartes' philosophy was his *Method of Doubt*. Descartes believed in the inherent superiority of reason over sensory experiences. *Any* sensory experience could be doubted, but pure deductive reasoning could not, so long as the premises were taken to be true. This mistrust of observational science may occur in unifiers, but does not transfer over to all those we could imagine. The work of James Joule resulted in reducing nature to a few "general principles which will explain everything", i.e. principles for understanding the translation of mechanical energy to heat energy, leaving the universe a little simpler than he found it, yet his approach was critically reliant on rigorous experimental observations.

On the other hand, Bacon was clear on his need for experimental observation, applying the inductive process to produce new knowledge based firmly on the real world. Bacon's view held little space for theories without some experimental grounding—he stated clearly that mathematics should be used *"only to give definiteness to natural philosophy, not to generate or give it birth."* (Novum Organum XCVI,

1620). This places him far from the unifier camp, where abstractions and mathematics are often used to motivate and give birth the next stage of investigation.

A further important aspect of Bacon's philosophy was the *economic impact* of science. Bacon's era was one where the British Empire was emerging, a time of immense economic growth throughout the 16th/17th century. He demands that natural philosophy (science) should be more than merely contemplative, but should be active, put to use to serve the state, not merely hedonistic but should be a platform for business and economic growth. He was a strong supporter that it could provide economic impact in this manner, though he had a long term viewpoint of returns happening in decades rather than short term engineering aims. So, a strong element of Bacon's philosophy appears to*require* economic impact. This seems to be a common diversifier trait, but by no means a requirement; the earlier example of John Wheeler serves to illustrate this, and many of Rutherford's early observations on the structure of the atom had no immediate application.

3.3. The analytic/synthetic distinction

A controversial idea of the past century in philosophy has been the distinction between*analytic* and *synthetic* statements [8]. Here we provide a brief discussion, though a fuller treatment is outside the scope of this article. A statement of the form "S is P", is *analytic* if the predicate P is contained within the subject S, that is, the statement *is true in virtue of its own meaning*. The example made famous by Kant was "all bachelors are unmarried"—the term bachelor *means* to be unmarried. On the other hand, a *synthetic*statement is one such as "all bachelors are unhappy", where the predicate is not*necessarily* contained in the subject, and to ascertain its truth requires some information beyond the meaning of the words.

Kant argued for a third category, *synthetic a priori* statements—here the predicate is not contained within the subject, but the statement is necessarily true and does not require any further information to confirm it as such. Kant asserts that all of mathematics is in this category. If we take an example from our own field—a Kalman filter is a special case of a Gaussian Process. Rephrasing this, we have that a "KF is a GP"—clearly true, and not requiring sensory experience to confirm. Additionally, the definition of a KF in no way uses a GP as a defining component, thus we consider this is a *synthetic a priori* statement.

Whomsoever was the first to notice this (KF = GP) could certainly be regarded as a "unifier"—re-interpreting one Machine Learning model as another, showing how a single principle can unite the two bodies of literature. Could it be that unifiers are more pre-disposed to making synthetic a priori statements? At present, the answer to this is unclear. Certainly if we take the strictest view of the work we do—it all comes down to a mathematical statement or set of statements (i.e. algorithm) executed on a computer.

Kant [8] referred to analytic statements as *clarifying or explicating* our knowledge, or in other words, making explicit what was once implicit. Similarly, he referred to synthetic statements as *augmenting* or *extending* knowledge, that is, introducing new information that was not contained in the subject S in any way. These two styles – clarifying versus extending – certainly bear a passing resemblance to the concepts of *unifying* versus*diversifying*. However, to categorise them strictly as such would be to say an act of unifying never extends our knowledge, and Einstein certainly did extend our understanding of the universe. A full in-depth treatment of the analytic/synthetic distinction is outside the scope of this article, but is certainly something worth pursuing in future work.

3.4. Summary: the balance between unifiers and diversifiers

Perhaps then, the unifier–diversifier split is best seen as a *spectrum*. The unifiers (e.g. Einstein) are following a direction that bears some similarities to Plato's worldview, though of course modern science bows to experimental tests of its validity—something Plato would never accept. The diversifiers are somewhat Baconian, though without Bacon's strict need for economic impact. The grey area between unifier/diversifier seems to be best characterised by the Aristotlean viewpoint.

If we look at the space of people holding the diversifier mindset, it seems it may be slightly more full of experimenters than theorists, probably slightly more engineers than scientists, and probably slightly more industrial than academic. The space of unifiers is roughly the complement, but none of these individual dichotomies is isomorphic to Dyson's concept.

However, Dyson does perceive a definite imbalance between unifiers and diversifiers in different fields, and this may well hold true for

Pattern Recognition also. He argues that the unifiers have dominated physics for most of the 20th century. In contrast, he believes that biology has enjoyed a "healthier balance," where although it is the case that diversifiers have dominated, when a unifier like Darwin or Hamilton comes along, he is not ignored, but celebrated. Dyson reminds us that in biology, Darwin's work is celebrated as a milestone unifying framework, but such occurrences are rare—the working lives of 99 out of 100 biologists consist of investigating and manipulating the complex behaviour patterns of particular species or biochemical pathways. A modern perspective on this divide is given by Jogalekar [9].

In a controversial point, Dyson states his belief that the unifiers are most likely to be remembered in history:

"it is true in general that the very greatest scientists in each discipline are unifiers. This is especially true in physics."

However, given his later comments, one posits that Dyson intends the term "greatest" here to mean in the sense of fame/notoriety, as opposed to ability or impact. He certainly does not try to downplay the significance of the diversifier stance and, in his own work, engages in both styles of work. He provides an interesting account referring to his work to unify the field of Quantum Electrodynamics:

"When I did my most important piece of work [...] *I had consciously in mind a metaphor to describe what I was doing. The metaphor was bridge-building. Tomonaga and Schwinger had built solid foundations on one side of a river of ignorance. Feynman had built solid foundations on the other side, and my job was to design and build the cantilevers reaching out over the water until they met in the middle."* [10]

So here, Dyson *explicitly* thinks of himself in a unifying role. In another communication[11] he recounts his discussions on Quantum ElectroDynamics with Richard P. Feynman, who was apparently obsessed with finding a unifying theory of the large (gravity) and small (nuclear forces). In contrast, Dyson was comfortable with more than one set of equations, each useful at different scales. Referencing Gödel's theorem says:

"in the last hundred years of physics, unifiers have had things too much their own way. [...] *I hope that the notion of a final statement of the laws of physics will prove as illusory as the notion of a formal decision process for all of mathematics. If it should turn out that the whole of physical*

reality can be described by a finite set of equations, I would be disappointed."

So here he is quite clear that he also emphasises with a slight diversifier viewpoint, that not everything can be brought under a single metaphorical umbrella. Whilst Dyson clearly thinks that the great advances of 20th century physics are due to the dominant trend of unifiers, he clearly states his final position,

"every science needs for its healthy growth a creative balance between unifiers and diversifiers"

With this more clearly elucidated, we will consider how some of these issues transfer to the Pattern Recognition field.

4. UNIFYING AND DIVERSIFYING IN PATTERN RECOGNITION

The previous sections have explored various subtle interpretations of the terms "unifier" and "diversifier". One element made very clear is that unifiers favour *simplicity* in their work. Dyson seems to equate this with a certain *beauty* in the theory or experimental setup—in physics, mathematical beauty is a key element in the pursuit of a Grand Unified Theory for the field. In this section we will address these issues for Pattern Recognition: firstly exploring the concept of beauty, and then the idea of a Grand Unified Theory. Finally, we will consider how these two competing pressures of unifying/diversifying balance against each other over long time periods.

4.1. The pursuit of beauty in our work?

Whilst Dyson does discuss the idea of beauty in theories, several prominent physicists have stated their belief more boldly:

"a beautiful or elegant theory is more likely to be right than a theory that is inelegant." [12]

In the field of physics, this pursuit of aesthetics has proved exceptionally fruitful. Dyson however does not believe this holds true for all fields of science:

"Mathematical beauty was key to the discovery of the laws of nature [...]That somehow seemed to work beautifully in physics, but it doesn't seem to work in biology [...] The fact is that mathematics is useful for biology only in a very humble way, essentially computer science [...] making simulations of complicated systems [...] not as a creator for insight." [13]

To explain the concept of mathematical beauty is challenging, just as it is challenging to explain the feeling an individual gets from a piece of artwork. The great physicist Murray Gell-Mann said that something is beautiful if it can be explained concisely in terms of mathematics we already have. Richard Feynman explained it as the quality of a result that fits like the last piece in a puzzle, either making everything else seem obvious in hindsight, or providing startling new predictions that are borne out in experiment.

Whilst it seems to be justifiable that in physics, mathematical beauty is the key to truth, in PR we are not necessarily always seeking *truth*—but sometimes simply *utility*. So, is mathematical beauty the key to progress: either to discovery of new truths, or new utility, in our field? Ockham's razor is the obvious discussion point here. The pursuit of simplicity has clearly been a useful practical rule for model selection. In terms of theories/concepts, it has also been a useful post hoc organisational tool—cleaning up areas after their invention, sometimes yielding small gaps for new work. However the principle has yet to prove its worth at the same magnitude observed in physics, a tool of discovery for entirely new areas of study.

Symmetry is a form of beauty which has been a crucial tool in the understanding of fundamental physics. The most recent high profile example of this is the discovery of the Higgs Boson, predicted to be observable in the Large Hadron Collider at a particular energy level. This prediction was made in 1964, for the simple reason that it would make for a beautiful mathematical symmetry. There may be algorithms we consider beautiful in retrospect—but this principle, of *discovery via aesthetics*, has not yet been so convincingly demonstrated in PR. There has not been a flood of predictions in the form*"there should exist a learning algorithm with generalisation error x% "*. The only instance even vaguely like this (that I know of) is the Boosting family of algorithms—the existence of which was predicted by studies in computational complexity theory [14], and discovered later by Schapire [15]. Our equivalent to the headline-grabbing Higgs prediction would be a prophecy of the form: *"if you create a deep neural network with between* 10^{15}*and* 10^{16}*connections, a phase transition should occur and enable a new level of machine intelligence"*. Thereafter, several billion of EU funding would be directed towards tunnelling under Switzerland to build a neural net big enough. But it has not happened.

It is arguable that a far more fruitful "tool of discovery" in our field has been *inter-disciplinarity*. Many of our best optimisation schemes come from mathematics (e.g. simplex) or physics (e.g. simulated annealing), many of our best models come from biological analogy (e.g. convolutional neural nets), and many of our best methodologies come from statistics (e.g. bootstrap). Of course, this may be an artefact of this stage in our (short) history, and in 50 years the pursuit of symmetry-breaking might turn out useful for artificial intelligence, but who knows.

Given this inherent interdisciplinarity, it is instructive to question whether our subject is on a path towards a 'unified theory' as many people believe is the case for physics. Or indeed, if it is 'unifiable' at all. Even if the answer to this is negative, are there individual elements of our *practice* that could be unified? What are the pros and cons of unifying/diversifying in our field?

4.2. A unified theory of pattern recognition?

Is it the case that there exists a *single* unified theory of Pattern Recognition, towards which we are converging? I believe this idea can be dismissed immediately almost without controversy. For one, even if a Grand Unified Theory exists for physics, we *know*that we are not describing that. It is true that we are in some sense using inference to predict the behaviour of the universe (e.g. whether a person will buy a book on Amazon or not), but we are *modelling* at a level of abstraction several dozen layers above where String Theory is working. And, multiple abstractions can hold true without problem, providing different overlapping and mutually reinforcing viewpoints. The best way to model something is not necessarily at the deepest level at which we understand it. For example, fluid mechanics is a well established discipline, allowing us to predict how water waves break against a wall; the calculations work almost perfectly, using the assumption that the water is a continuum, even though we understand the water to be made of atoms, or digging deeper, little vibrating strings in 11 dimensions.

There of course exist almost religious factions that try to convince everybody else that their method of data analysis and inference is the *One True Path*, but ultimately, with incisive questioning, they can usually be brought to a more pragmatic perspective, at least in the short term.

The pragmatic viewpoint says that different mechanisms, theories and implementations of intelligence will be useful in different scenarios. In this light, it can be believed that we may get pockets of unification, but no over-arching theory to unify us all. There is certainly no shortage of attempts—a quick Google search reveals recent papers in a common style:

- A Unifying Framework for Statistical Relational Learning
- Rule Evaluation Measures: A Unifying View
- A Unifying View of Multiple Kernel Learning
- A Unifying Framework for Information Theoretic Feature Selection

Just as Dyson believes that different sets of equations would be useful at different scales of experience, so it is likely that different theories of inference and data modelling will be appropriate for different problem scenarios, and at different scales and types of data, different aesthetics will become apparent.

4.3. Unifying/diversifying as part of an evolutionary process

In any field, unifying and diversifying behave according to a kind of evolutionary process,[3] where the units of evolution are *memes*: ideas, behaviours or styles that spread from person to person within a culture. In PR, the Bayesian and Kernel memes gained particular traction from about 2000 onwards, and are arguably of a *unifying*flavour. They have both successfully abstracted several techniques to special cases of their respective methodologies, enabling new insights, e.g. kernel PCA. Whilst these have proved immensely powerful, when a unifying meme does not serve to progress science as rapidly as it has in the past, its dominance in the culture is displaced, and diversifying memes appear. The recent meme of *deep learning* seems to be very much in a diversifying flavour, without a single aesthetically pleasing theory to explain it, yet clearly providing results of utility in several domains.

The evolutionary pressures are complex, existing at various *levels of granularity* in a field. Coarse-grained aspects of the field can be *unified* under a common societal challenge, such as the recent trend for *Big Data*, whilst at the same time finer-grained aspects of the field are *diversified* to cope with the new challenges. Sometimes results are rediscovered, but put in a new light given that other topics have progressed in the meantime—results once seen as diversifying, can later be seen to serve a unification. The field progresses only with the *blend* of these pressures: too much of either one will hinder progress.

Taking this long-term viewpoint, a meaningful diversification can be exceptionally healthy. The field of artificial intelligence underwent the ultimate diversification from the 1980s onward, documented well by Cristianini [16]. Looking back at the Dartmouth Conference [2], the primary goal was to create intelligent beings, and it was imagined this was only a decade or so away. Over half a century later, we have sub-sub-subfields—for example, *adversarial* classification, as a subfield of supervised learning, as a subfield of machine learning, as a subfield of AI. This diversification enabled questions we never imagined 1955, and created a generation of technology that has become indispensable to everyday life.

5. WHAT DO UNIFIERS/DIVERSIFIERS DO IN PR?

Unifiers like to explore the connectedness of ideas. They prefer to discover the relationships between existing scientific artefacts, rather than create new ones. In our case, these are algorithms, mathematical constructions, and their implementations, whether in hardware or software. When unifiers create, they create artefacts at the intersection of existing ones, so as to see their connection. As a consequence, they write papers which bring people together, cross discipline boundaries for the purpose of reinterpreting their primary field of study, and have a broad view of the research landscape. It could be conjectured that unifiers tend to publish less frequently than diversifiers, taking more time to integrate the various concepts they bring together.

Diversifiers on the other hand enjoy exploration and invention, they have a narrower focus on the research landscape at any one time, or multiple narrow foci. They push limits and figure out what is and is not possible. This was precisely Rutherford's achievement, pushing the boundaries of our understanding of the atom. As a consequence, they innovate more, posing questions not previously considered, often by importing ideas across a discipline boundary. They create artefacts with utility, not only in the immediate engineering sense but also in that they highlight problems, chinks in the armour of a theory.

Both groups have the capability to inspire new directions, create new fields—but they do it in different ways. Unifiers provide a new viewpoint on existing literature, showing gaps, enabling meaningful analysis of properties, providing new languages which can express computational artefacts at the junction of several others. Diversifiers address challenging new domains and questions that current work has simply not considered; they start slow, often with heuristic (but effective) approaches and accumulate a fan-base of loyal followers who slowly refine these, figuring out what works and what does not. As may be obvious, the two groups provide fuel for each other—one follows the other in a never-ending cycle of interleaving innovation. Where the unifier defines a framework, the diversifier finds an exception. When the diversifier finds sufficiently many exceptions, the unifier sees commonalities and patterns for a new framework.

As we have stated at the start of Section 2.3, unifying and diversifying are *styles of practice*. As such, each can be done *badly*, causing more harm than good. Whilst it is tempting in this essay to take the middle ground and avoid offence, here I will not, and outline downsides of each practice.

Novice unifiers[4] can be dangerous. They often stumble for a long time, seeing patterns where there are none, over-egging the significance of their 'frameworks'. Unification can be *sterile*—bringing several ideas under a common umbrella, but ending up with strained analogies and relationships between the ideas, and ultimately closing more doors than it opens. Claims to unification can be little more than a *categorisation* of the ideas: a literature review with a solid backbone, but not enabling invention of new ideas, or meaningful explanation of existing ones. There are downsides to the unifier stance in general, even if done "correctly". Why should we force others to adopt the same perspective as our own? If we attempt to cast everything into a single mould then, whilst aesthetically pleasing, it will mean compromises have to be made. In this way, doors will be closed on young minds exploring the literature for the first time.

As stated eloquently by Langley [17], too much diversification can also be bad for a field:

"...diversification also has its dangers. Subdisciplines can emerge that focus on one goal or evaluation scheme to the exclusion of others, and similarities among methods can be obscured by different notations and terminology." [17]

It is common to see papers offering 'novel' methods with an *immensely* complex computational pipeline, and many parameter settings left unjustified; or worse, nuances of the implementation left completely unreported. Though this article is focused on Pattern Recognition, it is fair to note that similarly vague work appears in related communities [18]. These papers can generally be characterised by the phrase *"my classifier gets higher accuracy than your classifier"*, though results often cannot be reproduced as they depend on those unspecified nuances. The best one can say in this situation is congratulations to the authors for finding the three or four datasets on which their method was successful. It is difficult to see what can be done to discourage this, apart from refining the unspoken rules of acceptable practice in our field. One can only hope that further standards of *reproducible research* will infiltrate the community, and allow genuine progress rather than illusory [19].

6. WHO DRIVES THE PARADIGM SHIFTS OF PATTERN RECOGNITION?

Kuhn [20] presents a treatise on the nature and reasons behind revolutions in scientific understanding. In this, he discusses how new scientific concepts bring about revolutions in a field. Kuhn proposes that all scientific revolutions follow a similar pattern, described by his 'paradigm shift' cycle (Fig. 1).

An interesting question is *who drives the transitions around this cycle?* Is it the unifiers, coming up with fundamental new theorems to unify the state of the art? Or the diversifiers, challenging popular opinion with new observations/phenomena?

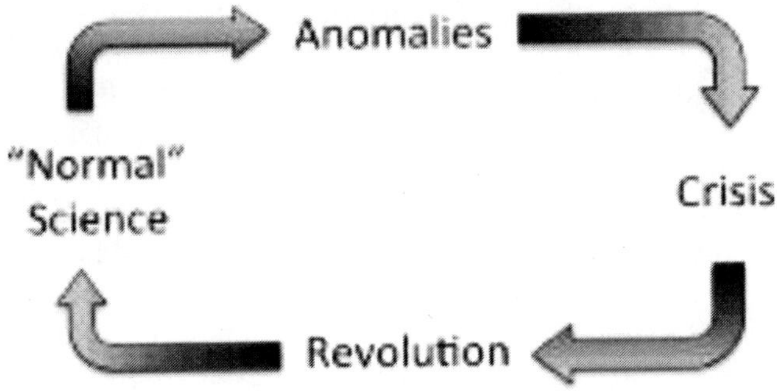

Figure. 1. Kuhn's paradigm shift cycle. So-called 'normal' science precedes anomalies in observation, followed by a crisis of understanding, then a scientific 'revolution' where new ideas are adopted by mainstream science, and a new paradigm begins.

Dyson claims that Kuhn's vision of this is too narrow—that transitions are brought into being only by unifiers, coming up with new theorems. He calls this a *concept-driven revolution*. He expands upon this view in a book titled *"The Sun, The Genome, and The Internet"*, [21], discussing how *tools* are an equal (if not greater) influence on the recent revolutions in science. Dyson takes a very broad viewpoint on the definition of a tool, as might be suggested by the book title, he considers the sun, the genome, and the internet, all as tools for science. In his own words:

"a scientific tool is not only considered to be something that strengthens our senses or is useful in taking measurements, but also as an aid to our understanding" [21, p. 51]

Dyson points out that new tools (created by diversifiers) enable observation of new phenomena, which possibly conflict with previous theories—pushing the field into the 'anomalies' and then 'crisis' phase. In addition, the transition back round to normal science is very often enabled by tools which observe and manipulate data to resolve the anomalies—the new theories play a relatively minor role in the process. He proposes that physics was dominated by concept-driven revolutions prior to the 20th century, but beyond the 1920s it was not possible to conduct experiments in isolation, and tool-driven revolutions took over—when tools like Electron Microscopes and the Large Hadron Collider enabled new paradigms of understanding.

Returning the discussion to Pattern Recognition, we had a concept-driven revolution in the early 1990s, when statistical and data-driven modelling began to dominate. We are possibly about to transition into a *tool-driven* revolution, with the availability of tools like Kinect, and a new wearable computing industry with the Apple Watch and imitators—using many embedded sensors that will make inferences based on observations during the day. Embedded sensors and computing are disappearing into the fabric of life, as so many Sci-Fi movies have it. This generation of embedded intelligent sensors will need software, and it will be the intellectual descendants of those reading this article that write it. Other non-obvious examples of ML tools are: approximate inference algorithms, multi-core computers and GPUs, Amazon's Mechanical Turk, toolkits such as Weka and libSVM, and of course APIs that open up sources of data unavailable to most people, such as Twitter feeds.

Very occasionally, single, powerful tools come along that drive an entire revolution. These enable the field to both ask and answer questions that would have been previously inconceivable, just as the physics of black holes would be inconceivable to the ancient Athenians without modern day radio telescopes. Dyson has recently speculated [13] that the progress of artificial intelligence is fundamentally limited until critical new tools (analogue computing machines) are properly developed.

7. RELATED WORK IN PATTERN RECOGNITION

Whilst we may never have a truly "unified theory of inference", there are a number of technical elements of our field which could benefit from a little unification; in classic papers, Breiman [22] and Langley [17] present ideas along this line. With over a decade since Breiman's paper, and a quarter-century since Langley's, it seems an interesting time to revisit their words.

7.1. Breiman's two cultures

Breiman [22] discusses two cultures of statistical modelling: *data* modelling versus*algorithmic* modelling. For Breiman, "data modelling" means considering the form of the problem/data one is faced with, then thinking of a parametric class of mathematical models, and fitting the parameters. This is epitomised by linear and logistic regressions, and procedures like LASSO. The models are mathematically tractable and elegant, and have direct (if questionable) mappings of their structure to phenomena in the problem domain—Breiman proposes that their use accounts for 98% of the working lives of all statisticians. The 'algorithmic modelling' culture is epitomised by decision trees, neural nets, SVMs and other terms familiar to us in Machine Learning. These models make no claim to reflect the structure of the problem in their own structure. A node in a neural net or an RBF kernel is simply a good way of fitting the data, as opposed to being a symbol for a particular real-world event. He claims that these account for 2% of all statisticians.

Breiman argues three main points, that the overuse of data models has: led to irrelevant theory and questionable conclusions; kept statisticians from using more suitable procedures; and kept statisticians from working on exciting new domains.

In the years since Breiman's paper, many of these boundaries have been crossed. Many of the techniques Breiman calls algorithmic models are now known as computational statistics, and are in common use in both communities. There is still the hardcore of both the statistics and ML communities that hold fast to the aesthetics of certain modelling approaches, and these are slowly dropping their restrictive assumptions, becoming just as strong in practice as any method. Nevertheless, Breiman's paper is a thought-provoking read over a decade later; and, with its pragmatic view, encourages these two communities to unify their goals and practices.

7.2. Langley's seven dichotomies

Langley [17] wrote a striking editorial for an issue of Machine Learning Journal, on the topic of unifying machine learning as it stood in the late 1980s. He discusses seven apparent dichotomies that had emerged at the time, stating that *"long term progress will only occur if we can find ways to unify these apparently competing views into a single whole"*.

For the interested reader, an online Appendix[5] to this article contains a detailed analysis of each of these seven dichotomies (from my own perspective) and the extent to which I believe they have been resolved over the past 25 years.

8. THE VALUE OF THE DICHOTOMY

What is the *value* of Dyson's unifier/diversifier dichotomy? Is it *predictive*, in the sense that it may inform profitable new directions in research? Does it give an understanding of our own actions, successes/failures? What *is* a healthy balance of the two for PR? To address these questions, it is in fact easier to first address the more abstract question—what is the value of philosophy in general? A powerful answer to this is presented by Russell [23, chapter XV].

"The study of physical science is to be recommended [...]*because of the effect on mankind in general. This utility does not belong to philosophy. If the study of philosophy has any value* [...]*it must be only indirectly, through its effects upon the lives of those who study it."*

Russell suggests that the benefits of philosophical thought show themselves firstly in the lives of those who study it, and only indirectly in the lives of others who they interact with. If philosophical reflection is undertaken by scientists, this enables more considered and reflective practice in whatever field they happen to occupy. Many years later, Russell summarised his views as,

"the man who has no tincture of philosophy goes through life imprisoned in the prejudices derived from common sense, from the habitual beliefs of his age or his nation, and from convictions which have grown up in his mind without the co-operation or consent of his deliberate reason." [24]

Can philosophy in general inform profitable new directions in PR research? Pelillo and Scantamburlo [25] present a post hoc example, discussing the *essentialist* viewpoint in philosophy. Essentialism is the view that entities in the world have inherent, *essential* and*immutable* properties, by which they can be described. Pelillo and Scantamburlo [25]discuss how *dissimilarity measures* in PR sit in direct opposition to this philosophical view, in that an entity is best described by its relation (similarities) to other entities. I suggest an speculative extension, that *evaluation metrics* in our field should be considered in the same manner. The evaluation metric is not something *essential* to a predictive model—it is something subjective, imposed by humans, for particular tasks, at a particular point in time, in a particular context. Perhaps merging some ideas from multi-objective optimisation with the theory of ranking measures might prove fruitful in this direction.

But, what benefit is the unifier/diversifier dichotomy? Can it give an understanding of our own actions, successes/failures? Possibly, yes.

This may come by reflections on previous successes/failures, and what character they have. If an individual sees on reflection that most of their successes have come from a diversifying mindset, they may be able to direct actions accordingly in the future. As in most areas of life, raising awareness of one's emotions and actions is usually profitable.

What is a healthy balance of unifying and diversifying? This is a difficult question. For one, a 'healthy balance' is ill-defined, and even if it wasn't, it would be different at different scales of organisation. The individual researcher, their research team, their academic school or institution, all the way up to a nation's research budget—each will have different emphases depending on complex factors. Even so, the dichotomy might be useful as an analytical tool—asking at each of these scales, how much effort is being placed into four different areas: unifying in science/engineering, and diversifying in science/engineering. Whilst this is sure to be a controversial point of view, and I do not suppose to know the best way to manage an entire country's research budget, it is a thought-provoking concept.

9. CONCLUSION

The question originally posed for this paper was "can Dyson's unifier/diversifier dichotomy apply in the Pattern Recognition field?". We conclude that the answer is *yes*, but in a subtly different way. There do exist *pure* unifiers and *pure* diversifiers, just as in physics, however, they are rare in our field. Most people in PR sit on the spectrum between the two: keen to expand the scope of our field (diversifying) but equally keen to find aesthetically pleasing results linking them to other researchers (unifying). Many researchers can adopt unifying perspectives one day, and be diversifying the next.

However, I conjecture that this situation may change with time. Dyson argued that both theories and tools drive scientific revolutions [21]. Physics has been maturing its arsenal of theories and tools for hundreds of years longer than us. As such, the *accessibility* of theories and tools is much more restrictive than in PR. It takes many years to master advanced physics, such as the mathematics of String Theory. Equivalently, to be an experimental physicist, tools such as electron microscopes cost hundreds of thousands of pounds; or, even more extreme, the Large Hadron Collider cost billions of Euros, and is inaccessible to most. In biology, an experimentalist spends many years learning just one tricky technique for refining biochemical reactions to observe their phenomenon of interest. In Pattern Recognition however, we all have Matlab, Python, Weka, and fast computers, the tools we need to do good work. The theory side is also not too obscure—a student in computational learning theory can start to contribute excellent work before they graduate. It is likely this will change with time as the field matures.

Experimental tools are maturing too. GPUs and multi-core machines are commonplace, but learning how to program them is non-trivial. Datasets such as Twitter-feeds are posing new challenges to us, and dealing with this data scale takes special skills, and increasingly, large budgets. Datasets too may become commodities; we are already seeing that only large industry practitioners can afford tackle certain types of problems. Take it further into the future—what happens when the tools of Machine Learning are custom built neural microchips, ala the *positronic net* of Commander Data in Star Trek? This is not such an implausible direction to head. Why should we not have computing devices that are by construction inherently suited to inference tasks, either deductive or inductive? It could be argued that such devices are at prototype stage already with*neuromorphic* computing [26].

As the theories in the field becomes more sophisticated, the techniques will take many years to learn. As the tools become more specialised, they will become more financially inaccessible. Although we have argued that theory/experiment is not an isomorphic dichotomy to unifier/diversifier, it is one factor. If theorists and experimenters become very distinct roles in PR, with theorists rarely (if ever) learning the tools of experimenters, and vice versa, then the gulf between unifier and diversifier may grow larger.

So, maybe we will never have a fully unified discipline of Pattern Recognition. It is likely however that we need *both* the forces of unification and diversification to move forward, summarised eloquently by Langley [17], referencing Dyson:

"Just as the twin forces of gravity and pressure hold a star in dynamic equilibrium while generating energy, so the joint processes of diversification and unification can hold a science together while fostering progress.

To conclude, in my own career to date, I have mostly been a unifier. However, Dyson defines diversifiers as those who like exploring the details of nature, and that unifiers prefer the broad brush, the big picture. I believe fruitful unifications only come from looking at the details—so maybe I am a bit of both, but it is fun to consider.

ACKNOWLEDGEMENTS

I would like to thank Fabio Roli for prompting and encouraging the thought processes that led to this work, and Joshua Knowles, Marcello Pelillo, Michael Lee and Henry Reeve for broadening my awareness of the philosophy literature. The research leading to these results has received funding from the EPSRC Anyscale project EP/L000725/1.

REFERENCES

1. F.J. Dyson **Manchester and Athens** Infinite in All Directions, Harper & Row Perennial (1988), pp. 35–53

2. J. McCarthy, M. Minsky, N. Rochester, C. Shannon, The Dartmouth Summer Research Conference on Artificial Intelligence, 1955, http://www-formal.stanford.edu/jmc/history/dartmouth/dartmouth.html.

3. C. Darwin The Autobiography of Charles Darwin, J. Murray, London (1887)

4. A. Thackray **Natural knowledge in cultural context: the Manchester model** Am. History Rev., 79 (3) (1974), pp. 672–709

5. M. Pelillo, T. Scantamburlo, V. Schiaffonati **Pattern recognition between science and engineering: a red herring?** Pattern Recognit. Lett. (2015)

6. R.P. Feynman, The Character of Physical Law (Messenger Lectures), 1964.

7. F.J. Dyson **Roundtable critique; hidden in plain: view, narrative and creative potentials in war and peace** J. Tolstoy Stud., 2 (1989), pp. 1–41

8. I. Kant Critique of Pure Reason (1781)

9. A. Jogalekar **Diversifiers of the world—unite!** Scientific American Blogs (April 15, 2014)

10. F.J. Dyson The Scientist as a Rebel, New York Review Books (1995)

11. F.J. Dyson Disturbing the Universe, Basic Books (1979)

12. M. Gell-Mann, TED Talk: Beauty, Truth and... Physics?, 2007.

13. F.J. Dyson, Are Brains Analogue or Digital?, School of Theoretical Physics, Dublin Institute for Advanced Studies, May 19, 2014.

14. M. Kearns, L.G. Valiant **Learning Boolean formulae or nite automata is as hard as factoring** Technical Report, Harvard University Aiken Computation Laboratory (1988)

15. R.E. Schapire **The strength of weak learnability** Mach. Learn., 5 (2) (1990), pp. 197–227

16. N. Cristianini **On the current paradigm in artificial intelligence** AI Commun., 27 (1) (2014), pp. 37–43

17. P. Langley **Toward a unified science of machine learning** Mach. Learn., 3 (4) (1989), pp. 253–259

18. K. Sörensen **Metaheuristics: the metaphor exposed** Int. Trans. Oper. Res. (2013)

19. D.J. Hand **Classifier technology and the illusion of progress** Stat. Sci., 21 (1) (2006), pp. 1–14

20. T. Kuhn The Structure of Scientific Revolutions, Univ. Chicago Press (1970) [21]

21. F.J. Dyson The Sun, The Genome, and the Internet: Tools of Scientific Revolutions, Oxford University Press (1999)

22. L. Breiman **Statistical modeling: the two cultures (with comments and a rejoinder by the author)** Stat. Sci., 16 (3) (2001), pp. 199–231

23. B. Russell The Problems of Philosophy, Oxford University Press (1912)

24. B. Russell **Philosophy for laymen** Univ. Q., 1 (1946), pp. 38–49

25. M. Pelillo, T. Scantamburlo **How mature is the field of machine learning?** Advances in Artificial Intelligence, Springer (2013), pp. 121–132

26. S. Furber, F. Galluppi, S. Temple, L. Plana **The SpiNNaker project** Proc. IEEE, 102 (5) (2014), pp. 652–665

9

VECTOR DISPARITY SENSOR WITH VERGENCE CONTROL FOR ACTIVE VISION SYSTEMS

Francisco Barranco [1,★], Javier Diaz [1], Agostino Gibaldi [2], Silvio P. Sabatini [2] and Eduardo Ros [1]

[1] Department of Computer Architecture and Technology, CITIC, ETSIIT, University of Granada, C/Daniel Saucedo Aranda s/n, E18071, Granada, Spain

[2] PSPC Group, Department of Biophysical and Electronic Engineering (DIBE), University of Genoa, Via Opera Pia 11A, I-16145, Genoa, Italy

ABSTRACT

This paper presents an architecture for computing vector disparity for active vision systems as used on robotics applications. The control of the vergence angle of a binocular system allows us to efficiently explore dynamic environments, but requires a generalization of the disparity computation with respect to a static camera setup, where the disparity is strictly 1-D after the image rectification. The interaction between vision and motor control allows us to develop an active sensor that achieves high accuracy of the disparity computation around the fixation point, and fast reaction time for the vergence control. In this contribution, we address the development of a real-time architecture for vector disparity computation using an FPGA device. We implement the disparity unit and the control module for vergence, version, and tilt to determine the fixation point. In addition, two on-chip different alternatives for the vector disparity engines are discussed based on the luminance (gradient-based) and phase information of the binocular images. The multiscale versions of these engines are able to estimate the vector disparity up to 32 fps on VGA resolution images with very good accuracy as shown using benchmark sequences with known ground-truth. The performances in terms of frame-rate, resource utilization, and accuracy of the presented approaches are discussed. On the basis of these results, our study indicates that the gradient-based approach leads to the best trade-off choice for the integration with the active vision system.

KEYWORDS

field programmable gate arrays; active vision; real time systems

1. INTRODUCTION

Depth perception is essential for an autonomous system that is moving in a dynamic environment. It is applied in multiple applications such as autonomous navigation [1], obstacle detection and avoidance [2], 3-D reconstruction [3], tracking [4,5], grasping [6,7], *etc*. For example, depth computation is used for obtaining 3D information of real-world scenarios with real-time implementations such as [8,9]. Many computer vision algorithms have been proposed for extracting depth information from multiple-view images [10,11].

An alternative for depth estimation is based on the correspondences of image features of a binocular system. Disparity computation models basically consist of a matching problem, finding correspondences between features or areas in both left and right images and taking into account some constraints based on the geometry of the stereo rig that may help to simplify the search process (due to the epipolar geometry constraint [10]). This model assumes that the geometry of the cameras is fixed and known (e.g., using a previous calibration stage that allows us to extract the intrinsic and extrinsic binocular cameras parameters [10]). Based on this assumption, in most of the literature contributions, the disparity is managed as a mono-dimensional matching problem of correspondences. They usually assume that images are calibrated or include a pre-processing stage for undistortion and rectification. This process consists of correcting the lens radial distortions and aligning the image planes with the epipolar lines, which simplifies the disparity estimation, reducing the problem to a matching only for the horizontal coordinates (see Figure 1). Nevertheless, the main problem is that the rectification process is required each time the camera configuration is modified. Therefore, this technique is not suitable for any active system that is able to modify the vergence of the cameras, which means that we need a different approach.

In our case, we select a system that adaptively controls the vergence of its binocular camera setup. The use of a static vergence angle cannot yield to a correct gazing position to a specific point. However, a solution for this problem is to use a vergence control that allows the modification of the relative position of the cameras in order to fixate a point. This bio-inspired solution achieves the best disparity results around the fixation point because it moves the image plane at the depth of this point and computes a very small range of disparities around it. In general, indeed, the highest accuracy of the disparity calculation kernel is obtained with the lowest disparity ranges.

On the other hand, our active binocular sensor acts depending on the target, which means that its fixation point is determined by three parameters: version, tilt, and vergence angles (see Section 2). There are some previous works that support the use of the disparity for guiding vergence eye movements in active vision systems [12–14]. The listed advantages allow us to explore the scene in detail, by changing gazing and fixation at different targets or areas of interest. In this work, we present the implementation of a system where vision and motion control act in a collaborative manner for solving the presented issue. With respect to the motion control strategy, our work is based on a separate control of version and vergence inspired by the Hering's law [15]. Hering proposed that the movement of one eye is coordinated with the other with a movement of equal amplitude and velocity, but it could be in opposite directions. This coordinated movements are specified in terms of version and vergence components. However, eyes only approximate this law, because saccadic movements may include additional vergence components [16]. More details are provided in the following subsection.

In the literature, we find different works that deal with the vector disparity estimation problem [17–19]. In this work, we propose a comparison between a gradient-based [20,21] and a phase-based [22–24] approach for the disparity computation. Phase-based approaches are more accurate and robust against variations in the illumination. On the other hand, gradient-based approaches may be implemented at a reduced cost, saving resources in comparison with the first one and presenting a good accuracy.

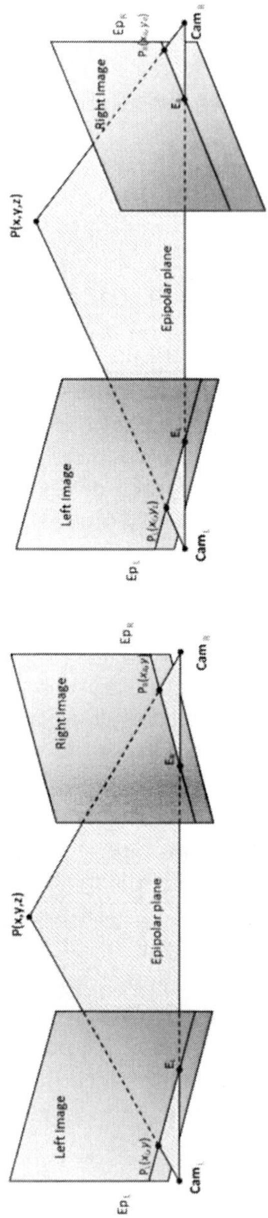

Figure 1. Epipolar geometry for a pair of cameras. **Left:** *P* corresponds to (x_L, y) and (x_R, y) coordinates for the left and right image planes respectively. **Right:** The same *P*point corresponds to different *x* and *y* coordinates on each image plane. Ep_L and $Ep_R$are the epipolar lines, Cam_L and Cam_R, the camera optical centers, and E_R and E_L stand for the epipoles.

FPGA is selected as the platform for our system because of the requirements of real-time performances and the suitability of the integration with the active vision system due to the reduced chip size and limited power consumption compared with other approaches as the one based on GPUs. For vision processing algorithms with a high-computational complexity, we need to exploit the maximum parallelism at different levels and in our case, this objective is matched using a fine-pipeline based architecture in an FPGA. In the case of the single-scale version of our disparity computation, we achieve up to 267 and 118 fps (frames per second) for the gradient- and the phase-based algorithms, respectively. For the multi-scale implementations, the reached frame rate is almost 32 fps. In both cases, the image resolution is VGA (640 × 480), although higher resolutions are possible at the cost of reducing the frame rate.

This paper is structured as follows: in Section 2, we present the vergence, tilt, and version control for our sensor; in Section 3, we describe the mathematical formulation of the used approaches for the disparity computation (gradient-based and phase-based); Section 4 analyzes the hardware implementations for both gradient-based and phase-based approaches detailing their mono- and multi-scale versions. This section also presents the performance analysis (accuracy and frame rate) and the resource utilization. Section 5 shows the motion control strategy for our binocular system and the integration of the system with the disparity computation. Finally, Section 6 presents the conclusions and the future work.

2. VERSION, TILT, AND VERGENCE CONTROL

In this section, we present a system that manages the vergence, version, and tilt control with a stereo pair of cameras to fixate a target object. This is possible thanks to the utilization of a vector disparity model and a camera setup endowed with a shared motor for the tilt control, and two motors for the independent control of the pan angle of each camera. The separate controls allow us to move the gaze toward the point of interest and to control the vergence angle to fixate the target.

The experiments described in Section 5 were performed using the iCub head platform designed by the RobotCub Consortium [25]. Figure 2 displays the real RobotCub head and the architecture scheme. This platform is composed by a stereo pair of FireWire cameras, two DSPs, and an inertial sensor connected to a PC. The communication between the elements and the PC is carried out through a CAN bus. The DSP controllers use Motorola 56F807 16-bit hybrid processors. The head consists of a binocular system with six degrees of freedom: the eyes have two rotational degrees of freedom but with a common tilt; the neck also has three degrees of freedom. The control of cameras and neck motors is performed separately by two DSP units. The main problem with such a platform is the sensitivity of the motors to the low velocities, or different friction for the motors which might cause oscillations in the fixation task. Finally, slower responses of the system yield more predictable results. More information about the mechanics is provided in [26,27]. Finally, cameras provide pairs of 15 fps with a 1,024 × 768 resolution, although we are able to compute up to 32 fps of 640 × 480 pixels of resolution, we crop and subsample the resolution to 320 × 240 for our experiments because it provides good results for the vergence control algorithm. Our disparity computation system is based on an adaptable architecture that allows us to set the image resolution using input parameters. In this way, it is possible to adopt the most appropriate resolution for the target application. A smaller resolution for the images in our experiments allows the tracking of the objects in a very controlled scenario, and helps us to avoid any possible problem that may be caused by the rapid movements of the head.

The voluntary fixation of the visual system is directly related with the fovea, the central area of the retinas, that provides high-resolution visual stimuli. In fact, in human vision, fixation movements have the task to register the target into the foveae, in order to maximize the perceptible details in the area of interest [28]. Version is defined as the rotation of the eyes about the vertical axis to maintain a constant disparity. Meanwhile, tilt is the rotation of each eye with respect to the horizontal axis. Finally, vergence is the rotation of each eye about the vertical axis to change the disparity. These parameterization of the system allows to define a unique fixation point with three angles [29]. In Figure 3, we observe the top and side views of our camera setup. In the figure, Θ_v defines the vergence angle, Θ_L and Θ_R stand for the pan angles (version) and finally, Θ_t is the tilt angle (displayed on the right). As we mentioned before, tilt angles are common for both right and left cameras. Due to the correlation between the angles, if the vergence angle is defined, we only need either Θ_L or Θ_R to define version.

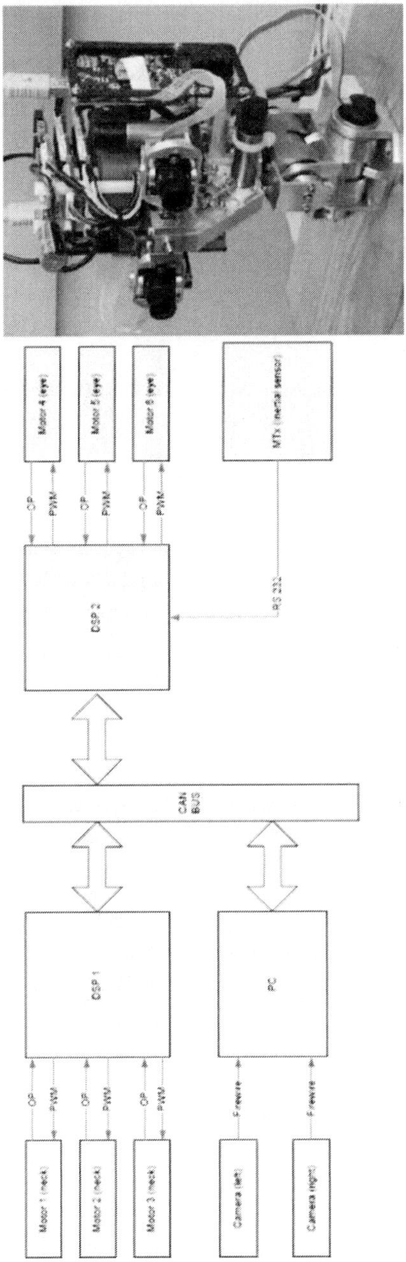

Figure 2. Hardware architecture of the iCub head. On the left, the architecture with the two DSPs, the PC connected to the CAN bus, and the inertial sensor are shown. An image of the head is shown on the right.

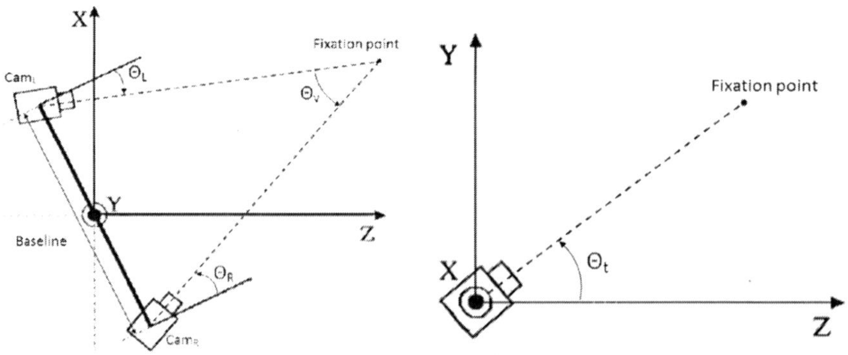

Figure 3. Version, vergence, and tilt angles for the stereo vision system. Top and side views of the camera configuration showing the version, vergence, and tilt angles for each camera.

Version might be determined monocularly using a master eye (camera in our case) for the gazing to the target object and the slave camera performs a vergence movement to fixate the point. In this case, we only have two separate controls. However, vergence has to be defined in terms of binocular disparity.

The selected joint control method combines version, vergence, and tilt as independent parallel movements. The performed control can be expressed by the following set of equations in Equation (1).

$$\begin{aligned} \Theta_{version} &= K_1(\mathbf{x}_L + \mathbf{x}_R) \\ \Theta_{tilt} &= K_2(\mathbf{y}_L + \mathbf{y}_R) \\ \Theta_{vergence} &= K_3 f(\mathbf{d}) \end{aligned} \quad (1)$$

where ($\mathbf{x}_L$, $\mathbf{y}_L$) and ($\mathbf{x}_R$, $\mathbf{y}_R$) are the coordinates of the target for the left and right images regarding the current fixation and$f(\mathbf{d})$ is a function of the disparity for the fixation point for almost similar vertical disparities that only avoids nullifying the vergence angle for the zero disparity and gives the disparity in other case. Finally, K_1, K_2 and K_3 are tuning gains. The area close to the fixation point is defined as "zero disparity" region. Vergence control allows us to fixate the gazed target by searching for this region.

We assume the computation of real-time disparity for the implementation of our control model. A fast vergence control can be computed using the information of the disparity of the target when the gazing is changing continuously, and our system is trying to reduce it to "zero" at this point.

There are also some different alternatives such as performing the fixation with several fixed setups for the cameras, constraining them to a set of more likely depths for the fixation point. This approach seems to save resources, since it avoids the computation of the real vector disparity (the undistortion and rectification stage has to be done, but the implementation is easy since the setups are fixed and known "a priori"). As our approach is also applied to autonomous mobile vehicles, vibrations may affect the setup, therefore a periodic evaluation of the rectification would be needed. From this perspective, the strategy of fixed setups is unsuccessful, since the rectification steps keep being mandatory. Another alternative may consist of using several fixed cameras with different vergence configurations, completely avoiding the rectification stage. This approach is similar to the previous one but it entails a high economic cost, which makes it unsuitable for a lot of applications.

3. COMPARISON OF VECTOR DISPARITY ALGORITHMS

The binocular disparity is usually defined as the difference in the *x* coordinates between the right and left images of a binocular vision system. This definition is useful because, even if in real-world applications the images are uncalibrated, binocular disparity systems usually include a preprocessing rectification stage that compensates for the difference in the *y*coordinate. This operation is related to the geometry of the cameras, and needs to be recomputed each time that the relative position of the cameras is modified. If the rectification is not applied (for instance, because the relative position of the cameras is continuously changing as in active vision systems), the disparity becomes a 2D problem, as we will discuss in the next subsections.

Disparity estimation techniques can be grouped into local and global methods. Local methods are centered in the surrounding neighborhood of a pixel to estimate its disparity. Global methods take into account the complete image. In our case we implement two different alternatives: a gradient-based technique, the well-known local algorithm of Lucas and Kanade [20,21] and a phase-based one detailed in [23] (also a local algorithm). The first technique estimates small local disparities assuming the intensity or brightness constancy of a pixel between left and right images, while the second one computes the disparity using the phase information for different orientations, in a contrast-independent way. In order to increase the working range for disparity detection, we use the multi-scale extension of the algorithms. Both implementations have been developed from the horizontal-disparity implementations (1D) but conveniently extended for the vector disparity (2D).

In order to validate our approach, we compare both the methods in terms of their different advantages and drawbacks. While the gradient-based method provides a good trade-off between efficiency and resource utilization, phase-based methods are very robust against variations in illumination and shadows, which makes them specially appropriate for real-world applications. In this paper, we avoid the use of global algorithms because they are not suitable for the on-chip implementation, at least with an affordable resource cost. This also explains why most of the current embedded implementations of disparity computation engines are based on local approaches [28,30–34].

3.1. Gradient-Based Lucas–Kanade Disparity Model

The disparity is defined as a 2-D problem as shown in Equation (2):

$$I^{right}(x, y) = I^{left}(x + d_x, y + d_y) \tag{2}$$

where I^{right} and I^{left} are the intensity of right and left images respectively and d_x and d_y are the disparity components. The solution of the system in this case is similar to the case of the optical flow in [35,36]. Applying the Taylor expansion inEquation (2), we obtain Equation (3)

$$d_x I_x^{left} + d_y I_y^{left} + I^{left}(x, y) - I^{right}(x, y) = 0 \tag{3}$$

where I_x^{left} and I_y^{left} are the partial derivatives of the left image. With this ill-posed system, additional assumptions need to be considered. The Lucas–Kanade algorithm supposes that pixels in the same neighborhood correspond to the same object and therefore, have a similar disparity.

And then, applying a least-square fitting for solving Equation (4) procedure, we obtain the system defined by Equations (5) and (6).

$$(d_x, d_y) = (A^T W^2 A)^{-1} A^T W^2 b \tag{4}$$

$$(A^T W^2 b) = \begin{bmatrix} \sum_{i\in\Omega} W_i^2 I_{xi}^{left}(I_i^{left} - I_i^{right}) \\ \sum_{i\in\Omega} W_i^2 I_{yi}^{left}(I_i^{left} - I_i^{right}) \end{bmatrix} \tag{5}$$

$$(A^T W^2 A) = \begin{bmatrix} \sum_{i\in\Omega} W_i^2 (I_{xi}^{left})^2 & \sum_{i\in\Omega} W_i^2 I_{xi}^{left} I_{yi}^{left} \\ \sum_{i\in\Omega} W_i^2 I_{xi}^{left} I_{yi}^{left} & \sum_{i\in\Omega} W_i^2 (I_{yi}^{left})^2 \end{bmatrix} \tag{6}$$

where W_i stands for the weighting matrix of the pixels in the neighborhood Ω. For the optical flow, Barron [20] computes the confidence of the computed estimation thresholding with the minimum of the eigenvalues of Matrix (6). We simplify it by using the determinant of this Matrix without a significant loss of accuracy, as shown in [36,37]. Finally, this algorithm also provides very computationally efficient solutions with a competitive accuracy as shown in [38,39].

3.2. Phase-Based Disparity Algorithm

Sabatini *et al.* proposed in [23] a multi-channel interaction algorithm to combine the phase information from multiple spatial scales (the multi-scale approach will be detailed in Section 3) and multiple orientations. The computation is performed combining multiple Gabor filter responses tuned at 8 orientations. Using the same formulation for Gabor filtering of [40], the vector disparity can be computed from the phase difference applying an intersection of constraint along different orientations, as in [41], assuming that points on an equi-phase contour satisfy $\phi(x, t) = c$, with c a constant. Differentiation with respect to time yields Equation (7):

$$\nabla\phi \cdot d + \psi = 0 \tag{7}$$

where $\nabla\phi = (\frac{\delta\phi}{\delta x}, \frac{\delta\phi}{\delta y})^T$ is the spatial phase gradient, $d = (d_x, d_y)^T$ is the vector disparity, and ψ is the phase difference between left and right images. The phase difference is computed without any explicit phase computation using the formulation proposed in [24]. In a linear model, the spatial gradient can be substituted by the radial frequency vector $(w_0 cos\theta_q, w_0 sin\theta_q)$ [23] where q indicates one of the eight orientations of the Gabor filter bank that we use. Next, Equation (7)can be rewritten as Equation (8)

$$w_0(cos\theta_q, sin\theta_q) \cdot d = -\psi_q \tag{8}$$

where · denotes scalar product. From this point, we can extract the component disparity and finally compute the disparity estimation solving the over-determined system defined in Equation (9)

$$d_x(\mathbf{x})w_0 cos\theta_q + d_y(\mathbf{x})w_0 sin\theta_q + \psi_q(\mathbf{x}) = 0 \tag{9}$$

3.3. Multi-Scale Generalization

As mentioned, our development is based on the multi-scalar generalization or coarse-to-fine scheme, inspired on Bergen's work [42], that increases the working range 30 times with respect to the mono-scalar implementation (using 5 scales). Moreover, it is a mandatory operation to achieve fully-operative systems on real-world scenarios. Our architecture is based on warping images, an approach that is usually avoided in the real-time embedded system literature because of its high resource costs (although it is more cost-effective than global methods).

The multi-scalar version implementation is simple. Firstly, we compute the pyramid for the input images (left and right) and they are stored (see [43]). In such a way, we have a bank of images sampled at different spatial resolutions (depending on the number of scales). The second step consists of iterating in a loop as many times as scales: for each iteration, we upsample the previous disparity estimation; then, we warp the previous upsampled results and the frames for the following finer scale; next, the new disparity estimation is computed using the previous results as input for the core; the final stage collects the new estimation and the partial previous, stored results to combine them in a new partial estimation for the next iteration. The first iteration only consists of the initialization, computes the estimation using as input the images computed in the pyramid for the first spatial resolution scale, and continues to the next iteration.

4. HARDWARE IMPLEMENTATION

The selected device for our hardware implementation is an FPGA. As mentioned in the introduction, the FPGA is a good candidate as a platform that allows us to exploit the maximum level of parallelism to achieve an embedded system able to work in real-time. Furthermore, the second key point is the possibility of integration with the motor control for our binocular system. The selected FPGA is a Xilinx Virtex4 chip (XC4vfx100). The board is a Xirca V4 [44] with a PCIe interface and four SRAM ZBT memory banks of 8 MB each one. This platform can work as a stand-alone platform or a co-processing board. This means that the platform can be used separately working alone or connected with a PC which facilitates the hardware implementation debugging and the result display.

Our super-scalar architecture was developed using fine-pipelined datapaths. The implementation of this ILP (Instruction Level Parallelism) provides high performances and low power consumption [36]. Our architecture is displayed as an adaptable design for different applications and requirements as is shown in some previous works [30,35,36,45]. The use of fixed-point arithmetic entails a high resource saving with an acceptable loss of accuracy (provided that the bit-width at different operations is carefully chosen).

Our design validation consists of evaluating the accuracy of this degradation with respect to a software floating-point version. We split the complete processing engine into different stages and test different bit-widths for the variables at each stage. The key point is to find the minimum bit-width that leads to a minimum loss of accuracy. Once our objective is reached, we continue with the following stage sequentially along the datapath. This process has been successfully adopted in other contributions as [30,35,36] and represents a good working methodology to allow the fixed-point implementation of floating point algorithms using digital hardware.

The development of the implementation was performed using two hardware description languages for two different abstraction levels.

Firstly, the implementation of the modules that perform the communication protocols and interfaces and the Memory Controller Unit (MCU [46]) are implemented in VHDL. The disparity computation and the multi-scale architecture was developed using Handel-C because this C-like language is better suited for algorithmic descriptions, without significantly degrading performances or increasing resources [47].

The hardware implementation of the multiscale extension is described in detail [35,40,45]. This multi-scale-with-warping architecture is usually avoided in the literature because of the high computational costs that imply in hardware implementations high resource costs. On the other hand, the multi-scale architecture that we implemented allows us to increase the working range 30 times with respect to the mono-scale implementation.

4.1. Lucas–Kanade Vector Disparity Core

The implementation of this core is based on previous approaches [35,36,48]. In the cited works, the authors implement optical flow gradient-based algorithms, for both mono- and multi-scale versions. In this work, the most important difference is the computation of the vector disparity or bidimensional disparity for uncalibrated images instead of the 1-D disparity for rectified and undistorted images.

In Figure 4, *Pixel In* denotes the input to the disparity core (in our case, 2 frames for the left and right images with a bitwidth of 8); *Control* represents the control word, with the parameters for the number of scales, confidence thresholds, and the input resolution. The output bitwidth is 24 bits: 12 bits for the vertical and the horizontal component of the disparity. The core is implemented in a segmented pipeline design with 5 stages:

- St_0: In this stage, the filtering of the inputs reducing the aliasing effects is performed. It convolves them with Gaussian filters whose kernels of 3 taps are $K = [1\ 2\ 1]/4$.

- St_1: It computes the left-right difference and applies a smoothing filter to the inputs.

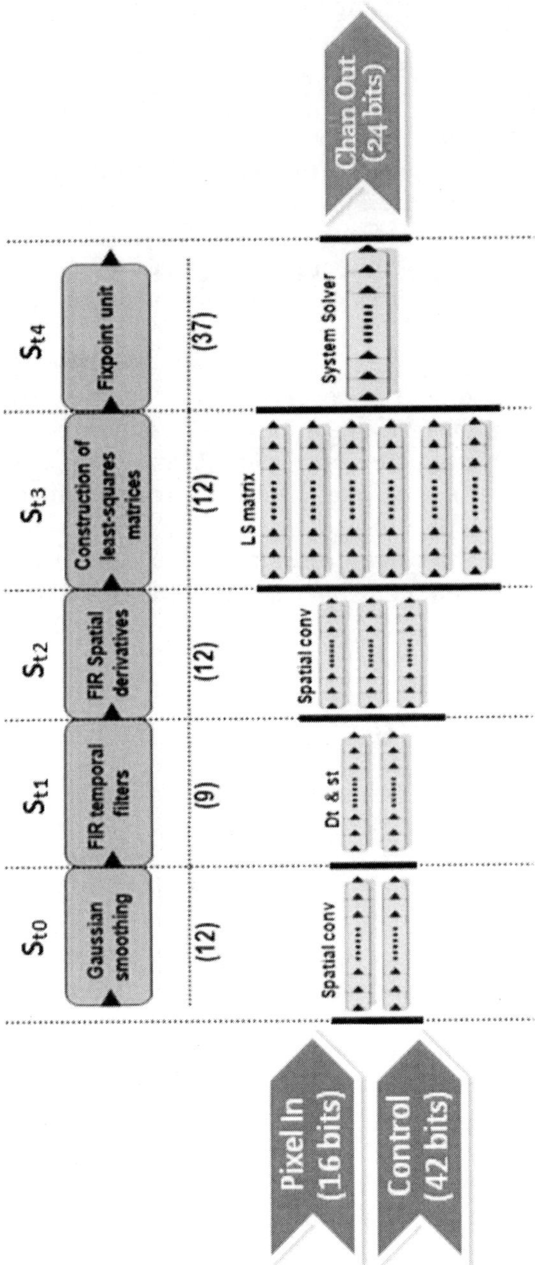

Figure 4. Scheme of the pipelined stages for the Lucas–Kanade vector disparity core. It describes the computation stages (from St_0 to St_4) indicating the pipelined stages (in brackets) and the number of parallel datapaths for each one of them.

- St_2: In this stage, we compute the spatial derivatives to the results of the previous stage: I_x, I_y, and filter again the results (including the left-right difference).

- St_3: This stage performs the calculation of the coefficients for the linear systems of 5 and 6. The weights W are set to a 5 × 5 separable kernel defined W = [1 4 6 4 1]/16 as in [36,37].

- St_4: The final stage computes the solution of the system using the previous results. It uses as confidence measure the determinant of this matrix.

For the computation of this core, we use 187 parallel processing units: stage St_0 has 2 paths (2 frames) for the Gaussian convolution, St_1 has 2 paths (for the left-right difference and the smoothing), St_2 has 3 paths (2 for the derivatives I_x and $I_y$and 1 for the left-right difference), St_3 has 6 paths (one for each coefficient in Equations (5) and (6)) and St_5, has only one path for the system resolution. The number in brackets in the figure denotes the micropipelined stages for each of them.

4.2. Phase-Based Vector Disparity Core

The design of this core is also based on a previous approach [30]. The main difference with respect to our case is that previous approaches implement a core for the computation of disparity for calibrated images, as in the previous core (as in [30,34]).

In Figure 5, we show a scheme of the design. Input parameters are the same as in the case of the previous core: *Pixel In*denotes the input data (2 frames for left and right images with 8 bits); *Control* for the control word (42 bits). The output bitwidth is 24 bits: 12 bits for each disparity component. In this case, the core is implemented in a segmented pipeline with 3 stages:

- St_0: This stage computes the odd and even filtering quadrature components for the image pair.

- St_1: It computes the disparity for each orientation (we use 8 orientations).

- St_2: The provided component disparities need to be combined to compute the final full disparity. They conform an equation system solved in this stage applying least-squares (see Equation (9)).

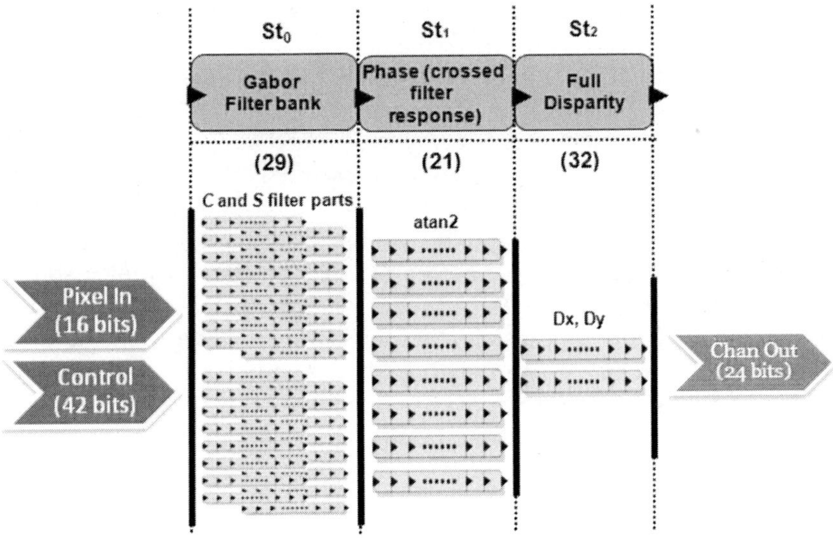

Figure 5. Scheme of the pipelined stages for the phase-based vector disparity core. It describes the computation stages (from St_0 to St_2) indicating the pipelined stages (in brackets) and the number of parallel datapaths for each one of them.

For the computation of this core, we use 1,160 parallel processing units: stage St_0 has 32 paths (2 frames) for the computation of the odd and even filter components (with 8 orientations, we have 16 different filters), St_1 has 8 paths for the*atan2* operations and finally, St_2 has 2 paths, one for each disparity component. The number in brackets in the figure denotes the micropipelined stages for each of them. We have used two IP cores from Xilinx Core Generator platform to compute complex arithmetic operations such as arctangent (St_1) and a pipelined division (St_2).

4.3. Multi-Scale Architecture

The implementation of the multi-scale architecture allows us the expansion of the working range of our disparity estimation more than 30× (using 5 scales) compared to the case of mono-scale versions. The design of this multi-scale architecture is the same as in previous works [30,45]. This approach is inspired by Bergen's work [42].

The multi-scalar version implementation is simple and it is displayed in Figure 6. Firstly, we compute the pyramid for the input images (left and right) and store them. In such a way, we have a bank of images sampled at the different spatial resolutions (depending on the number of scales). The second step consists of iterating in a loop as many times as scales: for each iteration, we upsample the previous estimation of the disparity; the next stage consists of the computation of the warping using the previous up-sampled results and the frames for the following finer scale; the warping operation compensates (removes) the apparent movement of scene elements due to the different points of view, allowing us the computation of disparity estimates in a valid range for that scale; the new disparity estimation is computed using the previous results as input for the core; the final stage collects both the new estimation and the partial previous stored results, combining them in a new partial estimation for the next iteration. The first iteration only consists of the initialization and computes the estimation using as input the images computed in the pyramid for the first spatial resolution scale and goes to the next iteration.

As a brief summary of this architecture, the design is divided into the following modules:

- Gaussian pyramid: This module implements the computation of the Gaussian pyramid of the left and right images for the disparity computation inspired in [43]. The number of levels of this pyramid depends on the number of scales with a downsampling factor of 2. It is built by a smoothing and a subsampling circuit. The main operations at this step are the 2D convolution with Gaussian filters of 5 taps (smoothing) and the sub-sampling. The kernel is a 5-by-5 matrix decomposed in two arrays $K = [\,1\;4\;6\;4\;1]/16$. Thanks to the use of separable filters, the convolution is performed in a parallel way for the x and y operations. Five image lines are stored in an embedded multi-port BlockRAM used like a FIFO for the convolution. Then, we send to the output (the external SRAM) a pixel every two clock cycles: one pixel is discarded (sub-sampling).

This sequential part of the processing is performed once and the results are stored/read to/from the RAM memory banks.

- Vector Disparity: This module has been explained in detail in previous subsections. Depending on the case, this module implements the vector disparity estimation based on the Lucas–Kanade or the phase-based algorithm.

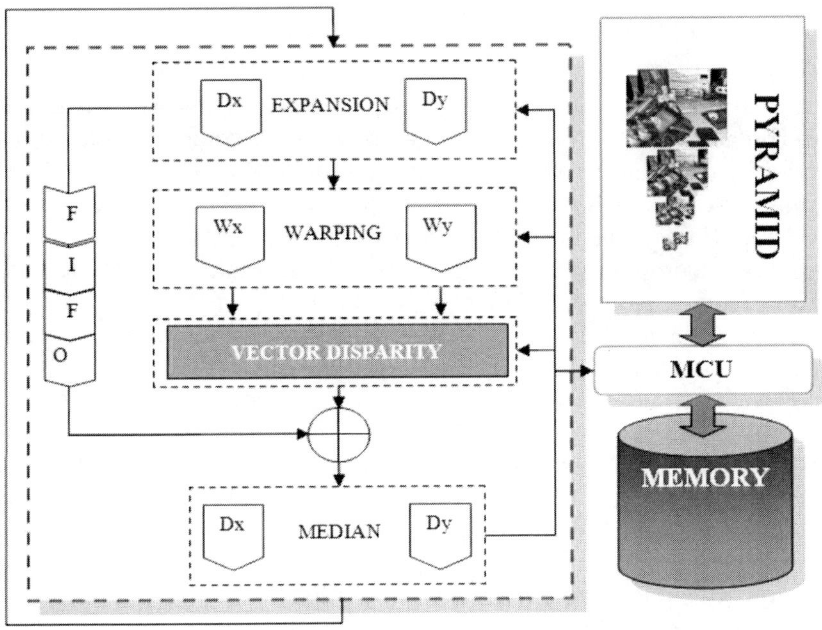

Figure 6. Hardware system architecture. Right side: the pyramid and its communication with memory. Left side: multi-scale computation (scaling, warping, merging, median filtering and vector disparity computation).

- Expansion: This module up-samples the current scale results to the resolution of the following finer scale (the up-sampling factor is also 2). In contrast with the mono-dimensional disparity, this module is duplicated for the vector disparity. We use one module for each component of the vector disparity that needs to be up-sampled to the next scale resolution.

- Warping: In the literature, this computationally expensive stage is usually avoided because of its high computational cost. In our case, it consists of a bilinear interpolation between left and right image (keeping the left frame and warping the right one with the estimation of the disparity computed for the previous scale). In Equation (10), the warping computation for the vector disparity computation is shown. Θ denotes the bidimensional scaling operator for **d**(*x*, *y*) (vector disparity) at the scale *s* with a factor of 2 and I^R stands for the right image.

$$I_R^s = Warp(I_R^{s-1}(x, y), \Theta(d^{s-1}(x, y))) \tag{10}$$

The warping operation for the vector disparity consists of a bilinear interpolation of the input images with the shift values which we have stored from the computed disparity in the previous scale. The computation of each warped pixel requires the reading of the pair (Δx, Δy) and the correspondent pixel *P*. Each pair (Δx, Δy) is used for retrieving from memory the four pixels of the original image for each *P* pixel. Then, the warped pixel is calculated performing a weighted bilinear interpolation with the obtained values. The warping process needs to perform four memory accesses per clock cycle to calculate one warped pixel to achieve the maximum throughput. This is one of the reasons for the choice of a specific MCU to manage data with different Abstract Access Ports (AAP) [46]. The warping architecture uses a reading AAP of the MCU for accessing the original image. The MCU provides a 36-bit bus allowing the access to four pixels per memory read. The X and Y matrices are provided from the expansion circuit through two blocking FIFOs. Warping requires a neighborhood of 4 pixels and the number of data available per memory access is limited to four in a same line. Thus, one access brings 2 pixels of the same line in the best case. Nevertheless, it is impossible to access the 4-pixel window in a single memory access. In the worst case, we access 4 different memory words (every 4 consecutive memory accesses). Therefore, the performance is constrained up to 4 pixels every 10 memory accesses.

- Merging: This module computes the addition of the previous feature estimation and the current one. The result is stored for the next iteration. The non-valid values are propagated from the coarsest scales to the finest ones. At the last scale, the finest one, we make the logical AND operation between its non-valid values and the propagated ones for the final estimation (the non-valid values obtained at the finest scale are the most reliable). The main problem of this module is the synchronization between the current and the stored results.

- Homogenization: This stage filters the results for each iteration with two 3 × 3 median filters in cascade. This filtering removes non-reliable values and homogenizes the results.

More details about the hardware implementation of this architecture can be found in [35,40,45].

5. DISCUSSION OF RESULTS

As explained in the Introduction, with an active sensor that changes the vergence, the rectification process is required each time that the camera configuration is modified. This fact makes the static rectification approach unsuitable for this kind of systems. Moreover, an adaptive vergence system allows gazing on a target or fixation point and it may obtain the optimal disparity estimations around the image plane that is set using the depth of that fixation point. This section analyzes the performances of the vector disparity computation and the comparison in resource costs between our system and the same system with the static rectification unit.

We present the comparison of the developed systems in terms of resource utilization, accuracy and density of the results. Firstly, we list the performances of our work and some state-of-the-art publications with different implementations and technologies. Next, we benchmark our work (both approaches) with the set of images of Middlebury [49]. All this dataset is addressed to work with horizontal disparity algorithms; therefore, it is only shown to illustrate the comparison of our 2D disparity performances with the 1D ones. As mentioned before, our approach is suitable for working with active vision systems. We also test our implementations with our own benchmark images especially plotted to test the vector disparity accuracy and some images from an on-line set of benchmarks available at [50]. The benchmarking is performed for the hardware and software approaches to compare also the accuracy degradation due to the fixed-point arithmetic adopted in the hardware implementation. The last part of the section is dedicated to present a summary of the resource utilization.

In the case of the mono-dimensional benchmarks, we compute the MAE (Mean Absolute Error) and the Density. We also compute the PoBP (percentage of bad pixels, *i.e.*, the percentage of pixels whose MAE is greater than 1, see [40]). For the vector disparity estimation, we compute the AAE (Average Angular Error), and the Density. Furthermore, we also compute the PoGP (percentage of good pixels, or the percentage of pixels whose AAE is less than 5, see again [40]).

5.1. State-of-the-Art Comparison

We mentioned in the Introduction that our aim is the development of a high-performance system that works in real time (in our case, it means a frame rate of at least 25 fps with VGA resolution). In Table 1, we find that our implementation reaches up to 32 fps with a resolution of 640 × 480. This result fulfills our requirements.

Table 1. Disparity performance comparison (works sorted by date of publication). For vector disparity implementations, two PDS values are given: the first considers only 1-D displacement performance and the second takes into account that 2-D matching of the vector methods have a search region that is the squared of the 1-D ones.

	Resolution	Frame rate (fps)	PDS ($\times 10^6$)	Architecture	Algorithm
Our phase-based mono-scale core	640 × 480	118	218/1,304	Xilinx V4 (36 MHz)	2D Phase-based
Our Lucas–Kanade mono-scale core	640 × 480	267	492/1,968	Xilinx V4 (82 MHz)	2D Lucas–Kanade
Our phase-based multi-scale system	640 × 480	32	1,887/7,122	Xilinx V4 (42 MHz)	2D Phase-based
Our Lucas–Kanade multi-scale system	640 × 480	32	1,132/4,528	Xilinx V4 (41 MHz)	2D Lucas–Kanade
Tomasi (2010) [30]	512 × 512	28	939	Xilinx V4 (42 MHz)	1D Phase-based
Chang (2010) [51]	352 × 288	42	273	UMC 90nm Cell	1D Semi-Census
Hadjitheofanous (2010) [31]	320 × 240	75	184	Xilinx V2 Pro	1D SAD

	Resolution	Frame rate (fps)	PDS ($\times 10^6$)	Architecture	Algorithm
Jin (2010) [32]	640 × 480	230	4,522	Xilinx V5 (93.1 MHz)	1D Census Transform
Calderon (2010) [33]	288 × 352	142	2,534	Xilinx V2 Pro (174.2 MHz)	1D BSAD
Chessa (2009) [17]	256 × 256	7	59/236	QuadCore Processor	2D Energy-based Pop. coding
Georgoulas (2009) [28]	800 × 600	550	21,120	Stratix IV (511 MHz)	1D SAD
Ernst (2009) [52]	640 × 480	4.2	165	GeForce 8800	1D SGM
Han (2009) [53]	320 × 240	144	707	ASIC (150MHz)	1D SAD
Gibson (2008) [54]	450 × 375	6	65	G80 NVIDIA	1D SGM
Diaz (2006) [34]	1,280 × 960	52	1,885	Xilinx V2 (65 MHz)	1D Phase-based
Gong (2005) [55]	384 × 288	16	30–60	ATI Radeon x800	1D GORDP

Table 1 shows a performance comparison between our four developments (mono- and multi-scale approaches, phase-based, and Lucas–Kanade) with the last works in the literature. Due to the lack of works for computing vector disparity, we summarize in the table the most important ones that compute horizontal disparity in the last years. Besides, the mono-scalar version achieves a frame rate calculated using the maximum working frequency. Finally, in the multi-scalar versions, the frame rate is empirically measured using the proposed architecture and taking into account the PCIe bandwidth restrictions for the communication with a PC.

Most of the listed works in Table 1 are mono-scalar developments except [30] and [17]. The performances depend on the algorithm, the architecture, and the optimization level. Algorithms with a lower computational cost as SAD-based implementations may obtain better speed performances but the accuracy results are also rather low. Furthermore, there are substantial differences between mono- and multi-scalar versions. On the other hand, we merge horizontal and vector disparity algorithms in the same table to easily compare the main performances, but this comparison is not completely fair, e.g., in the case of the PDS. The PDS (Points × Disparity measures per Second) is a metric that measures the number of operations performed by our algorithm per time taking into account the disparity range. With respect to this last measure, Georgoulas *et al.* [28] achieves impressive results with a PDS of 21120×10^6. Our PDS for the best multi-scalar version is 7122×10^6. The computation of the PDS depends on the disparity range and, for vector disparity algorithms, this range is squared compared with the horizontal disparity range. In the column, we show firstly the PDS using the simple range to check the magnitude differences with the 1D algorithms and the second values are the PDS for the 2D implementation.

To estimate the disparity at different spatial resolution levels, the multi-scalar architecture is revealed as essential. The Laplacian pyramidal approach for the multi-scale architecture [43] is the way to implement this multi-resolution analysis through a fine-to-coarse strategy. The objective is to estimate disparities larger than the filter support. The factor depends on the number of scales (determined by the target application). In the case of the mono-scalar versions, the main advantage is obviously a computation with a high frame rate. Moreover, multi-scalar versions obtain significant precision improvements due to its wide-range estimations.

5.2. Benchmarking for Horizontal Disparity

In this subsection, we briefly analyze the performances of our vector disparity algorithms with the well-known benchmark images of Middelbury [49], whose vertical disparity components are always zero. As vector disparity implementations are rare in the literature, we include this section for future comparisons with horizontal disparity algorithms. Actually, we do not expect better results than the proper 1D algorithms, any variation in the vertical disparity (that should be zero) adds error to the resolution of the 2D equation system. Moreover, the search space for the solution is developed from 1D to 2D (see Equations (3) and (9) respectively) which makes the solutions more unreliable.

Figure 7 and Table 2 show the performance analysis for the horizontal disparity computation. In the literature, besides the example which is being used in this paper, there are not many image benchmarks for vector disparity. Most of the works which we find in the literature test their algorithms and implementations with the classical horizontal disparity benchmark provided by Middlebury [49]. Firstly, we also show the efficiency and density of our approaches with some images of this benchmark, in particular: "*Tsukuba*", "*Sawtooth*", "*Venus*", "*Teddy*", and "*Cones*" (respectively called *bm*1 to *bm*5). We distinguish between the Lukas–Kanade and the phase-based version and between the hardware and the software implementations. In the figure, we notice that the error is similar for the different versions except in the case of *bm*4 and *bm*5 ("*Teddy*" and "*Cones*" cases). The increment in these cases of the errors for the phase-based hardware version is substantial and also entails an important loss of density. The Lucas–Kanade hardware version achieves even better results than the software version due to the use of homogenization stages. The table shows the best results for the Lucas–Kanade hardware version but, except for the last two cases, all the results are very similar and the degradation of the precision is not quite significant.

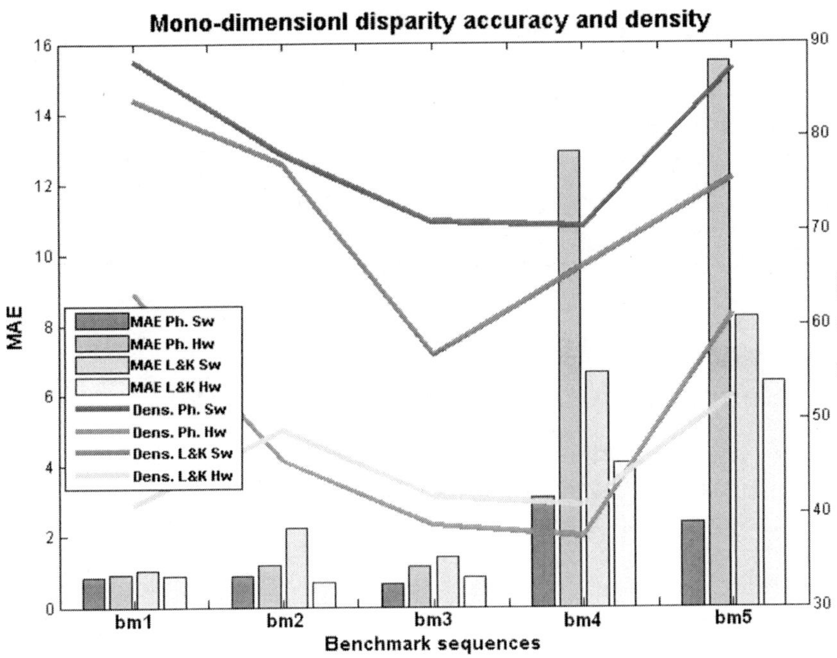

Figure 7. Horizontal disparity comparison: Lucas–Kanade *vs.* Phase-based and Hardware *vs.* Software versions (MAE and density).

The generalized loss of density is very significant and may be attributed to the loss of precision of both designs. But it is even worst in the case of the phase-based implementation constrained for the fixed-point arithmetic, especially in the complex operations such as divisions and arctangent modules and in computations for the Gabor filtering stage. Moreover, the use of the fixed-point arithmetic also affects the computation of the confidence measure that performs the thresholding operation. Finally, it is also worth regarding that hardware implementations in Figure 7 are generally more accurate than their correspondent software implementations (more accurate and reliable estimations entail discarding more estimations).

Table 2. Horizontal disparity performances: PoBP(%) percentage of pixels where MAE >1 and the density between parentheses.

	Phase-based		Lucas-Kanade	
	SW	HW	SW	HW
Tsukuba	16.65 (88.05%)	13.76 (63.42%)	21.77 (83.89%)	9.00 (40.89%)
Sawtooth	10.82 (78.11%)	10.58 (45.56%)	27.66 (77.10%)	5.90 (48.79%)
Venus	8.37 (70.99%)	7.84 (38.69%)	18.07 (56.83%)	7.57 (41.78%)
Teddy	25.73 (70.46%)	27.06 (37.55%)	40.91 (66.20%)	25.25 (40.85%)
Cones	27.18 (87.20%)	48.32 (61.10%)	58.06 (75.52%)	40.65 (52.45%)

5.3. Benchmarking for Vector Disparity

In this last subsection, we perform the benchmarking using the convenient set of images for the analysis for the performances of the vector disparity implementations. Figure 8 and Table 3 show the vector disparity results for the *"plane 0H 0V"*, *"plane 15H 15V"*, *"desktop00"*, and *"desktop09"* sequences (marked as *bv*1 to *bv*4). The first two sequences (*bv1* and*bv2*) were generated using an initial ground-truth, whereas *bv*3 and *bv*4 are active views of 3D acquired natural scenes generated by a virtual reality system [50] and available at [56]. In this case, differences between the software and hardware versions are more important. On the other hand, the differences between the phase-based and Lucas–Kanade have been shortened, although the Lucas–Kanade hardware implementation seems slightly better. This fact can be attributed, as in the previous section, to the loss of accuracy that affects the phase-based model due to the bit-widths and fixed-point arithmetic limitations. Table 3 also supports it, showing a PoGP that model is about 25% higher in the Lucas–Kanade than in the phase-based model.

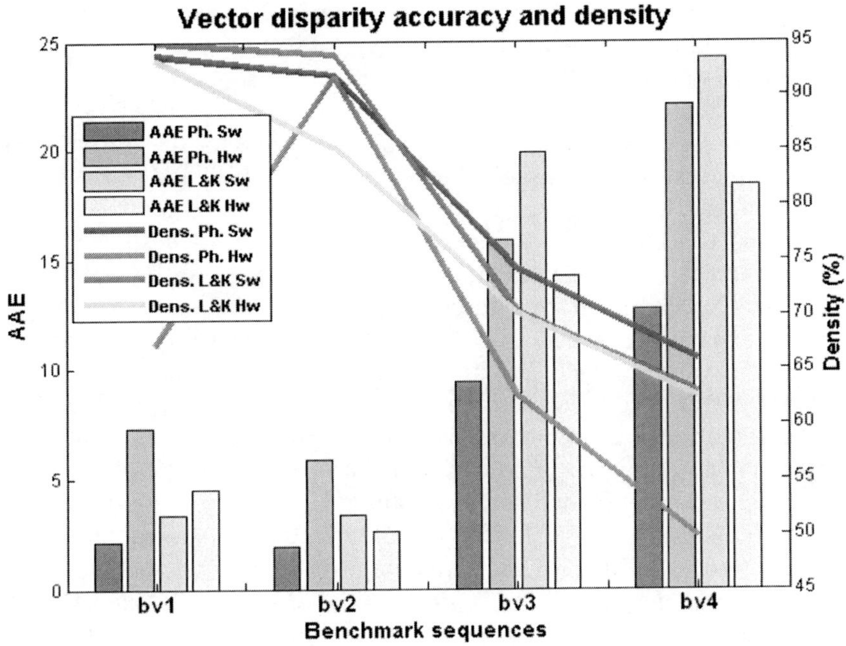

Figure 8. Vector disparity comparison: Lucas–Kanade *vs.* Phase-based and Hardware*vs.* Software versions (AAE and density).

Table 3. Vector disparity performances: PoGP(%), defined as the percentage of pixels where AAE < 5 deg. and the density between parentheses.

	Phase-based		Lucas–Kanade	
	SW	HW	SW	HW
plane 0H 0V	70.04 (93.66%)	93.77 (91.84%)	67.57 (74.17%)	68.67 (65.88%)
plane 15H 15V	69.99 (67.15%)	73.27 (91.73%)	67.82 (62.55%)	68.82 (49.76%)
desktop00	82.30 (94.84%)	80.48 (93.76%)	79.61 (70.29%)	80.68 (62.97%)
desktop09	84.24 (93.19%)	86.74 (85.26%)	82.92 (70.16%)	82.99 (62.57%)

In general, in the case of this benchmark, the density is quite similar in contrast with the previous subsection. The computation is not affected as dramatically as in the previous case because now we are using appropriately the confidence measure (implemented for the 2D model not for the 1D). For instance (except for the first sequence *bv*1), the maximum difference between hardware and software results in density is about 15%, with similar tendencies for all the sequences.

Finally, Figures 9 and 10 show the disparity results for the software and hardware versions for the sequences available at [56] and the ones that we generated. In the figures, we display the original images, the ground-truth, and the results for the software versions in the case of the first figure and the hardware results for the second one. All the estimations have a color-coding frame describing the direction of the estimated vector disparity. The values in black in the hardware column are the unreliable values (*NaN*). As it can be seen, the phase-based results present better results in the case of the software but, for the hardware implementation, the bit-width constraining degrades the final estimation in an appreciable way. On the other hand, the phase-based implementation presents some advantages for its use in real-world applications such as a better behavior against variations in the illumination [57,58]. This last advantage is illustrated in the figures, especially for "*desktop00*" and "*desktop09*". For a more detailed study of the robustness of phase-based implementations against illumination changes and affine transformations between the stereo pair images, cf. [57,59,60].

5.4. Hardware Resource Utilization

In computer vision, the selection of the best alternative is performed depending on the target application, searching for a good trade-off between the required accuracy (see previous subsections) and constraints about the maximum frequency and the resource utilization. Table 4 shows the resource utilization and the maximum working frequency of the implemented system. This table presents the information about the board resource utilization: total number of 4 input LUTs, Slice Flip Flops, Slices, DSPs, Block RAMs used, and finally, the maximum frequency (MHz).

The listed options include: the multi-scale vector disparity systems and the horizontal disparity systems with the rectification stage, for both approaches. More details about the resource cost of the different unit components of the multi-scale generalization can be found at [30,35,45].

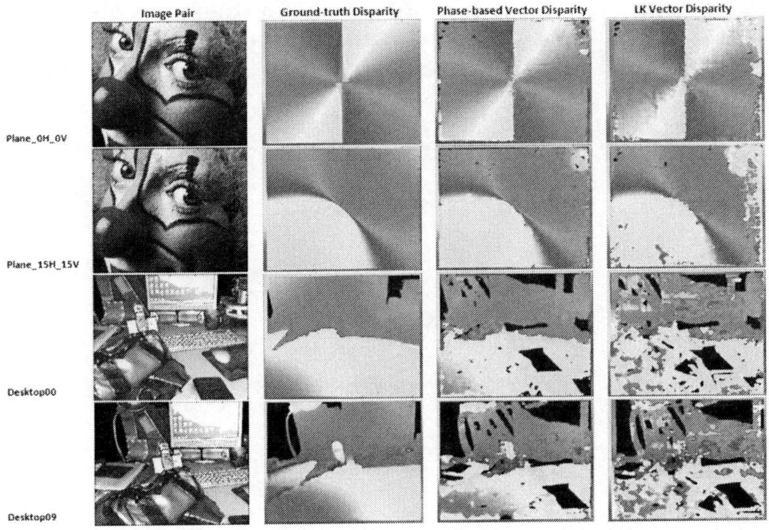

Figure 9. Software benchmark results for vector disparity. From left to right: original image, ground-truth, software results for phase-based, and Lucas–Kanade algorithms. The frame codes the vector disparity with a color.

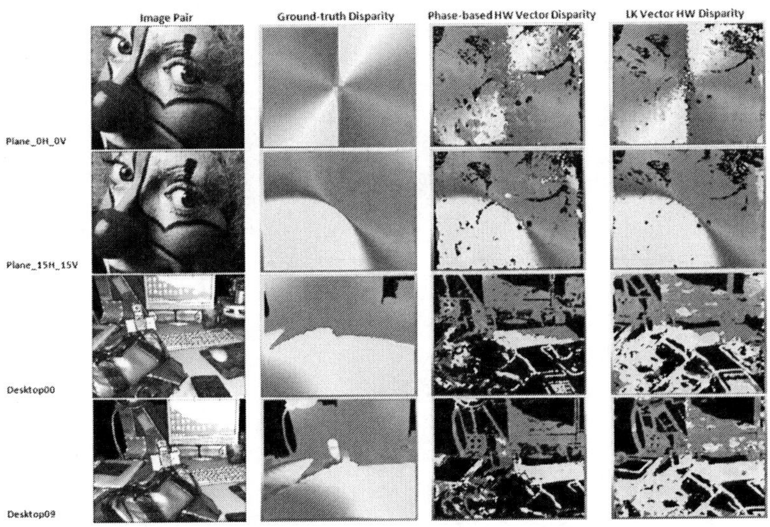

Figure 10. Hardware benchmark results for vector disparity. From left to right: original image, ground-truth, hardware results for phase-based, and Lucas–Kanade algorithms. The frame codes the vector disparity with a color.

Table 4. Hardware resource utilization for the presented complete architecture using a Virtex-4 FX100 FPGA (XC4vfx100).

	4 input LUTs (out of 84,352)	Slice Flip-Flops (out of 84,352)	Slices (out of 42,716)	DSP (160)	Block RAM (378)	Freq (MHz)
1D Phase-based system + Rectification	47,109 (56%)	27,221 (32%)	32,678 (76%)	159 (99%)	88 (23%)	44
1D Lucas–Kanade system + Rectification	55,152 (65%)	35,360 (41%)	38,560 (90%)	154 (96%)	100 (26%)	42
2D Phase-based Disp. system	55,445 (65%)	40,597 (48%)	37,383 (88%)	107 (66%)	126 (33%)	42
2D Lucas–Kanade Disp. system	33,039 (39%)	28,123 (33%)	27,749 (65%)	50 (31%)	148 (39%)	41

For the horizontal disparity systems, the Lucas–Kanade version uses about 9% more 4-Input LUTs, this is due to the difference in Block RAMs and DSPs and especially, to the optimization level. Tools for hardware implementations apply optimization techniques based on heuristics that cannot be completely controlled using the software parameters. A totally fair comparison can also be done with a more intensive use of resources.

On the other hand, focusing on the vector disparity computations, while the phase-based approach increases the resource utilization about 10%, the Lucas–Kanade approach achieves a remarkable reduction of about 25%. As the multi-scale architecture is the same for both approaches, the increment in resource costs for the phase-based approach is due to the 2D core. While the rectification unit is the bottle-neck for the Lucas–Kanade architecture, it is the proper 2D core for the phase-based scheme.

All these results support the idea of implementing the final system for motion control of our binocular system with the Lucas–Kanade approach taking into account also the low degradation of accuracy obtained in the previous subsection and the resource saving of more than 25% with respect to the phase-based approach.

6. CONTROL OF VERGENCE FOR A BINOCULAR SYSTEM

As described in the Introduction section, our final objective is the implementation of a system that, using the vector disparity (implemented according to the previous sections), manages the vergence, version, and tilt control.

Motor control is distributed using Digital Signal Processing (DSPs) boards, in this case, Freescale DSP-56F807, 80 MHz, fixed point 16 bits which perform a fast low-level control loop in real time. A CAN-bus line allows the communication between the boards and a remote PC. Motors are directly controlled by standard PID controllers. This DSP, due to its memory and computation limitations, implements simple operations such as pre-filtering, signal acquisition, and PID position control (using absolute position encoders). More details about the mechanics and the architecture of the ICub and RobotCub can be found in [26,27].

The algorithm that we use for the fixation consists of selecting a point of our object of interest and computing a centroid based on the color of this point, using a threshold for the RGB components (a range of [−5,5] for each component). Once we have the centroid computed, we firstly compute the distance between this point and the current position of the eye centers and send it via the CAN bus to the DSP-based control cards. The communication protocol allows four working modes: sending relative angles, absolute angles, relative pixel positions, or normalized relative position (see the documentation at [25]); as explained, we use the third alternative. The PID low-level control loop acts on the motors to modify version and tilt according to these coordinates of the color-based centroid and in this way, we set our eye centers in the object of interest. The last step is acting on the vergence motors and computing the vector disparity until it reaches a value near zero (we use a threshold of 5). Changing the vergence of the cameras means translating the image plane to the depth of the target. Once the object is fixated, we will obtain the optimal performances around this object (zero disparity plane).

Tracking adds the possibility of performing a smooth pursuit of the object gazing on several fixation points. It is worth noticing that, due to the huge backlash on the eyes pan movement [25] and the limits in the physical properties of the motors, the pursuit is not as smooth as it may be expected and there are some fluctuations shown in the second experiment.

One of the problems that might appear in this scenario is the motion blur between the left and right camera images. In our algorithm, we firstly have a master camera that moves to the color centroid (where the object of interest is) and fixates to this position, followed by the second camera. As explained, the tilt is common to the cameras, while the version is achieved to move the cameras towards the same orientation. Then, the second camera (the slave) achieves the vergence movement to fixate the object, according to the position of the first eye.

The blur may happen during this second step, since the disparity is now being computed. However, we partially avoid this situation by using the disparity after each movement when the rig setup of the cameras is steady and not constant. In addition, the multiscale process also provides robustness to this issue due to the coarse-to-fine process and the limited disparity range possible at each scale.

In this final section, we present the results for two real experiments: the fixation in a target object, in our case it is a red plastic bottle, and the fixation and tracking of a blue LED light.

6.1. Experiment 1: Red Plastic Bottle Fixation

The first experiment consists of making the system fixate at a red plastic bottle. Figure 11 displays the initial position of the system (left and right images of the cameras). The red cross shows the fixation point in each case. The processing begins with the selection of the fixation point and then, the system performs the fixation task with the static object. In the figure, we observe the initial horizontal disparity at the fixation point; after fixating the point, the horizontal disparity tends to zero (we use a threshold to avoid variations that might affect the stability of the system). The vertical disparity is also almost zero, and in our case, with a common tilt for both cameras, it is not possible to reduce it.

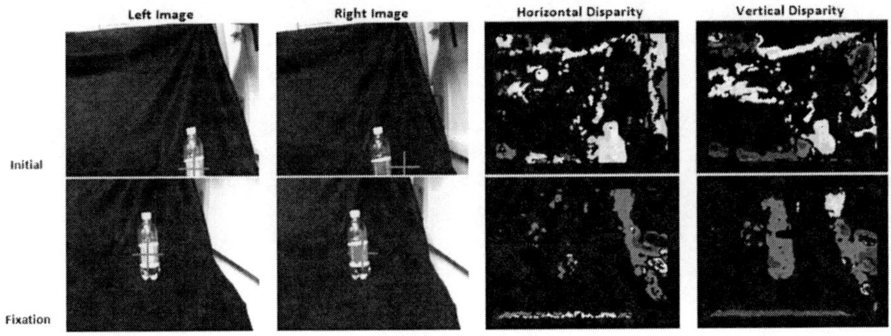

Figure 11. Initial position and fixation for the red plastic bottle example. Disparity components are displayed.

The evolution of the X and Y coordinates of the fixation point for both cameras and the component disparities are plotted in Figure 12. As we see, with an image resolution of 320 × 240, the fixation is finally performed in a very accurate and fast way. After 0.8 s, all the evolutions of the different parameters are stabilized (X and Y coordinates at 160 and 120 values respectively; component disparities around zero). The third row shows the evolutions for the vergence, version, and tilt. We plot the velocities for the different parameters that are the inputs of the DSP that controls the different motors of our system. After 0.8 s, all of them are also stable. Similar results are obtained for fixation in several works using other architectures: in [61], the fixation time is about 0.5–0.6 s and in [62], about 1.5 s. Our approach is shown as a very competitive alternative according to the fixation time and it has been also presented as one the most accurate ones.

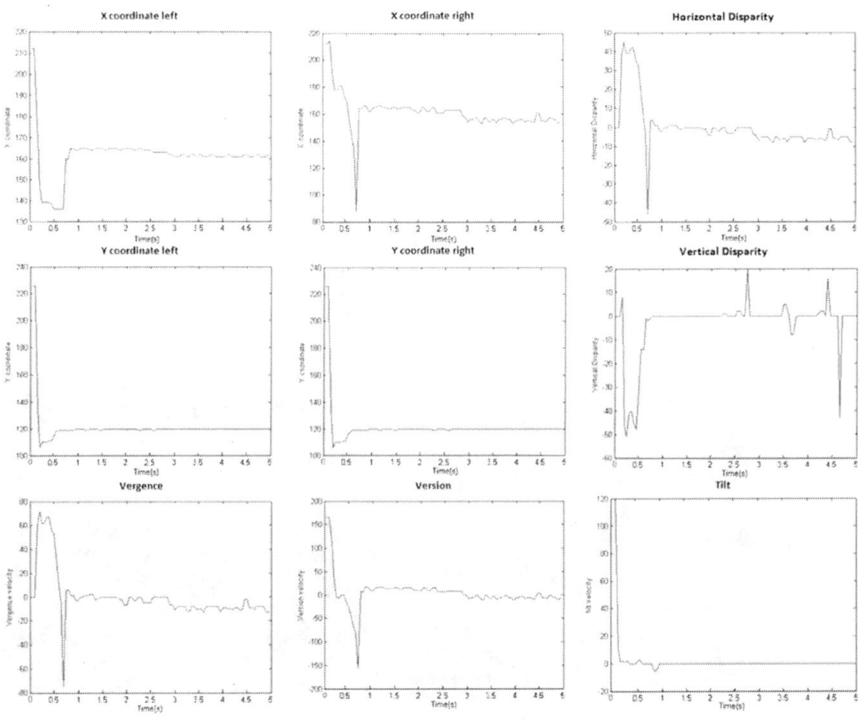

Figure 12. Red plastic bottle fixation example: X and Y coordinates for left and right images, horizontal and vertical component disparities and the evolution of version, vergence, and tilt velocities along the time (image resolution is 320 × 240).

6.2. Experiment 2: Smooth Pursuit

In this experiment, we show the smooth pursuit example with a blue object. Figure 13 shows the experiment performed for the pursuit of a blue object. The sequence shows the initial fixation and some subsequent captures of the cameras of our system tracking the object even at the limits of its physical properties. Once the object is detected, the system always performs the fixation again.

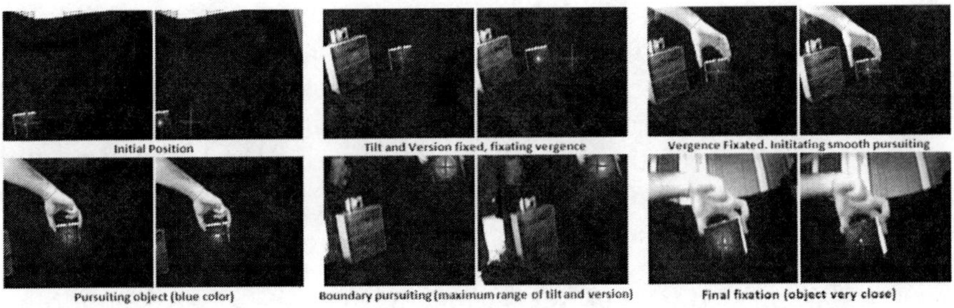

Figure 13. Blue LED smooth pursuit. At each different phase, we show the left and right images of our system, beginning with the fixation and then, with the pursuit of the target object.

It is worth noticing that the fixation point is not exactly the same point of the object in both cases, on the left and right camera images, because, as we mentioned, we use a threshold for the zero disparity region. In this way, our system is more stable and smoother trajectories are ensured.

7. CONCLUSIONS

The main contribution of this work is the implementation of a sensor for an active vision system with dynamic vergence control to explore dynamic environments using a scheme different to the common static camera configurations. The main problem of an active system is that the rectification process is required each time that the camera configuration is modified. Therefore, the use of a static rectification preprocessing stage technique is unsuitable for any active system that actively modifies the vergence angle of its camera setups. Our solution consists of using vector disparity estimations to control vergence. We have developed a SoC (system-on-a-chip) that integrates vector disparity estimation with vergence control on the same chip. This allows an embedded implementation with a low consumption at a single device that can be integrated on the i-Cub head (or any vision system including low level processing stages such as active stereo vision).

The first part of this work is dedicated to the design and implementation of an embedded system for the estimation of vector disparity. We have developed two different alternatives: a gradient-based one and a phase-based one. As mentioned, there are multiple examples for the horizontal disparity, while in the case of the vector disparity, as far as we know, the developments of this phase-based estimation in the literature are very seldom (see [13,17]), and their hardware implementation is even rarer. We have also designed a multi-scale generalization to increase the number of disparity levels 30× (using 5 spatial scales).

The requirements of a real-time system have been successfully fulfilled, since we are able to reach a working frequency of 32 fps with a VGA resolution (640 × 480) and, resorting on a multi-scale architecture, we are able to cope with large disparities. In the best case, the mono-scalar version of the system may achieve up to 267 fps for the same resolution, which shows the maximum level of parallelism provided by an FPGA (in our case, a Xilinx Virtex4 XC4vfx100 device). We have also analyzed the accuracy and density of our designs showing competitive results. By comparing different techniques with proper benchmark sequences, the Lucas-Kanade algorithm (including the homogenization stage) is revealed as the best choice, showing optimal efficacy *vs.* efficiency trade-off for vector disparity computation.

Hence, we have also compared the hardware and software versions of the algorithms; this comparison shows a low degradation for our hardware implementation which is affordable taking into account the use of fixed-point arithmetic instead of floating-point one. We have also compared the phase-based and the gradient-based algorithms and summarize the resource utilization. With the gradient-based algorithm, the resource cost is about 23% less than in the case of the phase-based one comparing the multi-scalar versions and 37% for the mono-scalar version. In terms of maximum working frequency, the gradient-based system is 2.3 times faster than the phase-based one.

The last section in this work deals with the implementation of the control model for a binocular camera system inspired by the Hering's Law. The control manages the vergence, version, and tilt angles of the system to modify the fixation point in order to focus on a target object using the real-time vector disparity computation. The easy integration with such a system and the low power consumption of the system [36] support the employment of the FPGA as well.

In the paper, we have also presented a fixation application and a tracking trajectory example for a real-world scenario. The implementation is tackled using the real-time vector disparity estimation, computed by the gradient-based algorithm. It consists of moving the cameras towards the position of an object of interest and afterwards, in moving the fixation point using the computed vector disparity to take advantage of the optimal computation that can be performed at the zero disparity plane. Once the proper fixation is ensured, we achieved a second experiment for a smooth pursuit movement towards an object of interest. As shown, we achieve fixating at the point of interest in approximately 0.8 s (it involves the gazing towards the object and the vergence control).

Finally, as future works, we will address the integration of the system on a robotic mobile platform for the implementation of real algorithms for autonomous navigation and scene mapping.

ACKNOWLEDGMENTS

This work has been supported by the National Grant (AP2007-00275), the projects ARC-VISION (TEC2010-15396), ITREBA (TIC-5060), MULTIVISION (TIC-3873), and the EU project TOMSY (FP7-270436).

REFERENCES

1. Bertozzi, M.; Broggi, A. GOLD: A parallel real-time stereo vision system for generic obstacle and lane detection. IEEE Trans. Image Process 1998, 7, 62–81.

2. El Ansari, M.; Mousset, S.; Bensrhair, A. A new stereo matching approach for real-time road obstacle detection for situations with deteriorated visibility. Proceedings of the 2008 IEEE Intelligent Vehicles Symposium, Eindhoven, The Netherlands, 4–6 June 2008; pp. 355–360.

3. Oisel, L.; Memin, E.; Morin, L.; Galpin, F. One-dimensional dense disparity estimation for three-dimensional reconstruction. IEEE Trans. Image Process 2003, 12, 1107–1119.

4. Lu, Z.; Shi, B. Subpixel resolution binocular visual tracking using analog VLSI vision sensors. IEEE Trans. Circuits Syst. II Analog Digit. Signal Process 2000, 47, 1468–1475.

5. Musleh, B.; Garca, F.; Otamendi, J.; Armingol, J.M.; de la Escalera, A. Identifying and tracking pedestrians based on sensor fusion and motion stability predictions. Sensors 2010, 10, 8028–8053.

6. Coelho, J.; Piater, J.; Grupen, R. Developing haptic and visual perceptual categories for reaching and grasping with a humanoid robot. Robot. Auton. Syst 2001, 37, 195–218.

7. Song, W.; Minami, M.; Yu, F.; Zhang, Y.; Yanou, A. 3-D hand amp; Eye-vergence approaching visual servoing with lyapunouv-stable pose tracking. Proceedings of the 2011 IEEE International Conference on Robotics and Automation (ICRA), Shanghai, China, 9–13 May 2011; pp. 5210–5217.

8. Diaz, J.; Ros, E.; Carrillo, R.; Prieto, A. Real-time system for high-image resolution disparity estimation. IEEE Trans. Image Process 2007, 16, 280–285.

9. Murphy, C.; Lindquist, D.; Rynning, A.; Cecil, T.; Leavitt, S.; Chang, M. Low-cost stereo vision on an FPGA. Proceedings of the 15th Annual IEEE Symposium on Field-Programmable Custom Computing Machines (FCCM '07), Napa, CA, USA, 23–25 April 2007; pp. 333–334.

10. Trucco, E.; Verri, A. Introductory Techniques for 3-D Computer Vision; Prentice Hall PTR: Upper Saddle River, NJ, USA, 1998.

11. Faugeras, O.; Luong, Q.T.; Papadopoulou, T. The Geometry of Multiple Images: The Laws that Govern the Formation of Images of A Scene and Some of Their Applications; MIT Press: Cambridge, MA, USA, 2001.

12. Samarawickrama, J.G.; Sabatini, S.P. Version and vergence control of a stereo camera head by fitting the movement into the hering's law. Proceedings of the 4th Canadian Conference on Computer and Robot Vision, Montreal, QC, Canada, 28–30 May 2007; pp. 363–370.

13. Theimer, W.M.; Mallot, H.A. Vergence Guided Depth Reconstruction Using a Phase Method; Neuro-Nimes '93; EC2 Publishing: Nanterre, France, 1993; pp. 299–308.

14. Gibaldi, A.; Canessa, A.; Chessa, A.; Sabatini, S.P.; Solari, F. A neuromorphic control module for real-time vergence eye movements on the iCub robot head. Proceedings of the 10th IEEE-RAS International Conference on Humanoid Robots (Humanoids), Nashville, TN, USA, 6–8 December 2011; pp. 543–550.

15. Semmlow, J.L.; Yuan, W.; Alvarez, T.L. Evidence for separate control of slow version and vergence eye movements: Support for Hering's law. Vis. Res 1998, 38, 1145–1152.

16. Enrights, J. Changes in vergence mediated by saccades. J. Physiol 1983, 350, 9–31.

17. Chessa, M.; Sabatini, S.P.; Solari, F. A fast joint bioinspired algorithm for optic flow and two-dimensional disparity estimation. Proceedings of the 7th International Conference on Computer Vision Systems: Computer Vision Systems (ICVS '09), Liege, Belgium, October 2009; pp. 184–193.

18. Xu, Y.; Zhou, J.; Zhai, G. 2D phase-based matching in uncalibrated images. Proceedings of the IEEE Workshop on Signal Processing Systems Design and Implementation, Athens, Greece, 2–4 November 2005; pp. 325–330.

19. Nalpantidis, L.; Amanatiadis, A.; Sirakoulis, G.; Gasteratos, A. Efficient hierarchical matching algorithm for processing uncalibrated stereo vision images and its hardware architecture. IET Image Process 2011, 5, 481–492.

20. Beauchemin, S.S.; Barron, J.L. The computation of optical flow. ACM Comput. Surv 1995, 27, 433–466.

21. Lucas, B.D.; Kanade, T. An iterative image registration technique with an application to stereo vision. Proceedings of the 7th International Joint Conference on Artificial Intelligence (IJCAI '81), Vancouver, BC, Canada, August 1981; pp. 674–679.

22. Fleet, D.J.; Jepson, A.D.; Jenkin, M.R. Phase-based disparity measurement. CVGIP Image Underst 1991, 53, 198–210.

23. Sabatini, S.P.; Gastaldi, G.; Solari, F.; Pauwels, K.; Hulle, M.M.V.; Diaz, J.; Ros, E.; Pugeault, N.; Krger, N. A compact harmonic code for early vision based on anisotropic frequency channels. Comput. Vis. Image Underst 2010, 114, 681–699.

24. Solari, F.; Sabatini, S.P.; Bisio, G.M. Fast technique for phase-based disparity estimation with no explicit calculation of phase. Electron. Lett 2001, 37, 1382–1383.

25. iCub Project. The EU iCub Project: An Open Source Cognitive Humanoid Robotic Platform. Available online: http://www.icub.org/ (accessed on 28 December 2011).

26. Beira, R.; Lopes, M.; Praga, M.; Santos-Victor, J.; Bernardino, A.; Metta, G.; Becchi, F.; Saltaren, R. Design of the robot-cub (iCub) head. Proceedings of the 2006 IEEE International Conference on Robotics and Automation (ICRA '06), Orlando, CA, USA, May 2006; pp. 94–100.

27. Ivaldi, S. From Humans to Humanoids: A Study on Optimal Motor Control for the iCub. Ph.D. Thesis,. University of Genoa, Genoa, Italy, 2011.

28. Georgoulas, C.; Andreadis, I. A real-time occlusion aware hardware structure for disparity map computation. Proceedings of the Image Analysis and Processing (ICIAP '09), Vietri sul mare, Italy, September 2009; 5716, pp. 721–730.

29. Hansard, M.; Horaud, R. Cyclopean geometry of binocular vision. J. Opt. Soc. Am 2008, 25, 2357–2369.

30. Tomasi, M.; Vanegas, M.; Barranco, F.; Diaz, J.; Ros, E. A novel architecture for a massively parallel low level vision processing engine on chip. Proceedings of the 2010 IEEE International Symposium on Industrial Electronics (ISIE '10), Bari, Italy, 5–7 July 2010; pp. 3033–3039.

31. Hadjitheophanous, S.; Ttofis, C.; Georghiades, A.; Theocharides, T. Towards hardware stereoscopic 3D reconstruction a real-time FPGA computation of the disparity map. Proceedings of the 2010 IEEE International Symposium on Design, Automation & Test in Europe Conference & Exhibition (DATE '10), Dresden, Germany, 8–12 March 2010; pp. 1743–1748.

32. Jin, S.; Cho, J.; Pham, X.D.; Lee, K.M.; Park, S.K.; Kim, M.; Jeon, J.W. FPGA design and implementation of a real-time stereo vision system. IEEE Trans. Circuits Syst. Video Technol 2010, 20, 15–26.

33. Calderon, H.; Ortiz, J.; Fontaine, J. High parallel disparity map computing on FPGA. Proceedings of the 2010 IEEE/ASME International Conference on Mechatronics and Embedded Systems and Applications (MESA '10), Suzhou, China, 8–10 July 2010; pp. 307–312.

34. Diaz, J.; Ros, E.; Pelayo, F.; Ortigosa, E.M.; Mota, S. FPGA-based real-time optical-flow system. IEEE Trans. Circuits Syst. Video Technol 2006, 16, 274–279.

35. Barranco, F.; Tomasi, M.; Diaz, J.; Vanegas, M.; Ros, E. Parallel architecture for hierarchical optical flow estimation based on FPGA. IEEE Trans. Very Large Scale Integr. (VLSI) Syst 2012. [CrossRef]

36. Diaz, J.; Ros, E.; Agis, R.; Bernier, J. Superpipelined high-performance optical-flow computation architecture. Comput. Vis. Image Underst 2008, 112, 262–273.

37. Brandt, J.W. Improved accuracy in Gradient-based optical flow estimation. Int. J. Comput. Vis 1997, 25, 5–22.

38. Barron, J.L.; Fleet, D.J.; Beauchemin, S.S. Performance of optical flow techniques. Int. J. Comput. Vis 1994, 12, 43–77.

39. Liu, H.; Hong, T.H.; Herman, M.; Chellappa, R. Accuracy vs. efficiency trade-offs in optical flow algorithms. InComputer Vision ECCV 96; Springer: Berlin, Germany, 1996; Volume 1065, pp. 174–183.

40. Pauwels, K.; Tomasi, M.; Diaz, J.; Ros, E.; Hulle, M.M.V. A comparison of FPGA and GPU for real-time phase-based optical flow, stereo, and local image features. IEEE Trans. Comput 2011. [CrossRef]

41. Gautama, T.; van Hulle, M. A phase-based approach to the estimation of the optical flow field using spatial filtering.IEEE Trans. Neural Netw 2002, 13, 1127–1136.

42. Bergen, J.; Anandan, P.; Hanna, K.; Hingorani, R. Hierarchical model-based motion estimation. In Computer Vision ECCV'92; Sandini, G., Ed.; Springer: Berlin, Germany, 1992; Volume 588, pp. 237–252.

43. Burt, P.J.; Adelson, E.H. The laplacian pyramid as a compact image code. IEEE Trans. Commun 1983, 31, 532–540.

44. Sevensols. Seven Solutions. Available online: http://www.sevensols.com/ (accessed on 28 December 2011).

45. Tomasi, M.; Vanegas, M.; Barranco, F.; Diaz, J.; Ros, E. High-performance optical-flow architecture based on a multiscale, multi-orientation phase-based model. IEEE Trans. Circuits Syst. Video Technol 2010, 20, 1797–1807.

46. Vanegas, M.; Tomasi, M.; Diaz, J.; Ros, E. Multi-port abstraction layer for FPGA intensive memory exploitation applications. J. Syst. Archit 2010, 56, 442–451.

47. Ortigosa, E.; Canas, A.; Ros, E.; Ortigosa, P.; Mota, S.; Diaz, J. Hardware description of multi-layer perceptrons with different abstraction levels. Microprocess. Microsyst 2006, 30, 435–444.

48. Tomasi, M.; Barranco, F.; Vanegas, M.; Diaz, J.; Ros, E. Fine grain pipeline architecture for high performance phase-based optical flow computation. J. Syst. Archit 2010, 56, 577–587.

49. Vision, M.C. Middlebury Computer Vision. Available online: http://vision.middlebury.edu/ (accessed on 28 December 2011).

50. Chessa, M.; Solari, F.; Sabatini, S.P. Virtual reality to simulate visual tasks for robotic systems. In Virtual Reality; Kim, J.J., Ed.; InTech: New York, NY, USA, 2010; pp. 71–92.

51. Chang, N.C.; Tsai, T.H.; Hsu, B.H.; Chen, Y.C.; Chang, T.S. Algorithm and architecture of disparity estimation with mini-census adaptive support weight. IEEE Trans. Circuits Syst. Video Technol 2010, 20, 792–805.

52. Ernst, I.; Hirschmüller, H. Mutual information based semi-global stereo matching on the GPU. Proceedings of the 4th International Symposium on Advances in Visual Computing, Las Vegas, NV, USA, December 2008; pp. 228–239.

53. Han, S.K.; Woo, S.; Jeong, M.H.; You, B.J. Improved-quality real-time stereo vision processor. Proceedings of the 22nd International Conference on VLSI Design, New Delhi, India, 5–9 January 2009; pp. 287–292.

54. Gibson, J.; Marques, O. Stereo depth with a unified architecture GPU. Proceedings of the IEEE Computer Society Conference on Computer Vision and Pattern Recognition Workshops (CVPRW '08), Anchorage, AK, USA, 23–28 June 2008; pp. 1–6.

55. Gong, M.; Yang, Y.H. Fast unambiguous stereo matching using reliability-based dynamic programming. IEEE Trans. Pattern Anal. Mach. Intell 2005, 27, 998–1003.

56. Virtual Reality Tool for Active Vision. Available online: http://www.pspc.dibe.unige.it/Research/vr.html (accessed on 28 December 2011).

57. Carneiro, G.; Jepson, A. Multi-scale phase-based local features. Proceedings of the 2003 IEEE Computer Society Conference on Computer Vision and Pattern Recognition, Madison, WI, USA, 18–20 June 2003; pp. 736–743.

58. Oppenheim, A.; Lim, J. The importance of phase in signals. Proc. IEEE 1981, 69, 529–541.

59. Tomasi, M.; Vanegas, M.; Barranco, F.; Diaz, J.; Ros, E. Real-time architecture for a robust multi-scale stereo engine on FPGA. IEEE Trans. Very Large Scale Integr. (VLSI) Syst 2011. [CrossRef]

60. Fleet, D.; Jepson, A. Stability of phase information. IEEE Trans. Pattern Anal. Mach. Intell 1993, 15, 1253–1268.

61. Bernardino, A.; Santos-Victor, J. Binocular tracking: Integrating perception and control. IEEE Trans. Robot. Autom 1999,15, 1080–1094.

62. Sapienza, M.; Hansard, M.; Horaud, R. Real-Time 3D Reconstruction and Fixation with an Active Binocular Head; Technical Report; INRIA: Le Chesnay Cedex, France, 2011.

INDEX